高等职业教育财经类规划教材（物流管理专业）

普通高等教育"十一五"国家级规划教材

物流专业英语

（第3版）

庄佩君　主　编

王晓萍　施　敏　副主编

电子工业出版社

Publishing House of Electronics Industry

北京·BEIJING

内 容 简 介

本书内容包括物流系统、供应链管理、货物运输、库存、物流信息、储存、搬运、配送、包装、物流单证、函电和电子商务各方面的专业基础知识和专业英语表述。

本书采用了“主、副”课文制。每章分三课,前两课为主课文,是该章的基本专业知识。对主课文从注解和练习两方面进行了重点处理,用做教师课内重点讲解的内容。第三课为副课文,介绍物流专业相关的新技术、新理念和一些国际著名企业的个案分析,主要供学有余力的学生课后自学或学生英文程度较好的学校选择授课,以便对主课文从语言和知识两方面起到巩固作用。

本教材可作为应用型本科院校、高职高专院校相关专业教材,也可供物流从业人员自学使用。

图书在版编目(CIP)数据

物流专业英语/庄佩君主编. —3 版. —北京:电子工业出版社,2011.1

高等职业教育财经类规划教材·物流管理专业

ISBN 978-7-121-12189-0

Ⅰ. 物… Ⅱ. 庄… Ⅲ. 物流-英语-高等学校:技术学校-教材 Ⅳ. H31

中国版本图书馆 CIP 数据核字(2010)第 213669 号

责任编辑:张云怡 特约编辑:李云霞

印　　刷:
北京京师印务有限公司
装　　订:
出版发行:电子工业出版社
　　　　　北京市海淀区万寿路 173 信箱　邮编 100036
开　　本:787×1092　1/16　印张:14.25　字数:466 千字
印　　次:2011 年 11 月第 3 次印刷
印　　数:2 000 册　定价:26.00 元

序

物流（Logistics）是一个控制原材料、制成品、产成品和信息的系统。物质资料从供给者到需求者的物理运动，是创造时间价值、场所价值和一定的加工价值的活动。物流是指物质实体从供应者向需求者的物理移动，它由一系列创造时间价值和空间价值的经济活动组成，包括运输、保管、配送、包装、装卸、流通加工及物流信息处理等多项基本活动，是这些活动的统一。

1990 年以来，全球互联网络以不可思议的速度迅猛发展，与之相生相伴的是贸易、物流、信息全球化的步伐开始加快。尤其是 WTO 取代 GATT 后，全球化的趋势更是不可遏止，由此，更带来了现代物流业的飞速发展。

互联网促进了全球化，同样，物流系统也可像互联网般，促进全球化。贸易上，若要与世界联系，必须倚赖良好的物流管理系统。市场上的商品很多是"游历"各国后才来到消费者面前的。产品的"游历"路线正是由物流师计划、组织、指挥、协调、控制和监督的，使各项物流活动实现最佳的协调与配合，以降低物流成本，提高物流效率和经济效益。

进入 21 世纪后，以新型流通方式为代表的连锁经营、物流配送、电子商务等产业在中国发展迅速，服务业对整个国民经济的发展越来越重要。物流服务业被誉为是"21 世纪最具发展潜力"的行业之一，并且已经成为中国经济新的增长点。

随着社会主义市场经济体制的建立，我国逐步建立了一个比较完整的物流教育体系。然而，随着社会对物流人才需求数量的急剧上升，人才供需矛盾日益显现。总体上看，我国高校大多仍处在自行设计课程与实践的阶段，与境外物流产业人才相比，差距主要体现在人员素质以及物流知识和技能与实践脱节等方面。

物流学科是一门综合学科，物流产业是一个跨行业、跨部门的复合产业，同时又具有劳动密集型和技术密集型相结合的特征。发展物流专业高等职业教育是完善物流教育多层次体系的需要，也是满足对物流人才需求多样化的需要。

2004 年 1 月，电子工业出版社组织全国各地 30 余所高职院校的优秀教师编写了"高等职业教育物流管理专业"系列规划教材，时隔 6 年，如今该系列教材大部分已经修订到第 3 版，在此期间，全国有百余所院校使用过这个系列的教材，获得了任课教师和学生的普遍好评。其中多种教材被评为"普通高等教育'十一五'国家级规划教材"，这更是对教材质量的肯定。

近年来，高等职业院校教学改革和课程改革稳步推进，不断深化。为使教材更好地适应市场，方便教师教和学生学，编者不断收集和征求一线教师的意见和建议，紧随物流行业发展趋势，认真调研并分析物流企业各个岗位的实际需求，不断修正和完善书中的内容，使教材内容最大限度的贴近实际岗位要求。

新版教材保留了上一版教材的精髓，同时弥补了上一版教材的不足。在内容方面体现了物流领域的新知识、新技术、新思想、新方法；在编写方法上坚持"岗位"引领、"工作过程"导向，突出"实用性、技能性"，提高学生动手能力，注重现实社会发展和就业的需求。

相信新版教材更加贴合学校教学，更为适应企业对技能型人才的需要，希望修订教材的出版和使用能为培养优秀的物流专业人才起到积极地推动作用。

黄有方

教育部物流专业教学指导委员会　副组长
中国物流学会　副会长
上海海事大学　副校长
2010 年 10 月

前　言

　　本书是物流专业英语教材，内容包括物流系统、供应链管理、货物运输、库存、物流信息、储存、搬运、配送、包装、物流单证、函电和电子商务各方面的专业基础知识和专业英语表述。根据物流业发展状况，本版对各部分内容进行了必要的更新和调整。

　　在前两版的基础上，编者进行了锤炼和完善。本书采用"主、副"课文制。每章分三课，前两课为主课文，是该章的基本专业知识。对主课文从注解和练习两方面进行了重点处理，用做教师课内重点讲解的内容。第三课为副课文，较主课文略有难度，介绍物流专业相关的新技术、新理念和一些国际著名企业的个案分析，主要供学有余力的学生课后自学或学生英文程度较好的学校选择授课。

　　每篇课文后的练习用以巩固专业英语的语言知识，提高学生的英语能力，思考题紧扣课文内容以促进对有关内容的掌握。教师可根据学生情况将思考题布置为口头练习或书面作业，以加强学生的口语和写作能力。课堂活动设计和新增的听力训练，有利于活跃课堂气氛，增强课堂互动性，既巩固了专业知识又培养了学生的英语交际能力。

　　本书紧密结合专业知识，结构严谨，内容新颖，知识面广，注重实践操作相关知识，是物流专业教师与英语教师合作的结晶，既保证了专业知识的系统性，也保证了英语语料的真实性。本书不仅是物流专业学生学习专业英语的优秀教材，也是高等学校工商管理类专业学生学习物流专业知识，提高专业英语水平不可多得的读本。本书附有详细的教师参考资料、多媒体课件和听力材料，以方便教师授课。

　　本书由宁波大学庄佩君任主编，王晓萍和施敏任副主编，参加编写的还有宁波工程学院陈金山老师。各位编者均长期从事物流管理课程的双语教学和专业英语教学，有着丰富的编写经验。

　　由于编写时间仓促，作者水平有限，书中难免存在不足之处，敬请广大读者批评指正。

编　者

前　言

Contents
目 录

Chapter 1 Logistics System

Chapter Outline ·· (1)
Part I Introduction to Logistics System ·· (2)
Part II The Relationship of Logistics Activities to Logistics Costs ··········· (7)
Part III Supplementary Reading
        Royal Caribbean Cruises Ltd. ·· (12)

Chapter 2 Supply Chain Management

Chapter Outline ·· (16)
Part I Concept of Supply Chain Management ··· (17)
Part II Supply Chain Strategies ·· (21)
Part III Supplementary Reading
        Supply-Chain Management of Volkswagen ······························· (27)

Chapter 3 Freight Transport

Chapter Outline ·· (32)
Part I Function and Modes of Transportation ··· (33)
Part II Container Transportation and Inter-modal Transport ···················· (37)
Part III Supplementary Reading
        Transport Participants ·· (41)

Chapter 4 Inventory Management

Chapter Outline ·· (46)
Part I Concept and Purposes of Inventory ·· (47)
Part II Inventory Types and Inventory Management ······························· (51)
Part III Supplementary Reading
        Just-In-Time Inventory Management ·· (56)

Chapter 5 Logistics Information

Chapter Outline ·· (60)
Part I Logistics Information System ··· (61)

Part II   Logistics Software ·· (66)
Part III   Supplementary Reading
           Cisco's E-commerce Connection ··································· (71)

Chapter 6   Warehousing

Chapter Outline ··· (74)
Part I   Warehousing Activities ·· (75)
Part II   Types of Warehousing ··· (79)
Part III Supplementary Reading
          Cross-docking ·· (83)

Chapter 7   Material Handling

Chapter Outline ··· (88)
Part I   Material Handling System ·· (89)
Part II   Mechanized Materials Handling Equipment ················ (93)
Part III Supplementary Reading
          Safety in Material Handling ··· (97)

Chapter 8   Packaging

Chapter Outline ··· (102)
Part I   Packaging Perspective ·· (103)
Part II   Packaging Design ·· (106)
Part III Supplementary Reading
          Packaging Materials ··· (110)

Chapter 9   Physical Distribution

Chapter Outline ··· (114)
Part I   Physical Distribution ··· (115)
Part II   Distribution Center ··· (119)
Part III Supplementary Reading
          An Integrated System of DC ·· (122)

Chapter 10   Correspondence

Chapter Outline ··· (126)
Part I   Business Letters ··· (127)
Part II   Electronic Correspondence ··· (131)
Part III Supplementary Reading
          Specimen Correspondence ·· (137)

Chapter 11   Logistics Documents 1

Chapter Outline ·· （142）
Part I   Government Documents ··· （143）
Part II   Commercial Documents (1) ··· （153）
Part III   Supplementary Reading
             Commercial Documents (2) ·· （162）

Chapter 12   Logistics Documents 2

Chapter Outline ·· （169）
Part I   Transport Documents (1) ·· （170）
Part II   Transport Documents (2) ·· （178）
Part III   Supplementary Reading
             Transport Documents (3) ·· （189）

Appendix I   Logistics Terms
··· （198）

Appendix II   World Famous Logistics Companies
··· （203）

Appendix III   Global Sea Ports
··· （209）

参考文献
··· （215）

Chapter 1 Logistics System

Chapter Outline

Part I   Introduction to Logistics System

The role of Logistics
The definition of Logistics
The definition of Logistics management
Components of a Logistics System

    Customer service
    Demand forecasting/planning
    Inventory management
    Logistics information
    Material handling
    Order processing

    Packaging
    Procurement
    Return goods handling
    Reverse logistics
    Transportation
    Warehousing

Part II   The Relationship of Logistics Activities to Logistics Costs

Customer Service Levels
Transportation Costs
Warehousing Costs
Order Processing /Information Systems Costs
Lot Quantity Costs
Inventory Carrying Costs

Part III   Supplementary Reading

Royal Caribbean Cruises Ltd.
    The Replenishment of Cruise Ships is Daunting
    Material Requirement of a Cruise Ship
    Distribution and Material Handling
    Purchasing and Supplier Management

Part I Introduction to Logistics System

The Historical Perspective of Logistics

Logistics starts from military

Logistics is a concept familiar to students of military history. Long associated with the distribution and supply of armed forces in wartime, logistics is proving to be a source of the victory of a campaign.

In the early part of 1991 the world was given a dramatic example of the importance of logistics. During the Gulf War it had been necessary for the United States and its allies to move huge amounts of material great distances in what were thought to be impossibly short time-frames. Half a million people and over half a million tones of material and supplies were airlifted 12,000 kilometers with a further 2.3 million tones of equipment moved by sea—all of this achieved in months.

Logistics in the Second World War

In the Second World War logistics also played a major role. The Allied Forces' invasion of Europe was a highly skilled exercise in logistics, as was the defeat of Rommel in the desert. Rommel himself once said that "…before the fighting proper, the battle is won or lost by quartermasters".

The Modern Perspective of Logistics

Logistics is recognized only recently

However while the Generals from the earliest times have understood the critical role of logistics, it is only in the recent past that business organizations have come to recognize the vital impact that logistics management can have in the achievement of competitive advantage.

This lack of recognition partly comes from the low level of understanding of the benefits of integrated logistics.

It has taken a further 70 years or so for the basic definition of logistics and the basic principles of logistics management to be clearly defined.

The Concept of Logistics

Logistics focus on customers

At its heart, logistics deals with satisfying the customer. A basic definition of logistics is the continuous process of meeting customer needs by ensuring the availability of the right benefits for the right customer, in the quantity and condition desired by that customer, at the time and place the customer wants them, all for a price the buyer is willing to pay.

The Definition of Logistics Management

Definition of Logistics Management by CLM

Then what is logistics management in the sense that it is understood today? There are many ways of defining logistics. The Council of Supply Chain Management Professionals (CSCMP) defines that: "Logistics management is that part of supply chain management that plans, implements, and controls the efficient, effective forward and reverse flow and storage of goods, services, and related information between the point of origin and the point of consumption in order to meet customers' requirements."

Components of a Logistics System

A logistics system can be made up of many different functional activities, some of which are described briefly below.

Customer service

● **Customer service**: Customer service is the output of a logistics system. It involves getting the right product to the right customer at the right place, in the right condition and at the right time, at the lowest total cost possible.

Demand forecasting /planning

● **Demand forecasting/planning:** Logistics usually becomes involved in forecasting how much should be ordered from its suppliers, and how much of finished product should be transported or held in each market. In some firms, logistics may even plan production.

Inventory management

● **Inventory management:** Inventory management involves the balance of the level of inventory held to achieve high customer service levels with the cost of holding inventory.

Logistics information

● **Logistics information:** Information links all areas of the logistics system together. Information processing is becoming increasingly automated, complex, and rapid. It is the key to the efficient functioning of system.

Material handling

● **Material handling:** Material handling is a broad area concerning all movements of raw materials, work in process, or finished goods within a factory or warehouse.

Order processing

● **Order processing:** Order processing is the system a firm has for getting orders from customers, checking on the status of orders and communicating to customers about them, and actually filling the order and making it available to the customer.

Packaging

● **Packaging**: Packaging can convey important information to inform the customer and provide protection during storage and transport. Pleasing packaging also can attract the customers' attention.

Procurement

● **Procurement**: Procurement is the purchase of materials and services from outside to support the firm's operations from production to marketing, sales, and logistics.

Return goods handling

● **Return goods handling**: Returns may take place because of a problem with the performance of the item or simply because the customer changed mind. Return goods handling is complex and costly.

Reverse logistics

● **Reverse logistics**: Reverse logistics is involved in removal and disposal of waste materials left over from the production, distribution, or packaging processes.

Transportation

● **Transportation**: Transportation involves selection of the mode, the routing of the shipment, compliance with regulations in the region of the country, and selection of the carriers.

Warehousing

● **Warehousing**: Warehousing and storage activities relate to warehouse layout, design, ownership, automation, training of employees, and related issues.

New Words and Expressions

Logistics [lə'dʒistiks]n.		物流，后勤
Familiar [fə'miljə]adj.		熟悉的，常见的
Military ['militəri]adj.		军事的，军用的
Associate [ə'səuʃieit]vt.		使发生联系，使联合
Ally [ə'lai, æ'lai] n.		同盟国
Airlift ['eəlift]vt.		空运
Quartermaster ['kwɔːtəmɑːstə(r)] n.		军需官
Critical ['kritikəl]adj.		危急的，临界的
Vital ['vaitl]adj.		重大的，至关重要的
Impact ['impækt]n.		碰击，影响
Availability [ə,veilə'biliti]n.		可用性，有效性，实用性
Implement ['implimənt]vt.		实施，执行
Conform [kən'fɔːm]vt.		使一致，依照，遵照
Forecast ['fɔːkɑːst]vt.		预测
Inventory ['invəntri]n.		存货，库存
Defective [di'fektiv]adj.		有缺陷的
Procurement [prə'kjuəmənt]n.		采购

NOTES

1. Rommel

隆美尔，纳粹德国陆军元帅，第二次世界大战时任北非战场德军司令官。

2．The Council of Logistics Management (CLM) of America

美国物流管理协会，是美国物流界的一个专业团体，1963 年成立。

3．A basic definition of logistics is the continuous process of meeting customer needs by ensuring the availability of the right benefits for the right customer, in the quantity and condition desired by that customer, at the time and place the customer wants them, all for a price the buyer is willing to pay.

物流的基本概念是按顾客期望的数量和条件，在顾客需要的时间和地点，以顾客愿意支付的价格，确保合适的顾客的合理利益的可获得性而满足顾客需要的连续过程。

4. Logistics management is that part of supply chain management that plans, implements, and controls the efficient, effective forward and reverse flow and storage of goods, services, and related information between the point of origin and the point of consumption in order to meet customers' requirements.

物流管理是对从初始点至消费点之间为了满足客户需求而对物品、服务和相关信息有效快速的前向或逆向的流动和储存所进行的计划、实施、控制的那部分供应链管理。

EXERCISES

I. Phrases translation

物流管理   零配件和服务支持

客户服务   工厂及仓库选址

物资搬运   存货管理

订单处理   逆向物流

需求预测   产出点

退货处理   消费点

II. Fill in the blanks and put the sentences into Chinese

1．A basic definition of logistics is the continuous process of _____by ensuring the availability of the _____benefits for the _____customer, in the quantity and condition desired by that customer, at the _____and place the customer wants them, all for a price the buyer is willing to pay.

2．Customer service involves getting the _____product to the right customer at the right place, in the ____condition and at the right time, at the lowest _____possible.

3．_____is key to the efficient functioning of system.

4. Order processing is the system a firm has for getting _____from customers, checking on the _____of orders and communicating to _____about them, and actually_____ the order and making it available to the customer.

5．Factory and warehouse site selection is a _____decision that affects the costs of _____, customer service _____and _____of response.

6．_____is involved in removal and disposal of waste materials left over from the production, _____, or packaging processes.

III. Fill out the following table according to the information you get from the text

Components of a logistics system	Important factors
Inventory management	
Logistics information	
Material handling	
Order processing	
Packaging	
Procurement	
Reverse logistics	
Transportation	
Warehousing	

IV. Listen to the conversation, and answer the question or complete the sentences

1. Who have become the most powerful companies in the global economy, big multi-national manufacturers or global retailers?

2. What is the secret for the success of Wal-Mart?

3. What was Sam Walton's formula?

4. Wal-Mart today is setting a new standard that other firms have to follow if they hope to compete. What is the new standard?

5. Wal-Mart was originally set up by _____ in _____(year) _____, Arkansas.

6. Wal-Mart is so powerful that it is referred as a _____.

V. Challenging questions for discussion

1. What is the logistics?
2. In your opinion, what is the importance of logistics?
3. Please give a definition of logistics management.
4. What activities may be considered part of the overall logistics process?
5. Why do we say determining the location of the company and warehouse is a strategic decision?
6. Why does return goods handling occur in a company?
7. What is reverse logistics?

Part II   The Relationship of Logistics Activities to Logistics Costs

Logistics costs are created by the activities that support the logistics process. Each of the major costs—customer service, transportation, warehousing, order processing and information, lot quantity and inventory carrying—is discussed below.

Customer Service Levels

The key cost associated with varying levels of customer service is the cost of lost sales. Monies that are spent to support customer service include the costs associated with order fulfillment, parts, and service support. They also include the costs of return goods handling, which has a major impact on a customer's view of the organization's service as well as the final level of customer satisfaction.

Cost of lost sale

The cost of lost sales includes not only the lost of the current sale, but also potential future sales from the customer and from other customers due to word-of-mouth negative publicity from former customers. A recent estimate indicated that every unsatisfied customer tells an average of nine others about his or her dissatisfaction with the product or service. It is no wonder that it is extremely difficult to measure the true cost of customer service!

The objective is to minimize total costs

Thus, the best approach is to determine desired levels of customer service based on customer needs. The idea is to minimize the total cost, given the customer service objectives. Because each of the other five major logistics cost elements work together to support customer service, good date are needed regarding expenditures in each category.

Transportation Costs

The activity of transporting goods causes transportation costs. Expenditures that support transportation can be viewed in many different ways. Costs can be categorized by customer, product line, type of channel such as inbound versus outbound, and so on. Costs vary with volume of shipment (cube), weight of shipment, distance, and point of origin and destination. Costs and service also vary with the mode of transportation chosen.

Warehousing Costs

Warehousing costs are created by warehousing and storage activities, and by the plant and warehouse site selection process. Included are all of the sites that vary due to a change in the number or location of warehouses.

Order Processing/Information Systems Costs

This category includes costs related to activities such as order processing, distribution communications, and forecasting demand. Order processing and information costs are a very important investment to support good customer service levels and control costs. Order processing costs include such costs as order transmittal, order entry, processing the order, and related internal and external costs such as notifying carriers and customers of shipping information and product availability. Shippers and carriers have invested a great deal in improving their information systems, to include technology such as electronic data interchange (EDI), satellite data transmission, and bar coding and scanning shipments and sales.

Lot Quantity Costs

The major logistics lot quantity costs are due to procurement and production quantities. Lot quantity costs are purchasing- or production-related costs that vary with changes in order size or frequency. Lot quantity costs must not be viewed in isolation because they also may affect many other costs. For example, a customer goods manufacturer that produces large production runs may get good prices from suppliers and have long efficient production runs, but requires more storage space to handle large runs. Customer service levels may suffer as order fulfillment declines because products are produced infrequently, in large batches, and with inventory going to zero and creating stockout situations in between runs. This may increase information and order processing costs, as customers frequently call to check on availability of back-ordered products, and cancel back orders.

Transportation costs also may rise as customers are sent partial or split shipments. Inventory carrying costs will rise as large quantities of inventory are held until used up, due to large batch sizes. The implication of one cost upon another must be carefully considered.

Inventory Carrying Costs

The logistics activities that make up inventory carrying costs include inventory control, packaging, and salvage and scrap disposal. Inventory carrying costs are made up of many elements. The relevant inventory costs are those that vary with the amount of inventory stored including the four major categories as following:

The relevant inventory costs are those that vary with the amount of inventory

1. **Capital cost**, which is the return that the company could make on the money that it has tied up in inventory.

2. **Inventory service cost,** which includes insurance and taxes on inventory.

3. **Storage space cost,** which includes those warehousing space-related costs which change with the level of inventory.

4. **Inventory risk cost,** including obsolescence, stealing, relocation within the inventory system, and damage.

New Words and Expressions

Expenditure [iks'penditʃə, eks-] *n.*	支出，花费	
Category ['kætigəri] *n.*	种类，类别	
Destination [ˌdesti'neiʃən] *n.*	目的地	
Inbound ['inbaund] *adj.*	入站，进货	
Outbound ['autbaund] *adj*	出站，出货	
Vary ['vɛəri] *vt.*	不同	
Communication [kəˌmju:ni'keiʃn] *n.*	信息，交流	

Forecast ['fɔ:kɑ:st] n. & vt.	预测
Transmittal [trænz'mitəl] n.	传送，传输
Order entry	订单输入
Internal cost [in'tə:nl] adj.	内部成本
External cost [eks'tə:nl] adj.	外部成本
Notify ['nəutifai] v.	通报，通知
Availability [ə,veilə'biliti] n.	可用性，可获得性
Satellite data transmission [trænz'miʃən]	人造卫星数据传输
Lot quantity	批量
Purchase ['pə:tʃəs] vt. n.	购买
Frequency ['fri:kwənsɪ] n.	频率，周率
Isolation [,aisəu'leiʃən] n.	隔绝，孤立
Order fulfillment [ful'filmənt]	履行订单
Decline [di'klain] v. & n.	降，下倾
Back order	延期交货
Stockout n.	缺货
Batch [bætʃ] n.	批次
Inventory carry cost	存货储存成本
Salvage ['sælvidʒ] v.	抢救
Scrap [skræp] v.	敲碎

NOTES

1. They also include the costs of return goods handling, which has a major impact on a customer's view of the organization's service as well as the final level of customer satisfaction.

它们（指用来支持客户服务的成本）还包括退货处理成本，这对客户对组织的印象及最终满意程度有重要影响。

2. The idea is to minimize the total cost, given the customer service objectives. Because each of the other five major logistics cost elements work together to support customer service, good date are needed regarding expenditures in each category.

其目标是在给定的客户服务水平下，实现总成本最小。由于其他五类主要的物流成本要素一起支撑着客户服务，因此需要知晓每类支出的信息。

3. Costs can be categorized by customer, product line, type of channel such as inbound versus outbound, and so on.

（运输）成本可以根据客户、生产线、渠道类型（如进货、出货）进行分类。

4. Order processing costs include such costs as order transmittal, order entry, processing the order, and related internal and external costs such as notifying carriers and customers of shipping information and product availability.

订单处理成本包括订单传送、订单输入、处理订单及相关的内外部成本（如告知承运人及客户有关运输信息和货物可获得性情况）。

5．…because products are produced infrequently, in large batches, and with inventory going to zero and creating stockout situations in between runs.

……由于产品生产不连续、批量大，并且库存趋于零而导致（订货）同期之间产生缺货。

6．This may increase information and order processing costs, as customers frequently call to check on availability of back-ordered products, and cancel back orders.

如果客户经常要求查询延迟订购货物的可获得性或取消延迟订货，那么会进一步引起信息及订单处理成本的增加。

EXERCISES

I．Phrases translation

物流成本	条码
销售损失	内部成本
退货处理成本	外部成本
潜在的销售	订单传输
运输成本	订单输入
进货渠道	批量成本
出货渠道	缺货
订单处理成本	库存持有成本
需求预测	资金成本
销售沟通	仓储空间成本
电子数据交换系统	风险成本
卫星数据传输	

II．Fill in the blanks and put the sentences into Chinese

1．Customer service cost are the monies spent to support customer service, include the costs associated with _____, parts and service support.

2．The cost of lost sales includes not only _____, but also potential future sales.

3．The objective of customer service management is to minimize_____, given the customer service level.

4．Transportation cost vary with _____, weight of shipment, _____, and point of origin and destination.

5．Order processing costs include such costs as _____, order entry, processing the order, and related internal and external costs.

6．Lot quantity costs are _____-related costs that vary with changes in order size or frequency.

III. Discuss with your partner and complete the following table on the main logistic costs and the factors that influence the costs

Main logistic costs	Important factors that influence the cost

IV. Challenging questions for discussion or writing training

1. Can you measure the true cost of customer service? Support your reply.
2. Explain the concept of the cost of customer service.
3. Give examples of order processing costs.
4. Explain the affect of lot quantity cost.
5. Explain the relevant inventory costs that vary with the amount of inventory.

Part III   Supplementary Reading

Royal Caribbean Cruises Ltd.

The Replenishment of Cruise Ships is Daunting

One of the most daunting logistics jobs in the world is planning and implementing the replenishing of a cruise ship. Literally thousands of items, ranging from fresh bed linen to engine parts to perishable foodstuffs, must arrive at the vessel by a hard-and-fast deadline. "Every week brings a new crisis," said Jim Walton, director of materials and logistics for Royal Caribbean Cruises Ltd. in Miami. "Recently, 1,500 pounds of lamb didn't make it to a vessel in time, so a chartered plane flew the lamb to the ship in Mexico." "Cruise ships are moving targets. You only have a short window to get what's critically needed to them. Otherwise, the captain doesn't wait around," he said.

Material Requirement of a Cruise Ship

As Cruises ship designers emphasized passenger amenities and cabin space over stowage space, the 90-day provisioning has been reduced to 14 days in all areas. This change transferred a huge responsibility to logistics to replenish ships in various out ports. On this basis, logistics have one opportunity to ensure all goods arrive within a six-to-eight hour window. The itinerary for each Royal Caribbean vessel is planed two years in advance. With that data in hand, Walton's logistics department publishes a container load schedule, which specifies vendor delivery dates, by commodity for each vessel, over a six-month period. For each ship there are delivery dates for chilled produce, frozen food, dry goods, bonded marine items, and gift shop and hotel items. The logistics department ships everything from blocks of ice to uniforms and tuxedoes; all manner of food stuffs; radar domes, navigation equipment, floral arrangement, spare parts for machinery in a vessel's engine room, even chemicals for each ship's photo—developing shop.

Distribution and Material Handling

Royal Caribbean owns 17 vessels—12 operated by Royal Caribbean International and five by Celebrity Cruises. Walton's 22-person staff handles logistics for all of the ship. "We work seven days a week, 24 hours a day. We load ships on weekends, working 10 to 12 hour days. We stagger our schedules so that some personnel are here all of the time, even on holidays. There are no days off for the logistics department." Walton's organization spends much of its time overseeing the physical handling of goods for the ships. A supplier may send a shipment covering eight different vessels. Walton's department segregates those goods by vessel and by service sector — beverage，hotel，gift shop, marine (meaning the functioning of the ship), entertainment, cruise programs, aquatics and hotel services. "We have to build specific pallets for each sector or department, and label them as such," he said. The reason is that goods are loaded on a cruise ship through different doors or hatches. When cargo arrives pier side, it must go aboard through the proper door. Royal Caribbean's cruise ships load at a rate of 40 pallets an hour, taking on a total of about 200 in five to six hours. At the same time, at least 2,000 passengers are boarding over other gangways.

Purchasing and Supplier Management

Royal Caribbean regularly uses a core group of about 400 vendors. The company buys through distributors, especially on the hotel and food and beverage side, but negotiates many of its contracts directly with manufactures. Distributors service the agreements, and maintain inventory stocks. "We try to keep as little inventory on hand as possible, and order on a just- in- time basis," Walton said. "If a vendor fails us, then they are charting a plane at their expense.

If they ship the wrong product, or something that wasn't according to specification, they have to get the right product to the vessel at the next port of call. If that means arranging for an aircraft immediately, then they have to do it."

(Source: Mottley, Robert "logistics for a floating city."
American shipper, December 1998, pp. 24-9)

New Words and Expressions

Cruise ship [kru:z]		邮轮
Daunting [ˈdɔːntiŋ] *adj.*		令人畏缩的
Implement [ˈimplimənt] *v.*		实施，执行
Replenish [riˈpleniʃ] *v.*		补给，补充
Amenity [əˈmiːniti] *n.*		舒适，便利
Cabin space [ˈkæbin] *n.*		客舱
Stowage space [ˈstəuidʒ]		货舱
Provision [prəˈviʒən] *n.*		供给
Outport [prəˈviʒən] *n.*		大港外的独立小港
Itinerary [aiˈtinərəri, iˈt-] *n.*		路线
Vendor [ˈvendɔː] *n.*		卖主
Chilled produce [tʃild] *adj.*		冷冻产品
Tuxedo [tʌkˈsiːdəu] *n.*		男士无尾半正式晚礼服
Radar dome [ˈreidə] [dəum] *n.*		天线屏蔽器，雷达天线屏蔽器
		雷达无线罩
Navigation equipment [ˌnæviˈgeiʃən] *n.*		导航设备
Floral arrangement [ˈflɔːrəl] *adj.*		插花艺术
Segregate [ˈsegrigeit] *v.*		隔离
Beverage [ˈbevəridʒ] *n.*		饮料
Pallet [ˈpælit] *n.*		托（货）盘
Hatch [hætʃ] *n.*		舱口，舱口盖
Pierside [piə] *n.*		码头
Distributor [disˈtribjutə] *n.*		经销商

NOTES

1. Cruise ships are moving targets. You only have a short window to get what's critically needed to them. Otherwise, the captain doesn't wait around.

邮船是一个活动目标，你只能通过一个窄小的窗口将他们最急需的东西送进去，否则，船长们是不会等候的。

2. As Cruises ship designers emphasized passenger amenities and cabin space over stowage space…

由于邮轮设计时，更强调乘客的舒适度，提高了客舱空间，而控制了货舱空间……

3. The reason is that goods are loaded on a cruise ship through different doors or hatches.

这是因为那些货物是通过不同的舱门或舱口而装入到邮轮上的。

4. At the same time, at least 2,000 passengers are boarding over other gangways.

与此同时，至少有 2000 名乘客正通过其他舷梯上岸旅游。

5. Distributors service the agreements, and maintain inventory stocks.

经销商执行协议，并且保持库存存量。

EXERCISES

Questions for discussion or writing

1. Explain why replenishment of a cruise ship is considered to be a most daunting logistics job.

2. Give some specific requirement of materials.

3. What logistics ctivities Royal Caribbean performing accrording to "the component parts of a logistics system" in Part I?

4. Explain the process of material handling abroad a cruise ship.

5. How does Royal Caribbean manage the suppliers and distributors?

6. Do you like the challenge of the logistic job of a cruise company? Defend your answer.

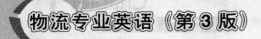

Chapter 2 Supply Chain Management

Chapter Outline

Part I   Concept of Supply Chain Management

Development of the concept

Definition of supply chain management

Strategic importance of the supply chain

Supply chain management is highly customer-oriented

Types of supply chain strategies

Market driven

Freshness oriented

Logistics optimizer

Operationally agile

Customer-guided

Trade focused

Part II   Supply Chain Strategies

Five supply chain strategy

Many-suppliers strategy

Few-suppliers strategy

Vertical integration

Keiretsu networks

Virtual companies

Part III   Supplementary Reading

Supply-Chain Management of Volkswagen

Redesign the Distribution Supply Chain in Volkswagen of America

Innovation of Manufacturing Supply Chain Management

Part I Concept of Supply Chain Management

Development of the Concept

SCM is an extension of logistics

The concept of supply chain management is relatively new. It is in fact the third phase of an evolution that started in the 1960s with the development of the physical distribution concept, which focused on the outbound side of a firm's logistics system. Logistics management is basically concerned with optimizing flows within the organization, while supply chain management extends such internal integration to the outside of the organization.

The initial focus on physical distribution or outbound logistics was logical since finished goods were usually higher in value, which meant that their inventory, warehousing, materials-handling, and packaging costs were relatively higher than their raw materials inputs. In U.S.A., a national organization, the National Council of Physical Distribution Management (NCPDM), was organized to foster leadership, education, research, and interest in the area of physical distribution management.

Supply chain management came into vogue during the 1990s and continues to be a focal point for making organizations more competitive in the global marketplace. Supply chain management can be viewed as a pipeline for the efficient and effective flow of products/materials, services, information, and financials from the supplier's suppliers through the various intermediate organizations/companies out to the customer's customers (see Fig. 2.1) or the system of connected networks between the original suppliers and the ultimate final consumer.

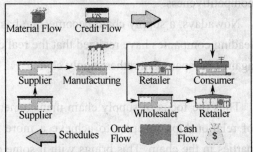

Fig.2.1 An Integrated Supply Chain

Definition of Supply Chain Management

Definition of SCM

Supply chain management (SCM) is viewed by some individuals to be narrowly focused and/or focused upon supplies and materials, not demand for finished products.

Broadly and comprehensively, SCM is the art and science of integrating the flows of products and materials, information (as order and schedules), and financials (as credit and cash) through the entire supply pipeline from the supplier's supplier to the customer's customer. It could be argued that supply chain, demand chain, value network, value chains, etc., can be used as synonyms.

Practically, Supply chain management is the integration of the activities that procure materials and services, transform them into intermediate goods and final products, and deliver them to customers. These activities include purchasing and outsourcing activities, plus many other functions that are important to the relationship with suppliers and distributors.

Strategic Importance of the Supply Chain

Role of SCM

The concept of supply chain management provides a perspective to view the total system of interrelated companies for increased efficiency and effectiveness. The supply chain arrangement links a firm and its distributive and supplier network to end customers. The integrated value-creation process must be managed from material procurement to end-customer product delivery.

The integrated supply chain management shifts traditional channel arrangements from loosely linked groups of independent businesses that buy and sell inventory to each other toward a coordinated initiative to increase market impact, overall efficiency, continuous improvement, and competitiveness.

Competition between supply chains

Nowadays, a supply chain becomes the basic unit of competition. The leading companies have realized that the real competition is not company against company but rather supply chain.

SCM focus on the channel relationship management

Thus the focus of supply chain management is upon the management of relationships in order to achieve a more profitable outcome for all parties in the chain. This brings with it some difficulties since there may be occasions when the narrow self-interest of one party has to be included for the benefit of the chain as a whole.

The context of an integrated supply chain is the firms' relationship management within a framework as capacity limitations, information, core competencies, capital, and human resource problems.

SCM is highly Customer-oriented

Integration of SCM depends on technology

Supply chain management is highly customer-oriented. "supply chain integration really begins with the goal of satisfying consumer demand," says LaHowchic, the President and CEO of Limited Logistics Services Co., "This fundamental belief impacts everything we do in the supply chain. We seek to raise the level of quality throughout the chain to more effectively respond to consumer demand. And to do this, we need to optimize information and product flows through interdependent linked business processes—from the sourcing of raw materials all the way to the sale of the finished products."

Transportation and information play important role in SCM

Technology is an essential tool of this supply chain integration process. Limited Logistics Services Co. has implemented a transportation management system to handle the worldwide flow of goods and a warehouse management system for inventory management and replenishment operations.

In LaHowchic's opinion, information systems will play an even more prominent role in enabling the firm's total supply chain capabilities. He believes that supply chain management can add value in a number of important ways.

SCM Strategies

With the numerous advantage of supply chain integration, its management can be a complex challenge. A recent study revealed six different, but equally successful, supply chain strategies.

Six strategies for SCM

- **Market Driven**: Focusing on generating high profit margins through strong brands and ubiquitous marketing and distribution.
- **Operationally Agile**: Configuring assets and operations to react nimbly to emerging consumer trends along lines of product category or geographic region.
- **Freshness Oriented**: Concentrating on earning a premium by providing the consumer with product than competitive offerings.
- **Consumer-guided**: Building and maintaining close relationships with end consumers through direct sales.
- **Logistics Optimizer**: Emphasizing a balance of supply chain efficiency and effectiveness.
- **Trade Focused**: Prioritizing "low price, best value" for the consumer (as with the logistics optimizer strategy but focusing less on brand than on dedicated service to trade customers).

New Words and Expressions

Foster ['fɔstə] *vt.*		培养，促进
Vogue [vəug] *n.*		时尚，流行样式
Intermediate [,intə(:)'mi:diət] *adj.*		中间的，中级的
Procure [prə'kjuə] *vt.*		取得，获得
Prominent ['prɔminənt] *adj.*		突出的，显著的
Capability [,keipə'biliti] *n.*		能做某事的素质；能力
Ubiquitous [ju:'bikwitəs] *adj.*		普遍存在的；无处不在的
Agile ['ædʒail] *adj.*		灵活的，机敏的
Nimbly ['nimbli] *adj.*		灵活的，敏捷的
Premium ['primjəm] *n.*		保险费，奖金
Offering ['ɔfəriŋ] *n.*		提供，献礼

NOTES

1. SCM is the art and science of integrating the flows of products and materials, information (as order and schedules), and financials (as credit and cash) through the entire supply pipeline from the supplier's supplier to the customer's customer.

供应链管理是从供应商的供应商到客户的客户的整个供应管道中，对产品流、信息流（如订单和时间表）、资金流（如信用卡和现金）予以整合的艺术和科学。

2. The integrated supply chain management shifts traditional channel arrangements from loosely linked groups of independent businesses that buy and sell inventory to each other toward a coordinated initiative to increase market impact, overall efficiency, continuous improvement, and competitiveness.

集成的供应链管理将传统的渠道安排转变成协调的行动，来增加市场影响力，提高整体效率，持续改进以及提高竞争力；传统的渠道安排则是一群松散地联系着的买卖库存品的独立企业。

3. The context of an integrated supply chain is the firms' relationship management within a framework as capacity limitations, information, core competencies, capital, and human resource problems.

集成供应链的内涵是公司的公共关系管理，包括能力限制、信息、核心竞争力、资金以及人力资源问题。

EXERCISES

I. Phrases translation

供应链	人力资源
最终用户	上游供应商
供应链管理	供应链整合

货物流   下游企业

核心能力   物资供应

信息流

II. Fill in the blanks and put the sentences into Chinese

1．Supply chain management is the system of connected networks between the _____ and the ultimate _____.

2．Supply chain management is the integration of the activities that _____materials and services, _____ them into intermediate goods and final products, and _____ them to customers.

3．_____will play an even more prominent role in enabling the firms' total supply chain capabilities.

4．Supply chain integration really begins with the goal of _____.

5．The six supply chain strategies include market driven, _____, freshness oriented, consumer-guided, _____ and _____ .

III. 🎧Listen to the interview, and answer to the following questions

1．What is the push system?

2．What is the pull system?

3．What was set up by the manufacturers in Bentonville?

4．What should the manufacturers pay attention to when bargaining with Wal-Mart buyers?

5．Why is Wal-Mart said to have changed a 100-year history?

6．What can Wal-Mart achieve in the one-sided business practices?

IV. Challenging questions for discussion:

1．What is the supply chain?

2．What definition will you give for supply chain management?

3．Discuss the difference between logistics and supply chain management.

4．Why is supply chain management highly customer-oriented?

5．What does a recent study reveal supply chain strategies?

Part II Supply Chain Strategies

Five Supply Chain Strategies

For those items to be purchased, companies must decide upon a supply-chain strategy. One such strategy is the traditional approach of negotiating with many suppliers and playing one supplier against another. A second strategy is to develop long-term, "partnering" relationships with a few suppliers. A third strategy is vertical integration, where firms may buy the supplier. A fourth strategy is keiretsu, in which suppliers become part of a company coalition. Finally, a fifth strategy is virtual companies. We will discuss each of these strategies.

Many Suppliers

With the many-supplier strategy, the supplier responds to the demands and specifications of a "request for quotation", with the order usually going to the low bidder. This strategy plays one supplier against another and places the burden of meeting the buyer's demands on the supplier. Suppliers aggressively compete with one another. Although many approaches to negotiations can be used with this strategy, long-term "partnering" relationships are not the goal. This approach holds the supplier responsible for maintaining the necessary technology, expertise, and forecasting abilities, as well as cost, quality, and delivery competencies.

Few Suppliers

A strategy of few suppliers implies that rather than looking for short-term attributes, such as low cost, a buyer is better off forming a long-term relationship with a few dedicated suppliers. Long-term suppliers are more likely to understand the broad objectives of the procuring firm and the end customer. Using few suppliers can create value by allowing suppliers to have economies of scale that yields both lower transaction costs and lower production costs.

Advantages of few-suppliers strategy

Few suppliers, each with a large commitment to the buyer, may also be more willing to participate in JIT systems, as well as provide innovations and technological expertise. However, the most important factor may be the trust that comes with compatible organization cultures. A champion within one of the firms often promotes a positive relationship between purchase and supplier organizations by committing resources toward advancing the relationship, further strengthen the partnership.

DaimlerChrysler's few-suppliers strategy

Many firms have moved aggressively to incorporate suppliers into their supply system. DaimlerChrysler, for one, now seeks to choose suppliers even before parts are designed. Motorola also evaluates suppliers on rigorous criteria, but in many instances has eliminated traditional supplier bidding, placing added emphasis on quality and reliability.

Downsides of few-suppliers strategy

Like all strategies, a downside exists. With few suppliers, the cost of changing partners is huge, so both buyer and supplier run the risk of becoming captives of the other. Poor supplier performance is only one risk the purchaser faces. The purchaser must also be concerned about trade secrets and suppliers that make other alliances or venture out on their own.

Vertical Integration

Purchasing can take the form of vertical integration. By vertical integration, we mean developing the ability to produce goods or services previously purchased or actually buying a supplier or a distributor. As shown in Fig. 2.2, vertical integration can take the form of forward ro backward integration.

Backward integration

Forward integration

Backward integration suggests a firm purchase its suppliers, as in the case of Ford Motor Company deciding to manufacture its own car radios. Forward integration, on the other hand, suggests that a manufacturer of components make the finished product. An example is Texas Instruments, a manufacturer of integrated circuits that also makes calculators and computers containing integrated circuits.

Advantage of vertical integration

Vertical integration can offer a strategic opportunity for the operations manager. For firms with the necessary capital, managerial talent, and required demand, vertical integration may provide substantial opportunities for cost reduction. Other advantages in inventory reduction and scheduling can accrue to the company that effectively manages vertical integration or close, mutually beneficial relationships with suppliers.

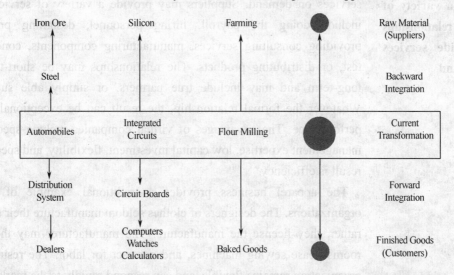

Fig.2.2   Vertical Integration Can Be Forward or Backward

Many organizations find interest in vertical integration nowadays. Vertical integration can yield cost reduction, quality adherence, and timely delivery. Vertical integration appears to work best when the organization has large market share or the management talent to operate an acquired vendor successfully. However, backward integration may be particularly dangerous for firms in industries undergoing technological change if management cannot keep abreast of those changes or invest the financial resources necessary for the next wave of technology.

Keiretsu Networks

Keiretsu is Japanese term to describe suppliers who become part of a company coalition

Many large Japanese manufacturers have found a middle ground between purchasing from few suppliers and vertical integration. These manufacturers are often financial supporters of suppliers through ownership or loans. The supplier then becomes part of a company coalition known as a keiretsu. Members of the keiretsu are assured long-term relationships and are therefore expected to function as partners, providing technical expertise and stable quality production to the manufacturer. Members of the keiretsu can also have suppliers further down the chain, making second-and even third-tier suppliers part of the coalition.

Virtual Companies

Virtual companies rely on a variety of supplier relationships to provide services on demand

Virtual companies rely on a variety of supplier relationships to provide services on demand. Suppliers may provide a variety of services that include doing the payroll, hiring personnel, designing products, providing consulting services, manufacturing components, conducting test, or distributing products. The relationships may be short-term or long-term and may include true partners, or simply able suppliers. Whatever the formal relationship, the result can be exceptionally lean performance. The advantages of virtual companies include specialized management expertise, low capital investment, flexibility, and speed. The result is efficiency.

The apparel business provides a traditional example of virtual organizations. The designers of clothes seldom manufacture their designs; rather, they license the manufacture. The manufacturer may then rent rooms, lease sewing machines, and contract for labor. The result is an organization remains flexible, and can respond rapidly to the market.

New Words and Expressions

Vertical ['və:tikəl]*adj.*	垂直的，纵向的
Integration [,inti'grei∫ən] *n.*	集成，整合
Backward ['bækwəd]*adj.*	后向的，倒向的
Coalition [,kəuə'li∫ən] *n.*	联盟，联合
Virtual ['və:tjuəl, -t∫uəl] *adj.*	虚拟的
Quotation [kwəu'tei∫ən]*n.*	报价，行情
Bidder ['bidə]*n.*	投标者
Aggressive [ə'gresiv]*adj.*	激进地
Attribute [ə'tribju(:)t]*n.*	特性，属性
Economy of scale	规模经济
Foster ['fɔstə]*v.*	培养
Alignment [ə'lainmənt] *n.*	结盟
Incorporate [in'kɔ:pəreit] *v.*	把……合并
Rigorous ['rigərəs] *adj.*	严密的，严格的
Downside ['daun,said] *n.*	缺陷
Alliance [ə'laiəns] *n.*	联盟，同盟
Forward ['fɔ:wəd] *adv.*	向前的，向末端的
Integrated circuit ['sə:kit] *n.*	集成电路
Substantial [səb'stæn∫əl]*adj.*	大量的，可观的
Undergo *v.*	经历，遭受
Keep abreast of [ə'brest]	与……并进，跟上，不落后
Fluid ['flu(:)id] *adj.*	不固定的，易变的
Payroll *n.*	工资单
Lean *adj.*	精益的，精细的
Apparel [ə'pærəl] *n.*	服装

NOTES

1. …and playing one supplier against another.

（竞争中）一家挤兑另一家。

2. With the many-supplier strategy, the supplier responds to the demands and specifications of a "request for quotation," with the order usually going to the low bidder .

在多供应商战略中，各供应商对采购方的询价中的需求和规格做出回应，订单往往为报价较低者所获得。

3. Motorola also evaluates suppliers on rigorous criteria , but in many instances has eliminated traditional supplier bidding, placing added emphasis on quality and reliability.

摩托罗拉公司也用严格的标准来评价各供应商，但很多时候，出于质量和可信度考虑，它不采用传统的投标方法来选择供应商。

4. By vertical integration, we mean developing the ability to produce goods or services previously purchased or actually buying a supplier or a distributor.

纵向整合是指本企业发展生产那些之前需要从企业外部购买的产品和服务，或者直接收购供应商或分销商。

5. Other advantages in inventory reduction and scheduling can accrue to the company that effectively manages vertical integration or close, mutually beneficial relationships with suppliers.

能够有效地进行纵向整合并和供应商保持亲密、互利合作关系的企业也将获得在降低库存和订货方面的优势。

6. Vertical integration appears to work best when the organization has large market share or the management talent to operate an acquired vendor successfully.

如果企业占有很大的市场份额并能很好地操控供应商，在这种情况下纵向整合将会发挥其最大的效益。

7. Members of the keiretsu can also have suppliers further down the chain, making second-and even third-tier suppliers part of the coalition.

企业集团成员也可以联合供应链更下游的供应商，让第二、甚至第三层供应商成为联盟的一员。

EXERCISES

I. Phrases translation

供应链战略   虚拟企业

多供应商战略   前向整合

少数供应商战略   后向整合

纵向整合战略   规模经济

企业集团   成本降低

II. Fill in the blanks and put the sentences into Chinese

1. With the many-supplier strategy, the supplier responds to the _____ and _____ of a "request for quotation," with the order usually going to the _____. This strategy plays one supplier against another and places the burden of meeting the buyer's demands on the _____.

2. Long-term suppliers are more likely to understand the _____ of the procuring firm and end customer. Using few suppliers can create value by allowing suppliers to have _____ that yields both lower _____ and lower _____.

3. With few suppliers, both buyer and supplier run the risk of becoming _____ of the other. Poor supplier performance is only one risk the purchaser faces. The purchaser must also be concerned about _____ and suppliers that make other alliances or venture out on their own.

4. Vertical integration can take the form of _____ or _____ integration.

III. Please complete the following table and discuss with your partner the advantages and disadvantages of five supply chain strategies

Supply chain strategy	*Advantages*	*Disadvantages*
Many suppliers		
Few suppliers		
Vertical integration		
Keiretsu networks		
Virtual companies		

IV. Challenging questions for discussion

1. Explain the main strategies for supply-chain management, and their objective?
2. Explain the basic approach of many-supplier strategy.
3. What is the advantage and downside of few-suppliers tactic?
4. Give examples of backward and forward vertical integration.
5. What do you know about Japanese company coalition?
6. Explain the virtual companies strategy with an example.

Part III   Supplementary Reading

Supply-Chain Management of Volkswagen

Redesign the Distribution Supply Chain in Volkswagen of America

VoA works with 750 dealer sites across USA

Volkswagen of America (VoA), a wholly owned subsidiary of Volkswagen AG, imports, markets and distributes Volkswagen and Audi vehicles in the United States. The vehicles are assembled in Mexico or Germany and distributed to a network of approximately 750 dealer sites across the United States. In 1995, VoA management appointed a project team with the mandate to review vehicle distribution process and develop new concepts or supply chain management.

The existing SCM takes dealer as customer, not the end user

POS carries significant inventory

The existing vehicle distribution process had served the organization over a number of years. The existing system had been developed around two implicit assumptions. The first is that the dealer (retail operator) is the "customer" of the VoA distribution process, not the end user. The logic was that Volkswagen of America distributes to the dealer and the dealer distributes to the end user. The second assumption was that, significant vehicle inventory (60-90 days of sales) carried by the dealer operator creates an incentive (financing cost avoidance) to increase the rate of sales. Thus the distribution system operated as a "push" system. Efficiency was the key performance criteria. These assumptions, in fact, reflect the dominant logic of vehicle distribution the U.S. auto industry.

Limitation of Push System

Different interests of the dealer and the end users

The push system does have significant limitations. One is that not all customers are able to purchase their first choice configuration of vehicle color and optional equipment. Many manufacturers offer many more vehicle configurations than individual dealers are able to inventory (even carrying 60-90 days of sales). Dealers, who are interested in completing sales transactions as quickly as possible generally offer customers the selection vehicles from their current inventory. If the current inventory does not contain the customer's first choice configuration the dealer may offer a price discount as incentive for the customer to accept a non first choice vehicle. Although this process often does result in a consumer purchasing a vehicle, the transaction is inefficient. Both parties have compromised to a common date of an inventory shortfall. The end user has not received his choice of vehicle and the dealer has unnecessarily discounted the price.

Higher logistic costs

A second limitation of the push system is the high system (importer + dealer) costs of transportation, financing and storage. Vehicles are inventoried at point of sale, the most expensive location in the entire distribution chain. In short, the push system is only coincidentally responsive to customer choices and it maintains large inventories at point of sale.

The project team at VoA was searching for a means to deal with these limitations. As a design principle for the new distribution system, the project team had rejected both of the above mentioned assumptions. The new system had to serve the end user's requirements as its key performance measure. The new system would have to be, first and foremost, responsive to end user choices and simultaneously more efficient than the current system. From these new principles the following performance criteria were established that the reengineered process would have to meet:

New criteria for performance

1. Maximize the percentage of customers who received their first choice of vehicles.

2. If a customer's first choice was not in a dealer's inventory, a first choice vehicle would be delivered to the dealer from VoA inventory within 48 hours.

3. Significantly reduce the total system (dealers and VoA) costs associated with transportation, financing and storage primarily through inventory reduction.

The project team developed a number of logistics concepts that alternatively managed where inventory might be aggregated and how it might be transported. However, they did not have an effective means of testing the concepts. The complexity and scope of the system made static analysis of limited value. Simulation was identified as a potentially effective means of testing the concept and various scenarios of implementation.

Innovation of Manufacturing Supply Chain Management

In its new Brazilian plant 100 miles northwest of Rio de Janeiro, Volkswagen is altering its supply chain. With this experimental truck factory, Volkswagen is sure that it has found a system that will reduce the number of defective parts, cut labor costs, and improve efficiency. Because VW's potential market is small, this is a relatively small plant, with scheduled production of only 100 trucks per day with only 1,000 workers. However, only 200 of the 1,000 work for Volkswagen. The VW employees are responsible for over quality, marketing, research, and design. The other 800, who work for suppliers such as Rockwell International, Cummins Engines, Delga Automotiva, Remon, and VDO, do the assembly work.

Tasks of VW's employee

The objective of the new supply chain

Volkswagen's innovative supply chain will, it hopes, improve quality and drive down costs, as each subcontractor accepts responsibility for its units and worker compensation. With this strategy, Volkswagen subcontractors accept more of the direct costs and risks.

As the schematic shows, at the first stop in the assembly process, workers from Lochpe-Maxion mount the gas tank, transmission lines, and steering blocks. As the chassis moves down the line, employees from Rockwell mount axles and brakes. Then workers from Remon put on wheels and adjust tire pressure. The MWM/Cummins team installs the engine and transmission. Truck cabs, produced by the Brazilian firm Dlga Automotiva, are painted by Eisenmann and then finished and upholstered by VDO, both of Germany. Volkswagen employees do an evaluation of the final truck.

Outsourcing and supply chain integration

Because technology and economic efficiency demand specialization, many firms, like Volkswagen, are increasing their commitment to outsourcing and supply-chain integration. At this Volkswagen plant, however, VW is buying not only the materials but also labor and the related services. Suppliers are integrated tightly into VW's own network, right down to the assembly work in the plant.

Because purchase costs in the auto industry exceed 60% of the sales dollar, even modest reductions in these costs could make Volkswagen's payoff substantial. The results are not in yet, but VW is already trying a similar approach in plants in Buenos Aires, Argentina, and with Skoda, in the Czech Republic. Volkswagen's new level of integration in supply-chain management may be the wave of the future.

Emphasis on procurement and supplier relationships

Most firms, like VW, spend more than 50% of their sales dollars on purchases. Because such a high percentage of an organization's costs are determined by purchasing, relationships with suppliers are becoming increasingly integrated and long-term. Joint efforts that improve innovation, speed design, and reduce costs are common. Such efforts, when part of an integrated strategy, can dramatically improve both partners' competitiveness. This changing focus places added emphasis on procurement and supplier relationships which must be managed. The discipline that manages these relationships is known as supply-chain management.

New Words and Expressions

Subsidiary [səb'sidjəri] *n.*　　　　　　附属事物，子公司
Mandate ['mændeit] *n.*　　　　　　　授权
Implicit [im'plisit] *adj.*　　　　　　无疑问的
Criteria [krai'tiəriə](criterion 的复数) *n.*　　标准，准则
Configuration [kən,figju'reiʃən] *n.*　　构造，形状，轮廓
Incentive [in'sentiv] *n.*　　　　　　激励，刺激，动机
Shortfall ['ʃɔ:tfɔ:l] *n.*　　　　　　　不足之量，差额
Simultaneously [siməl'teiniəsli]*adv.*　　同时地
Aggregate ['ægrigeit]*vt. & vi.*　　　　（使）聚集
Static ['stætik] *adj.*　　　　　　　不发展的，静止的
Simulation [,simju'leiʃən]*n.*　　　　模仿，模拟

Chassis [ˈʃæsi] *n.*   底盘，底架
Upholster [ʌpˈhəulstə] *vt.*   装潢
Schematic [skiˈmætik] *adj.*   纲要的，概略的

NOTES

1. Thus the distribution system operated as a "push" system. Efficiency was the key performance criteria.

因此，分销系统作为一个"推式"系统而运作。效益是关键绩效指标。

2. The new system would have to be, first and foremost, responsive to end user choices and simultaneously more efficient than the current system.

首先也是最重要的是，新的系统将必须对最终用户的选择做出反应，同时比现行系统更为有效。

3. Because purchase costs in the auto industry exceed 60% of the sales dollar, even modest reductions in these costs could make Volkswagen's payoff substantial.

在汽车行业，由于采购成本超过销售金额的 60%，即使对这些费用进行很小的削减就可以使大众汽车获得可观的收益。

4. Volkswagen of America (VoA)

美国大众公司（简称 VoA）

EXERCISES

I. Phrases translation

Distribution process	Distribution chain
Existing system	Design principle
The end user	User's requirements
Vehicle configurations	Supply-chain integration
Inventory shortfall	Supply-chain management

II. Challenging questions for discussion

1. What are the limitations of the push system?
2. What are the characteristics of the new system under design?
3. Why do Volkswagen subcontractors accept more of the direct costs and risk?
4. What are the advantages of the supply-chain integration?
5. Discuss the supply-chain management of VW.

Chapter 3 Frieight Transport

 **Chapter Outline**

Part I   Functions and Modes of Transportation

Introduction to transportation

Functions of transportation

  Product movement

  Product storage

Five modes of transportation：

  Rail transport   Road transport

  Pipeline transport   Air transport

  Water transport

Part II   Container Transportation and Inter-modal Transport

Container transportation

The business courses in container transport

  The course of full container load

  The course of less container load

Inter-modal transportation

Containers

  The advantage of container

  The disadvantage of container

Part III   Supplementary Reading

Transport Participants

  Carrier agents Government

  Shipper and Consignee

  Internet

  Public

Part I   Function and Modes of Transportation

Introduction

Overview of transportation

Transportation is one of the most significant areas of logistics management because of its impact on customer service levels and the firms' cost structure. Transportation refers to the physical movement of goods from a point of origin to a point of consumption and can involve raw materials being brought into the production process/or finished goods being shipped out to the customer. Transportation is a very visible element of logistics. Consumers are accustomed to seeing trucks and trains transporting product or parked at business facilities. Few consumers fully understand just how dependent our economic system is upon economical and dependable transportation.

Functions of Transportation

Transport Functionality

Transportation enterprises provide two major services: product movement and product storage.

Product Movement

Whether in the form of materials, components, work-in-process, or finished goods, the basic value provided by transportation is to move inventory to the next stage of the business process. The primary transportation value proposition is product movement up and down the supply chain. The performance of transportation is vital to procurement, manufacturing, and market distribution. Transportation also plays a key role in the performance of reverse logistics. Without reliable transportation, most commercial activity could not function. Transportation consumes time, financial, and environmental resources.

Transportation performance is vital

Product Storage

A less visible aspect of transportation is product storage. While a product is in a transportation vehicle, it is being stored. Transport vehicles can also be used for product storage at shipment origin or destination, but they are comparatively expensive storage facilities. Since the main value proposition of transportation is movement, a vehicle committed to storage is not otherwise available for transport. A trade-off exists between using a transportation vehicle versus temporarily placing products in a warehouse. If the inventory involved is scheduled to move within a few days to a different location, the cost of unloading, warehousing, and reloading the product may exceed the temporary charge of using the transportation vehicle for storage.

So although costly, product storage in transportation vehicles may be justified from a total cost or performance perspective when loading or unloading costs, capacity constraints, and ability to extend lead times are considered.

Five Modes of Transportation

Five modes of transportation

The five primary modes of transportation are rail, road, pipeline, water, and air. Each has different economic and service characteristics. The logistics manager must consider a number of trade-offs when selecting a mode of transportation: cost versus speed, packaging expense versus risk of damage, flexibility versus dependability. These are all very complex issues. For example, if hazardous material is to be moved by air, it may require more and different kinds of packaging than would be required by a motor carrier. Furthermore, most movements involve the services of more than one mode of transport.

Rail transportation

Railroads offer the logistics manager cost-effective, energy-efficient transport of large quantities of goods over long distances. Though often associated with the movement of low-value/high-volume cargo like coal, railroads also move a large number of containers in inter-modal movements. Rail movements are virtually unconstrained with respect to size, weight, or volume, but fixed tracks can limit their ability to provide complete customer support. For example, if both the shipper and receiver possess railroad sidings, then door-to-door service can be provided. However if no sidings are available, the movement of goods must be completed by some other mode. Similarly, on-time delivery and frequency of service may not be as responsive as with other modes simply because multiple handlings are more common in rail movements.

Road transportation

Road transport offers more flexibility and versatility to the shipper than virtually any other form of transportation. This mode tends to be used for higher-value/lower-volume cargo than that moved by rail and can offer essentially door-to-door service from seller to buyer. However, the global logistics manager will find that trucking can vary dramatically from country to country.

Pipelines

Pipelines are primarily used to move petroleum, natural gas, and chemicals. For suitable commodities, pipelines are the most efficient mode of transport. They offer a closed system with little risk of loss or damage to the products moved, and extremely low costs because minimal labor is involved in their operation. However, they typically serve a limited area over fixed routes. In addition, they only offer one-way service, although product can move 24 hours per day, seven days per week. Though naturally limited in their application, pipelines have been utilized to move coal and are being evaluated for other types of freight as well.

Air transport

Air transport is often viewed as a premium, emergency-type service that is used when all else fails. The most expensive of all the modes, airfreight offers the logistics manager fast, on-time service, but at a relatively high price. However, for firms supporting global markets, air may in fact be the most cost-effective mode of transport when inventory and customer service issues are considered.

Air transportation is best suited to moving relatively small high-value/low-volume items long distances, although things as diverse as livestock and automobiles routinely move by air as well. Like trucking, the air transport industry is made up of many small companies dominated by a few large airlines. Many of the world's air carriers are government owned or controlled to some degree situation that is slowly changing as governments are moving to put their airlines into private hands.

Water transport

Water transport occurs on inland waterways (i.e. rivers, lakes, and canals) and oceans. Though slower than other modes, this form of movement is also relatively inexpensive. Traffic moving on inland waterways tends to be low value high volume: coal, building materials, agricultural products, etc. However, in countries like Germany, with its vast network of navigable rivers, the variety of freight moved by water carriers may include bulk products, containers, and motor-vehicles.

In general, domestic water carriers compete with railroads for freight, relying on their price advantage to offset the slow transit time. Ocean-going ships, on the other hand, carry all types of cargo, although increasingly that freight moves in containers that are stacked on top of each other aboard the vessel. Air transport competes with ocean shipping, but the high cost and limited carrying capacity make air movement prohibitive for many items. In fact, rail may also compete via land-bridge services such as that provided by the Trans Siberian railway, which moves containers from the Far East across Russia to Western Europe that would otherwise go by ship.

New Words and Expressions

Dependable [di'pendəbl] adj.	可靠的	
Diversion [dai'vəːʃən] n.	转移，转向	
Unconstrained ['ʌnkən'streind] adj.	非强迫的，出于自然的，未受约束的	

Premium ['primjəm] *n.*	奖金，佣金，保险费
Cost effective	节省成本的，划算的
Dominate ['dɔmineit] *v.*	支配，控制，
Prohibitive [prə'hibitiv, prəu-] *adj.*	禁止的，抑制的
Inaccessible [,inæk'sesəbl] *adj.*	达不到的，难得的

NOTES

1. its impact on customer service levels
它对顾客服务水平的影响

2. in the performance of reverse logistics
在逆向物流性能的表现中

3. A trade-off exists between using a transportation vehicle versus temporarily placing products in a warehouse.
在利用交通工具（储存）与将产品暂时存入仓库之间要权衡选择。

4. Rail movements are virtually unconstrained with respect to size, weight, or volume.
铁路运输事实上是不受尺寸、重量和体积方面的限制的。

5. Air may in fact be the most cost-effective mode of transport when inventory and customer service issues are considered.
在考虑到库存和客户服务时，航空运输实际上是最节省成本的运输模式。

EXERCISES

I. Form Phrases

产品移动　　　　　　　　　　　门到门
product _____　　　　　　Door-to-_____
在途库存　　　　　　　　　　　有效利用能源
in-transit _____　　　　　　　_____-efficient
危险品　　　　　　　　　　　　灵活性和通用性
_____ material　　　　　　　_____ and versatility
远洋运输　　　　　　　　　　　建筑材料
_____ ships　　　　　　　　　_____ materials
价格优势　　　　　　　　　　　跨西伯利亚铁路
Price _____　　　　　　　　　_____ railway

II. Fill in the blanks and put the sentences into Chinese

1. Consumers are accustomed to _____ at business facilities.

2. Transportation cost results from _____, and

36

administration.

3. They offer a closed system with _____ moved, and extremely low costs because minimal labor is involved in their operation.

4. However, for firms supporting global markets, air may in fact be _____ when inventory and customer service issues are considered.

III. Group work (Work in a group of five)

Design a shipping business, suppose each of you were the representative of specific carrier of a transportation mode, explain the advantages of your mode and your company.

IV. Challenging questions for discussion

1. Explain the important role transportation plays in logistics system.
2. Why is transportation one of the most costly elements in logistics?
3. Describe the function of transportation as product storage.
4. Describe the five modes of transportation and their characteristics.

Part II   Container Transportation and Inter-modal Transport

Container Transportation

What is container transport

The transportation of international trading is nowadays frequently carried out in containers. Scheduled ocean container operations now provide the key liner cargo services between the main markets of the industrialized world. Roll-on/roll-off operations are also flourishing on long-haul routes due to their "flexibility", while this same factor is similarly contributing to the important growth of unitized services to developing areas of the world. Other forms of unitized services, such as pallets and LASH barges, are also used.

Advantage of containers

Containers are particularly suitable for inter-modal transport. If the goods have to pass through three stages of transportation, viz., they are first carried by land, then by sea, and finally again by land, they will travel in the same container from the place of loading to that of discharge and the physical labor as well as the cost of conveying them from one vehicle of transportation to the next are saved. In addition, the danger of theft and pilferage is reduced.

The Business Courses in Container Transport

The business courses in container transport is that the exporter, having made arrangements with a forwarder or directly with the office of a

The course for FCL

container shipping line, sends his goods to the nearest container loading depot of the forwarder or shipping line. These depots, called container freight stations (CFSs), are situated in all major industrial centers inland or at the ports.

If the exporter intends to fill a full container load (FCL), the forwarder or shipping line will be prepared to send an empty container to the exporter for loading. If the exporter has arranged for the delivery of the goods to the overseas buyer's place of business, the container would be a door-to-door container. It is important that the door-to-door container is properly sealed with the carrier's seal, this is sometimes done by the shipper, and in other cases by the driver of the collecting vehicle. The exporter should make sure of this because, if there is a claim for shortage of or damage to the cargo carried in the container, the state of the carrier's seal may allow an inference of what has happened. If it is broken, it would indicate that the cargo has been tampered with during the transport.

The course for LCL

If the cargo is less than a full container load (LCL), the exporter sends it to the container freight station, where it will be consolidated with the goods of other exporters in a groupage container. On arrival at the place of destination it will be taken to a container freight station, where it will be "de-grouped", i.e., the parcels contained therein will be separated and delivered to the various consignees.

Inter-modal Transportation

Concept of inter-modal transport

Inter-modal transportation refers to the movement of a shipment from origin to destination utilizing two or more different modes of transport. At its heart, however, the term refers to how goods are moved between those modes. Certainly the transfer could be done by hand. That is, each individual box is unloaded from, for example, a ship, and reloaded piece by piece onto a railroad car. This manual technique is time consuming, and increases the chance of theft, loss, and damage. Today the term inter-modal transportation denotes a systematic transfer of goods from one mode to another in a way that minimizes handling and total transit time. (This definition implies that freight being shifted from mode to mode in some non-systematic fashion is really not being handled inter-modally rather it is moving multi-modally via two or more different forms of transportation.) This exchange may mean placing a trailer onto a rail flatcar for onward movement. But general inter-modal systems are structured around the use of containers.

Containers

Container sizes

A container is a metal box that resembles a trailer without wheels. It generally measures 8 feet by 8.5 feet by 20 or 40 feet, although larger containers are becoming more common. In fact the 20-foot container has become the standard unit of measure, with ship capacities, for example, quoted in terms of "TEUs" or twenty-foot equivalent units. (One 40-foot container equates to two TEUs: six 20-foot and five 40-foot containers equal 16TEUs, and so on.) The container can be mounted onto a frame with wheels facilitating truck movement: cranes lift the container off the frame so that the boxes can then be stacked aboard ships or rail cars.

The advantage of containers

The advantage of containers from the shipper's point of view is that freight can be loaded and the box sealed before it leaves the warehouse. From this point on, only the container is handled: the goods themselves are not touched again until the customer receives the container and opens it.

The disadvantage of containers

Containers, however, have a restricted application in inland transport. Because containers on ships must be stacked, they must be sturdy in construction. In turn, this makes them heavy—too heavy for road transport since they unduly restrict payloads. Consequently, in Europe the preferred technologies for combined transport restricted to inland movements are unaccompanied road-rail transport, and accompanied road-rail transport.

The whole intent of inter-modal transport is to allow the shipper to take advantage of the best characteristics of all modes: the convenience of motor freight, the long-distance movement efficiency of rail, and the capacity of ocean shipping.

New Words

Flourishing [ˈflʌriʃiŋ] *adj.*		繁荣的
Inter-modal transport		多式联运
Forwarder [ˈfɔːwədə] *n.*		代理人
Unitize [ˈjuːnitaiz] *v.*		使成为一电位或一整体
Pilferage [ˈpilfəridʒ] *n.*		偷窃，赃物
Groupage *n.*		使成组，拼箱
Shortage *n.*		短缺
Equate [iˈkweit] *vt.*		使相等，同等对待
Unduly [ʌnˈdjuːli] *adv.*		过度地，不适当地
Shipper [ˈʃipə] *n.*		托运人
Carrier [ˈkæriə] *n.*		承运人

Consignee [kənsai'ni:] *n.* 　　　　收货人

NOTES

1. Scheduled ocean container operations now provide the key liner cargo services between the main markets of the industrialized world.

现在定期的远洋集装箱班轮运营在工业化世界的主要市场之间提供了重要的班轮货运服务。

2. Roll-on/roll-off operations

滚装运输

3. LASH: lighter abroad ship

一种将驳船放在大船上的运输方式

4. The term inter-modal transportation denotes a systematic transfer of goods.

多式联运这个词表示货物的系统化转运。

5. This exchange may mean placing a trailer onto a rail flatcar for onward movement.

这种变换意味着把拖车放到火车平板车厢上继续运输。

EXERCISES

I. Form Phrases

多式联运	工业中心
_____ transport	_____ center
空箱	装货地
Empty _____	Place of _____
拼箱	系统化转运
_____ container	_____ transfer
公铁运输	长距离运输
_____ transport	_____ movement

LASH: _____ 　　　　　　　　CFS: _____

FCL: _____ 　　　　　　　　　LCL: _____

TEU: _____

II. Fill in the blanks and put the sentences into Chinese

1. In addition, the danger of theft and _____ is reduced.

2. These depots, called container freight stations (CFSs), are _____ or at the ports.

3. But general inter-modal _____ of containers.

4. Containers, however, have a restricted _____ transport.

5. The advantage of containers from the shipper's _____ before it leaves the warehouse.

III. Challenging questions for discussion

1. Explain the concept of container.
2. What are the advantages of container transportation?
3. Describe the meaning of inter-modal transportation.
4. Describe the advantage of inter-modal transportation.

Part III Supplementary Reading

Transport Participants

Overview of Transport Participants

Overview of transport participants

The transportation environment impacts the decisions that can be implemented in a logistical system. Transportation decisions are influenced by six parties: (1) shipper; (2) destination party, traditionally called the consignee; (3) carriers and agents; (4) government; (5) Internet; and (6) the public.

The following figure illustrates the relationship among the involved parties. To understand the complexity of the transportation environment, it is useful to review the role and perspective of each party.

The relationship of the participants

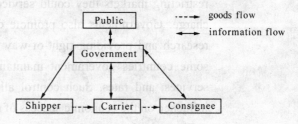

Shipper and Consignee

The interests of the shipper and consignee

The shipper and consignee have a common interest in moving goods from origin to destination within a given time at the lowest cost. Services related to transportation include specified pickup and delivery times, predictable transit time, and zero loss and damage as well as accurate and timely exchange of information and invoicing.

Carrier Agents

Why carrier agents are needed

The carrier, a business participant that performs a transportation service, desires to maximize its revenue for movement while minimizing associated costs. As a service business, carriers want to charge their customers the highest rate possible while minimizing labor, fuel, and vehicle costs required to complete the movement. To achieve this objective, the carrier seeks to coordinate pickup and delivery times in an effort to group or consolidate many different shippers' freight into movements that achieve economy of scale and distance. Brokers and freight forwarders are transport agents that facilitate carrier and customer matching.

Government

Why government is interested in transportation

The government has a vested interest in transportation because of the critical importance of reliable service to economic and social well-being. Government desires a stable and efficient transportation environment to support economic growth.

A stable efficient transportation environment requires that carriers provide essential services at reasonable cost. Because of the direct impact of transportation on economic success, governments have traditionally been more involved in the practices of carriers than in most other commercial enterprises. In some situations, such as the United States Postal Service, government is directly involved in providing the transportation service. Government traditionally regulated carriers by restricting markets they could service and regulating prices they could charge. Governments also promote carrier development by supporting research and providing right-of-way such as roadways and airports. In some countries government maintains absolute control over markets, services, and rates. Such control allows government to have a major influence on the economic success of regions, industries, or firms.

The overall nature of transportation regulation has changed significantly over the past three decades.

Internet

Internet-based communication

Marketplaces of Web-based enterprises

A recent development in the transportation industry is a wide assortment of Internet-based services. The primary advantage of Internet-based communication is the ability of carriers to share real time information with customers and supplies. In addition to direct Internet communication between businesses engaged in logistical operations, a wide variety of Web-based enterprises have been launched in recent years. Such Web-based enterprises typically provide two types of marketplaces. The first is a marketplace to exchange information for matching carrier freight capacity with available shipments. These Web-based services may also provide a marketplace to facilitate transactions.

Beyond freight matching a second form of Internet-based information exchange relates to the purchase of fuel, equipment, parts, and supplies. Information exchange operating over the Internet provides carriers the opportunity to aggregate their purchasing and identify opportunities across a wide range of potential vendors.

Real time information exchange

Finally, the use of the Internet as a communications backbone is rapidly changing the nature of transportation operations. The availability of real time information is improving shipment visibility to the point where tracing and tracking are no longer a challenge. In addition to real time visibility, the Internet can be used to share information concerning scheduling and capacity planning.

Public

What is the public concerned with?

The final participant of transportation system, the public, is concerned with transportation accessibility, expense, and effectiveness as well as environmental and safety standards. The public indirectly creates transportation demand by purchasing goods. While minimizing transportation cost is important to consumers, concerns also involve environmental impact and safety. The effect of air pollution and oil spillage is a significant transportation-related social issue even though there have been tremendous strides in pollution reduction and consumer safety during the past two decades. The cost of reducing the risk of environmental or vehicle accidents is passed on to consumers, who must collectively judge how much safety is necessary.

Air pollution and oil spillage

New Words

Consolidate [kən'sɔlideit] v.		巩固，加强，合并
Broker ['brəukə] n.		经纪人
Invoicing ['invɔisiŋ] n.		开发票，开清单
Freight forwarder		货运代理人
Well-being		福利
Marketplace		市场
Backbone ['bækbəun] n.		支柱，主要部分，骨干
Accessibility [ˌækəsesi'biliti] n.		易接近性，易受影响性，可理解地
Aggregate ['ægrigeit] adj. & v.		聚集的，总的

NOTES

1. The carrier, a business that performs a transportation service, desires to maximize its revenue for movement while minimizing associated costs.

承运人，即履行运输服务的商家，希望其运输收入最大化，同时相关的成本最小化。

2. Brokers and freight forwarders are transport agents that facilitate carrier and customer matching.

经纪人和货运代理人是促进承运人和客户（业务）相配的运输代理人。

3. Governments also promote carrier development by supporting research and providing right-of-way such as roadways and airports.

政府还通过支持研究和提供诸如公路和机场用地的方式以促进运输商的发展。

4. The cost of reducing the risk of environmental or vehicle accidents is passed on to consumers, who must collectively judge how much safety is necessary.

降低环境风险或交通事故的成本被转嫁到消费者。消费者必须判断多大的安全性是必要的。

EXERCISES

I. Form phrases

商业交易
Co_____ transactions

运输环境
Transportation en_____

信息流
In_____ flow

服务业务
Service b_____

合理的费用
Re_____ cost

潜在的卖主
Potential vendors

主要优势
Primary ad_____

商业企业
Commercial en_____

安全标准
Safety st_____

运输需求
Transportation de_____

II. Fill in the blanks and put the sentences into Chinese

1. The transportation environment impacts _____ in a logistical system.

2. Government desires _____ support economic growth.

3. Such control allows _____ success of regions, industries, or firms.

4. These Web-based services may _____ transactions.

5. Finally, the use of the Internet as a communications _____ operations

6. There have been tremendous strides _____ during the past two decades.

III. Challenging questions for discussion

1. How many participants are involved in transportation? What are they?
2. What does a carrier agent do in transportation?
3. Why the government has vested interest in transportation?
4. Describe the utilization of Internet in transportation.

Chapter 4 Inventory Management

Chapter Outline

Part I   Concept and Purposes of Inventory

Concept of inventory

Purpose of inventory：

    Facilitates economies of scale

    Offers a means of balancing supply and demand

    Provides protection from uncertain demand

    Specialization

    Inventory as a buffer

    Excessive inventory

Part II   Inventory Types and Inventory Management

Inventory is risky

Inventory Types：

    Manufacturer inventory

    Wholesaler inventory

    Retailer inventory

Inventory Management

New Trends of Inventory Management

    MRP & DRP

Part III   Supplementary Reading

Just-In-Time Inventory Management

    Introduction of Just-In-Time

    JIT Concept

    Advantage and Disadvantage of JIT

    Zero Inventory

Part I   Concept and Purposes of Inventory

Concept of Inventory

Inventory is costly

Inventory is a large and costly investment. Better management of firm inventories can improve cash flow and return on investment.

The inventory requirements of a firm depend on the network structure and the desired level of customer service. Theoretically, a firm could stock every item sold in a facility dedicated to serve each customer. Few business operations could afford such a large inventory commitment because the risk and total cost would be prohibitive. The objective is to achieve the desired customer service with the minimum inventory, consistent with lowest total cost.

Purposes of Inventory

Economies of scale

Facilitates economies of scale. Management may decide, for example, to purchase large quantities of an item in order to qualify for a discount. Or lower transportation costs may be realized by shipping larger quantities at one time. Similarly, a long production run may significantly reduce manufacturing costs. In every case, inventory is being utilized as a way to obtain savings in other parts of the logistics system.

Balancing supply and demand

Offers a means of balancing supply and demand. Some firms can only sell their products at certain times of the year. In order to utilize their fixed investment in buildings and equipment and maintain a skilled labor force, managers may decided to produce all year and store the finished goods until the selling season arrives.

Ensuring customer demands

Provides protection from uncertain demand. Despite management's best forecasting efforts, demand can never be known with absolutely certainty. Similarly, transport vehicles break down, raw materials may suddenly be unavailable. And manufacturing lines may stop. For all of these reasons, inventory is utilized to ensure that customer needs are met even when the production process itself is interrupted.

Inventory enables specialization

Specialization. Inventory makes it possible for a firm's plants to specialize in the products that it manufactures. The finished products can be shipped to field warehouses where they are mixed to fill customer orders. The economies that result from the longer production runs and from savings in transportation cost more than offsets the cost of additional handling.

Inventory is held throughout the supply chain

Inventory as a buffer. Inventory is held throughout the supply chain to act as a buffer for the following critical interfaces:

- Supplies-procurement (purchasing)
- Procurement-production
- Production-marketing
- Marketing-distribution
- Distribution-intermediary
- Intermediary-consumer/user

Symptoms of poor inventory management

Excessive inventory. Excessive inventories may compensate for deficiencies in basic design of a logistics network and to some degree inferior management. However, excessive inventory used as a crutch will ultimately result in higher than necessary total logistics cost. Symptoms of poor inventory management are described as following:

- Loss of customers
- Increasing number of back-orders
- Increasing investment in inventory with back-orders remaining constant
- Increasing number of orders canceled
- Periodic lack of sufficient storage space
- Deteriorating relationships with intermediaries, as typified by dealer cancellations and declining orders
- Large quantities of obsolete items

New Words and Phrases

Customer service		客户服务
Dedicated to [ˈdedikeitid] adj.		专用于
Prohibitive [prəˈhibitiv, prəu-] adj.		禁止的，抑制的，太贵的
Transport vehicles		运输工具
Specialization n.		专门化，专业化
Buffer [ˈbʌfə] n.		缓冲器
Interface [ˈintə(ː),feis] n.		界面
Procurement [prəˈkjuəmənt] n.		获得，采购
Intermediary [ˌintəˈmiːdiəri] n.		中间人，中间商
Excessive [ikˈsesiv] adj.		过量的
Deficiency [diˈfiʃənsi] n.		短缺，缺少
Compensate for [ˈkɔmpənseit]		补偿，弥补
Crutch [krʌtʃ] n.		拐杖，支撑
Symptom [ˈsimptəm] n.		症状，象征

Back order	迟延订单
Cancel *v.*	取消
Periodic [piəri'ɔdik] *adj.*	周期性的
Deteriorate [di'tiəriəreit] *v.*	恶化
Obsolete ['ɔbsəli:t] *adj.*	过期的，过时的，已废弃的

NOTES

1. The objective is to achieve the desired customer service with the minimum inventory commitment, consistent with lowest total cost.

其目标是以最小的库存保证，获得期望的客户服务，且不能与总成本最低相矛盾。

2. For all of these reasons, inventory is utilized to ensure that customer needs are met even when the production process itself is interrupted.

由于所有这些原因，库存被用于确保顾客需求得以满足，即使在生产过程本身被中断时亦然。

3. The economies that result from the longer production runs and from savings in transportation cost more than offsets the cost of additional handling.

由较长的生产运行期和运输成本节省所产生的经济效果多于补偿额外的处理费用。

4. However, excessive inventory used as a crutch will ultimately result in higher than necessary total logistics cost.

然而，被作为支撑的过量库存最终将导致不必要的物流总成本。

EXERCISES

I. Form phrases

资金周转	网络结构
cash f____	network st_____
运输成本	运输工具
tr____ cost	transport ve____
现场仓库	延期交货订单
fi____ warehouse	ba____ order
中间商	客户服务
in___	c_____ service

II. Fill in the blanks and put the sentences into Chinese

1. The inventory requirements of a firm _____ on the network structure and the _____ of customer service.

2. Similarly, transport vehicles _____, raw materials may suddenly be _____.

3. _____ these reasons, inventory is utilized to _____ customer needs are met even when the production process itself is interrupted.

4. The finished products can _____ field warehouses where they are mixed to fill customer orders.

5. Excessive inventories may _____ deficiencies in basic design of a logistics network and to some degree _____ management.

III. Complete the following table according to the given key words to get familiar with the purposes of inventory both in Chinese and English

Key word	Purposes (in English)	Purposes (in Chinese)
Economies	1.	2.
Supply and demand	3.	4.
Customer service	5.	6.
Specialization	7.	产品制造实现专业化
As a buffer	Inventory is held throughout the supply chain to act as a buffer	8.
Symptoms of poor inventory	9.	10.
Specialization	7.	产品制造实现专业化

IV. 🎧Listen to the interview, answer the following questions and complete the sentences

1. What types of inventory does Frioto Lay have?

2. What is the main raw material Frioto Lay holds?

3. How is raw material of potato changed to products in process?

4. What is MRO?

5. Frioto Lay has _____ product lines.

6. Frioto Lay has the following inventory: _____days of corn, _____ days of cornmeal, _____days oil, _____days seasoning, _____days packing film.

V. Challenging questions for discussion

1. What are the purposes of inventory?

2. When is inventory utilized?

3. Why is inventory used as a buffer?

4. What are symptoms of poor inventory management?

Part II Inventory Types and Inventory Management

Inventory Is Risky

Inventory management is risky, and the risk varies depending on a firm's position in the distribution channel. The typical measures of inventory commitment are time duration, depth and width of commitment.

Manufacturer Inventory

Manufacturer's inventory is long term

For a manufacturer, inventory risk is long term. The manufacturer's inventory commitment starts with raw material and component parts, includes work-in-process, and ends with finished goods. In addition, finished goods are often positioned in warehouses in anticipation of customer demand. In some situations, manufacturers are required to consign inventory to customer facilities. In effect, this practice shifts all inventory risk to the manufacturer. Although a manufacturer typically has a narrower product line than a retailer or wholesaler, the manufacturer's inventory commitment is deep and of long duration.

Wholesaler Inventory

Wholesaler's inventory has a economic function

A wholesaler purchases large quantities from manufacturers and sells smaller quantities to retailers. The economic function of a wholesaler is the capability to provide retail customers with assorted merchandise from different manufacturers in specific quantities. When products are seasonal, the wholesaler may be required to take an inventory position far in advance of the selling season, thus increasing depth and duration of risk. One of the greatest challenges of wholesaling is product-line expansion to the point where the width of inventory risk approaches the retailers, while depth and duration of risk remain traditional for the wholesalers. In recent years, retail clients have also forced a large increase in depth and duration by shifting inventory responsibility back to wholesalers.

Retailer Inventory

Retailer inventory risk is wide

For a retailer, inventory management is about buying and selling speed. The retailer purchases a wide variety of products and assumes a substantial risk in the marketing process. Retailer inventory risk can be viewed as wide but not deep. Due to the high cost of store location, retailers place prime emphasis on inventory turnover and direct product profitability. Inventory turnover is a measure of inventory velocity and is calculated as the ratio of annual sales divided by average inventory.

Although retailers assume a position of risk on a variety of products, their position on any one product is not deep. Risk is spread across more than 30,000 stock keeping units (SKUs)in a typical supermarket. A discount store offering general merchandise and food often exceeds 25,000 SKUs. A full-line department store may have as many as 50,000 SKUs.

How does retailer try to avoid risk

Faced with this width of inventory, retailers attempt to reduce risk by pressing manufacturers and wholesalers to assume greater and greater inventory responsibility. Specialty retailers, in contrast to mass merchandisers, normally experience less width of inventory risk as a result of handling narrower assortments; however, they must assume greater risk with respect to depth and duration of inventory holding.

If a business plans to operate at more than one level of the distribution channel, it must be prepared to assume related inventory risk. For example, the food chain that operates a regional warehouse assumes risk related to the wholesaler operation over and above the normal retail operations.

Inventory Management

What is inventory management

Inventory management is the integrated process that operates the firm's and the value chain's inventory policy. The reactive or pull inventory approach uses customer demand to pull product through the distribution channel. In other words, it is the planning which schedules product movement and allocation through the channel according to forecasted demand and product availability. Thirdly, inventory management is also the policy responding to product and market environments.

New Trend of Inventory Management

Material Requirements Planning (MRP)

How does MRP work

MRP deals specifically with supplying materials and component parts whose demand depends upon the demand for a specific end product. Essentially, MRP begins by determining how much of the final product customers desire, and when they need it. Then MRP breaks down the timing and need for components (all of which could have different lead times) based upon that scheduled end-product need. An MRP system consists of a set of logically related procedures, decision rules, and records, which are designed to translate a master production schedule into time-phased net inventory also re-plans net requirements as a result of changes. MRP minimizes inventory to the extent that the master production schedule accurately reflects what is needed to satisfy customer demand. If the production schedule does not match demand, the company will have too much of some items and too little of others. Because the master production schedule drives the need for parts, MRP is said to be a pull system. In other words, the production schedule "pulls" components through the system in order to meet manufacturing needs.

Distribution Requirements Planning (DRP)

How does DRP work

DRP is a more sophisticated planning approach that considers multiple distribution stages and the characteristics of each stage. DRP is the logical extension of manufacturing requirements planning, although there is one fundamental difference between the two techniques. MRP is determined by a production schedule that is defined and controlled by the enterprise. On the other hand, DRP is guided by customer demand, which is not controllable by the enterprise. So, while MRP generally

Comparing DRP with MRP

operates in a dependent demand situation, DRP operates in an independent environment where uncertain customer demand determines inventory requirements. The manufacturing requirements planning component coordinates the scheduling and integration of materials into finished goods. MRP controls inventory until manufacturing or assembly is completed. DRP then takes coordination responsibility once finished goods are received in the plant warehouse.

New Words and Phrases

Distribution channel	分销渠道
Duration [djuəˈreiʃən] *n.*	持续期
Component [kəmˈpəunənt] *n.*	组成部分
Consign [kənˈsain] *v.*	把……委托给，把……交付给
Inventory turnover [ˈtəːnˌəuvə]	库存周转率
Stock keeping units (SKUs)	存货单位
Typical [ˈtipikəl] *adj.*	典型的
Assortment [əˈsɔːtmənt] *n.*	分类

Setup cost	（生产）准备成本
Holding cost	持有成本
Withdraw [wið'drɔː] v.	撤退，撤回
Material Requirements Planning (MRP)	物料需求计划
Labor-hours	工时
Distribution Requirements Planning (DRP)	分销需求计划，配送需要计划
Plant warehouse	工厂仓库
Hybrid ['haibrid] n.	混合物
Assumption [ə'sʌmpʃən] n.	假设
Lead time	前置期，提前期

NOTES

1. The manufacturer's inventory commitment starts with raw material and component parts, includes work-in-process, and ends with finished goods.

生产商的库存投入起始于原材料和产品零部件，包括生产过程中的在制品，终止于制成品。

2. For a retailer, inventory management is about buying and selling velocity.

对零售商来说，库存管理与买卖的速度相关。

3. Inventory turnover is a measure of inventory velocity and is calculated as the ratio of annual sales divided by average inventory.

库存周转率是库存流通速度的一种衡量方式，计算为年销售量与平均库存的比率。

4. Inventory management is the integrated process that operates the firm's and the value chain's inventory policy.

库存管理是一个执行企业和价值链的库存政策的整合过程。

5. Purchasing, production scheduling, capacity planning, and warehouse management are a few examples of this data integration.

采购、生产进度安排、容量规划以及仓储管理是此类信息整合的少许例子。

EXERCISES

I. Form phrases

分销渠道	主生产计划
Distribution ch_____	Master_____schedule
库存周转率	前置期
Inventory _____	L_____ time
库存管理	搬运成本
Inventory m_____	C_____ cost
持有成本	容量规划

H_____ cost   Ca____ planning
生产进度安排   撤回

Production s_____   W___
工作进程中的   分类

Work-in-pr_____   A_____
存货单位

Stock _____

II. Fill in the blanks and put the sentences into Chinese

1. The typical measures of inventory commitment are time ____, ____, and ___ of commitment.

2. A wholesaler purchases ____ quantities from manufacturers and sells ____ quantities to retailers.

3. _____ the high cost of store location, retailers _____ inventory turnover and direct product profitability.

4. _____ this width of inventory, retailers attempt to reduce risk by pressing manufacturers and wholesalers to assume greater and greater _____ responsibility.

5. _____ (shortages) can be completely avoided if orders are placed at ____ time.

6. In _____, the production schedule "pulls" components through the system ____ meet manufacturing needs.

7. DRP is a _____ planning approach that considers _____ stages and the characteristics of each stage.

III. Group work

Work in a group of four. Three students play the role of a manufacturer, wholesaler and retailer respectively to discuss the risk and operations management of inventory, and one student works as a judge to mark the others' performance. You may develop your statements based on the key words given below:

Manufacturer: long term, raw material and component, work-in-process, finished goods, warehouse, customer facility
Wholesaler: assorted, seasonal, product-line expansion
Retailer: wide variety, buying and selling speed, inventory turnover

IV. Challenging questions for discussion

1. Why inventory management is risky?
2. How do retailers shift inventory responsibility to wholesalers?
3. Why is MRP called a pull system?
4. What is DRP?

Part III   Supplementary Reading

Just-In-Time Inventory Management

Introduction of Just-In-Time

**Overview of
Just-In-Time**

In the early 1970s, Toyota Motor Manufacturing developed a new production strategy that used little inventory, shortened cycle times, improved quality, and eliminated waste and costs in the supply chain.

This Just-In-Time (JIT) manufacturing management requires manufacturers to work in concert with suppliers and transportation providers to get required items to the assembly line at the exact time they are needed for production. The concept was also adopted by American and European automakers in response to the growing success of their Japanese competitors. The JIT concept then spread to other industries such as computers, and became popular in manufacturing strategies around the world.

JIT Concept

Meaning of JIT

Just-In-Time is a philosophy of continuous and forced problem solving. With JIT, supplies and components are "pulled" through a system to arrive where they are needed when they are needed. When good units do not arrive just as needed, a "problem" has been identified. This makes JIT an excellent tool to help operations managers add value by driving out waste and unwanted variability. Because there is no excess inventory or excess time in a JIT system, costs from unneeded inventory are eliminated and throughput improved. Consequently, the benefits of JIT are particularly helpful in supporting strategies of rapid response and low cost.

Advantages of JIT

Advantages

More inventory turns   Because there is less stock on hand, the inventory that is maintained stays for a shorter period of time.

Better quality   As was mentioned earlier, high quality products must be received with a JIT system, otherwise the entire benefit production process collapses.

Less warehouse space needed   When there is less inventory, fewer and/or smaller warehouses are required.

Disadvantages of JIT

Disadvantages

Risk of stock-outs   When firms eliminate inventory, the risk of stocking out can rise. Managers attempt to minimize this occurrence by demanding very high levels of service from their vendors and logistics service providers.

Increased purchasing costs   Purchasing discounts are generally associated with buying large quantities at one time. Theoretically, JIT means foregoing those price-breaks in favor of obtaining smaller amounts more frequently.

Small channel members may suffer   JIT is sometimes criticized as a system that allows strong organizations to shift their inventory to smaller firms in the channel.

Environmental issues   JIT can lead to higher levels of traffic congestion and air pollution because additional transportation is often required to maintain customer service levels in the absence of inventory.

Zero Inventory

Just-In-Time tactics are still being incorporated in manufacturing to improve quality, drive down inventory investment, and reduce other costs. However, JIT is also established practice in restaurants, where customers expect it, and a necessity in the produce business, where there is little choice.

JIT case in restaurant

Pacific Pre-Cut Produce, a $14-million fruit and vegetable processing company in Tracy, California, holds inventory to zero. Buyers are in action in the very early hours of the morning. At 6 a.m., production crews show up. Orders for very specific cuts and mixtures of fruit and vegetable salads and stir-fry ingredients for supermarkets, restaurants, and institutional kitchens pour in from 8 a.m. until 4 p.m.

Shipping begins at 10 p.m. and continues until the last order is filled and loaded at 5 a.m. the next morning. Inventories are once again zero, things are relatively quiet, and then the routine starts again. Pacific Pre-Cut Produce has accomplished a complete cycle of purchase, manufacture, and shipping in about 24 hours. VP Bob Borzone calls the process the ultimate in mass-customization. "We buy everything as a bulk commodity, then slice and dice it to fit the exact requirements of the end user. There are 20 different stir-fry mixes. Some customers want the snow peas clipped on both ends, some just on one. Some want only red bell peppers in the mix, some only yellow. You tailor the product to the customer's requirements. You're trying to meet the need of a lot of end users, and each restaurant and retailer wants to look different."

New Words and Expressions

Eliminate [i'limineit] *v.*	消除，消灭
Automaker ['ɔ:təu,meikə] *n.*	汽车制造商
Throughput ['θru:put] *n.*	产量，生产能力
Stock [stɔk] *n.*	存货
On hand	在手头上的，现有的
Traffic congestion [kən'dʒestʃən]	交通堵塞
Mass customization	大量客户化
Tactics ['tæktiks]	策略，战术
Bulk *n.*	大量，大块
Slice [slais] *v.*	切成薄片
Dice [dais] *v.*	切成小方块
Stir-fry [stə:] *n.*	用旺火炒，煎炒
Clip [klip] *n.*	修剪

NOTES

1. The JIT concept then spread to other industries such as computers, and became firmly entrenched in manufacturing strategies around the world.

准时制生产的概念推广到其他行业，诸如计算机行业，并且牢固地植根于全球制造业战略之中。

2. Because there is no excess inventory or excess time in a JIT system, costs associated with unneeded inventory are eliminated and throughput improved.

因为在准时制系统里没有多余的库存或多余的时间，所以与不必要的库存相关的成本被消除了，产量得到了提高。

3. Because there is less stock on hand, the inventory that is maintained stays for a shorter period of time.

因为在手上的存货较少，所持有的库存也只维持一较短的时间。

4. JIT can lead to higher levels of traffic congestion and air pollution because additional transportation is often required to maintain customer service levels in the absence of inventory.

在无库存条件下，经常需要增加额外的交通以保持客户服务的水平，这样准时制将导致更严重的交通堵塞和空气污染。

5. You tailor the product to the customer's requirements.

按照客户的要求，（提供）对产品进行量身定制式（的服务）。

EXERCISES

I. Form phrases

装配线   与……联合

A___ line   As___with

在手上   交通堵塞

On h_____   Traffic co_____

大量客户化   裁剪

Mass_____   Tailor

II. Fill in the blanks and put the sentences into Chinese

1. The concept was _____ by American and European automakers _____ the growing success of their Japanese competitors.

2. _____ is a philosophy of continuous and forced problem solving.

3. Consequently, _____ of JIT are particularly helpful in supporting strategies of rapid response and _____.

4. When there is _____ inventory, fewer and _____ warehouses are required.

5. JIT is sometimes _____ as a system that allows strong organizations to _____ on smaller firms in the channel

III. Challenging questions for discussion

1. What is the concept of JIT?

2. Please express advantages and disadvantages of JIT.

3. What do you think of zero inventory?

4. Tell the class a JIT story you know.

Chapter 5 Logistics Information

Chapter Outline

Part I   Logistics Information System
Functionality of logistics information
Logistics information management
Forecasting method
Forecasting logistics needs
Order processing system

Part II   Logistics Software
Warehouse Management Systems (WMS)
Transportation Management Systems (TMS)
Enterprise Resource Planning Systems (ERP)

Part III   Supplementary Reading
Cisco's E-commerce Connection
Starting of Cisco's E-commerce System
Virtual Order of the System
Advantages of the E-commerce System
Benefits from the Cisco's E-commerce-connection

Part I Logistics Information System

Functionality of Logistics Information

What is a logistic information system?

Part of an organization's ability to use logistics as a competitive weapon is based on its ability to assess and adjust actual logistics performance real time. This means the ability to monitor demands and inventory levels as they occur, to act in a timely manner to prevent stock-outs, and to communicate potential problems to customers. This requires excellent, integrated logistics information systems. These systems impact all of the logistics activities presented earlier, and must be integrated and take into account marketing and production activities. Such systems also must be integrated with other members of the supply chain, to provide accurate information throughout the channel from the earliest supplier through the ultimate customer.

How a logistics information system works

Logistics information systems (LIS) may link a variety of information technologies, as is the case with Wal-Mart. Wal-Mart uses EDI to communicate with suppliers, receiving information such as shipment, timing, quantities, and even invoicing. It uses bar coding to scan sales as customers make their purchases. The bar-code information is thus captured at the point of sale. Wal-Mart then downloads the information to suppliers. Suppliers use these data to determine the orders they need to supply to Wal-Mart, rather than having Wal-Mart create the orders. This system provides suppliers with rapid feedback on sales, so that they can anticipate production requirements based on accurate, near real-time sales data. Wal-Mart also benefits because it no longer has to place orders with many suppliers, and it can keep its inventory levels to a minimum.

Logistic Information Management

Managers faces with too much information

One of the by-products of the computer era is that managers are often faced with more information than can be effectively used for decisions. This abundance of data has several detrimental effect, among which are slower decisions, confused decisions, and the obscuring of important information.

Unnecessary data shall be screened out

For example, a warehouse manager at a consumer products company receiving weekly reports from corporate management. If a computer

61

output of great bulk is delivered with important and unimportant information mixed, inexpert managers will have difficulty finding the data that they really need. Expert managers will find the decision-relevant information, but will lose time developing the search expertise to do so. Both novice and experienced managers may simply stack the report in a corner of the office, to read when they have time. Of course, the managers will continue making decisions based on some other source of information and when reading time becomes available much of the formerly relevant information will be obsolete. Decision support systems screen out irrelevant information, so managers can have the precise data they need to deal with the issue at hand.

Forecasting Methods

LIS aids forecasting

One management task that is greatly aided by an LIS is forecasting. By having better data available, analysts can generate more timely and accurate forecasts that more closely reflect environmental realities. A number of standardized forecasting methods are available. These have been categorized into three groups: qualitative, historical projection, and causal. Each group differs in terms of the relative accuracy in forecasting over the long run versus the short run, the level of quantitative sophistication used, and the logic base (historical data, expert opinion, or surveys) from which the forecast is derived.

Needs for logistics forecasting

Generally, the logistician need not be directly concerned with the broad spectrum of available forecasting techniques. Because forecasted information, especially the sales forecast, is needed by various segments of the organization, the forecasting activity is often centralized in the marketing, planning, or business analysis area of the firm. Forecasts of medium-term or long-term time periods usually are provided to the logistician. Unless there is a need to develop specific long-term forecasts, the logistician's need is limited to the short-term forecasts that assist in inventory control, shipment scheduling, warehouse load planning, etc. Indeed, "simple" models of the time-series variety often predict as well or better than more sophisticated complex versions.

Order Processing System

One way that an order can be placed is for the customer to write it up by hand and mail or give it to a sales representative who takes it back to

Automatic way to place an order

the firm. Alternatively, the buyer could fax or telephone the order to a clerk who then writes it. Another approach is for the customer to place his or her order over the phone to a salesperson who simultaneously inputs it directly into the computer. Finally, by utilizing some preprogrammed criteria, orders can be placed automatically by the buyer's computer directly to the seller's system without human involvement. There are clear trade-offs in each situation between cost and information quality. When the ordering process is completely manual, the cost is relatively low but the procedure is slow and prone to errors. As the order placement activity becomes more automated, customer requests can be handled more quickly and with fewer mistakes, but the initial costs increase with the sophistication of the system.

Information of processing an order

Processing an order requires the flow of information from one department to another, as well as the referencing or accessing of several files or databases, such as customer credit status, inventory availability, and transportation schedules. The information system may be fully automated or manual, most are somewhere in between.

Functions of an order processing system

The order processing system sets many logistics in motion, such as:
- Determining the transportation mode, carrier, and loading sequence.
- Inventory assignment and preparation of picking and packing lists.
- Warehouse picking and packing.
- Updating the inventory file, subtracting actual products picked.
- Automatically printing replenishment lists.
- Preparing shipping documents (a bill of lading if using a common carrier).
- Shipping the product to the customer.

New Words and Phrases

Customer demand	客户需求
Stock-out	缺货
Feedback [ˈfiːdbæk] *n.*	反馈
Real-time	实时
Detrimental [ˌdetriˈmentl] *adj.*	有害的，不利的
Obscure [əbˈskjuə] *v.*	遮掩，搞混
Decision- relevant information	决策相关信息
Logistician	物流从业人员，物流管理人员，物流师
Novice [ˈnɔvis] *n.*	新手，初学者
Inventory control	库存控制
Obsolete [ˈɔbsəliːt] *adj.*	过时的，已不用的，废弃了的

Standardized ['stændədaiz] *adj.*　　　　标准化了的

Medium- or long-term time periods　　　中期或长期

Shipment scheduling　　　　　　　　　运输时间安排

Warehouse load planning　　　　　　　仓库积载计划

Prone to errors [prəun]　　　　　　　易出错的

Sophistication [səˌfɪstiˈkeiʃ ən] *n.*　　复杂，高级，先进

NOTES

1. to assess and adjust actual logistics performance real time.

实时评估和调整实际的物流运作。

2. This abundance of data has several detrimental effects.

这大量的信息有若干有害的效果。

3. Giving managers more than they need to know can be very dangerous when it keeps them from effectively receiving and using the information relevant to their current problems.

给经理们的信息多于他们所需知道的，这使他们不能有效地接收、利用那些与当前问题相关的信息，那就可能很危险了。

4. Managers can have the precise data they need to deal with the issue at hand without examining a lot of extraneous and irrelevant information.

经理们可获得处理手头问题所需的准确的资料，而无须检验大量无关紧要的和不相关的信息。

5. These have been categorized into three groups: qualitative, historical projection, and causal.

这些（预测方法）分为三类：定性预测、趋势预测、因果预测。

6. Indeed, "simple" models of the time-series variety often predict as well or better than more sophisticated complex versions.

事实上，各种时间序列法的"简单"模型通常能预测得同更高级的复杂的模型一样好或更好。

7. The initial costs increase with the sophistication of the system.

初始成本随着系统复杂性的提高而增加。

8. Updating the inventory file, subtracting actual products picked.

更新库存资料、减去实际已分拣好的产品。

EXERCISES

I. Form Phrases

竞争武器　　　　　　　　　　　　　物流信息系统

_____ weapon　　　　　　　　_____ information system

库存水平　　　　　　　　　　　　　实时销售信息

_____ levels　　　　　　　　　_____ sales data

潜在的问题　　　　　　　　　　　　决策相关信息

_____problem   _____-relevant information

物流活动   决策支持系统

_____activities   Decision _____

最终顾客   长期预测

_____customer   Long-term _____

信息技术   库存控制

_____technologies   _____control

II. Fill in the blanks and put the sentences into Chinese

1. This requires _____ logistics systems.

2. Decision support systems screen out _____ use of the important data.

3. Both _____ in a corner of the office, to read when they have time.

4. By having better data available, analysts can generate _____ environmental realities.

5. Such systems also must be _____ the channel from the earliest supplier through the ultimate customer.

6. Wal-Mart also benefits because _____ to a minimum.

III. True or false statement

Identify the main functions of an order processing system

(   ) 1. Warehouse picking and packing

(   ) 2. Connecting to the internet

(   ) 3. Updating the inventory file, subtracting actual products picked

(   ) 4. Automatically printing replenishment lists

(   ) 5. Preparing shipping documents

(   ) 6. Inventory assignment and preparation of picking and packing lists

(   ) 7. Sales forecasting

(   ) 8. Shipping the product to the customer

(   ) 9. Evaluating the customers

(   ) 10. Determining the transportation mode, carrier, and loading sequence

IV. ✎Listen to the conversation, answer the following questions and complete the sentences

1. What is one of the Wal-Mart's most important tools?

2. What are the functions of a Telxon?

3. Why is the barcode so important?

4. How many items do they have in a store of Wal-Mart?

5. With its own supercomputer, Wal-Mart streamlined its_____, _____from plant to store shelf.

6. Wal-Mart became a world leader in_____and promoted greater efficiency among its _____.

V. Challenging questions for discussion

1. Why an excellent, integrated logistics information system is required in a logistics system?
2. What are the information technologies in Wal-Mart's information system?
3. Why is the LIS so important to a logistics manager?
4. Explain the order processing procedure.
5. What are the three groups of standardized forecasting methods?

Part II   Logistics Software

This part is going to review the development of some software applied in warehousing, transportation and resource planning. The functionalities/benefits are detailed in relation to logistics and supply chain management.

Warehouse Management Systems (WMS)

Role of WMS

WMS are providing real time views on material flows within the warehouse, i.e. tracking and keeping note of the movement and storage of material within a warehouse facilitating the optimal use of space, labor, and equipments. From the managers' point-of-view, this means that a WMS enables to optimize transactions to and from warehouse operators, recognize problem areas and major shifts in activity levels and patters, while making it possible continuously determine performance indicators, such as productivity, shipping and inventory accuracy, warehouse order cycle time, and storage density.

WMS connect to other activities

WMS software producers

Typical WMS systems are well connected to material handling automation and transportation systems. Some WMS systems also include a route planning functionality that makes them related with the TMS systems. Some of the large suppliers of these software products are, amongst others, Marc Global Services, PeopleSoft, SSA Global, Microsoft Business Solutions, Oracle Corporation, JD Edwards, and PULSE Logistics Systems. Table 5-1 lists some key functionality of WMS systems and the claimed benefits of using the software.

Table 5-1 Functionality and benefits for WMS

Functionality	Claimed benefits
Inventory management Maintain items, groups, orders	Real time enterprising in material management
Order flow Retrieval orders Storage orders Track and trace	Improved operations in terms of accuracy; reduced paper work. Integration to automated warehouses

Transportation Management Systems (TMS)

Role of TMS

Transportation management systems (TMS) are software applications that facilitate the procurement of transportation services, the short-term planning and optimisation of transportation activities, and the execution of transportation plans with continuous analysis and collaboration. They typically provide route planning, transportation control features and advanced reporting. These software packages also automate the work of traffic controllers and provide a systematic way to generate documents and labels. Table 5-2 presents the functionality provided by typical TMS systems and claimed benefits for business.

Table 5-2 Functionality and benefits for TMS

Functionality	Claimed benefits
Optimize delivery routes for retailers	Improve processes drive saving and manage more business without increasing resources
Operational transportation control: booking, labeling and document printing, track and trace	Improve operational costs in collecting goods from suppliers and delivering to distribution centers. Improved utilization of fleet
Transportation business control: load tending	Reduced costs improved invoicing and tendering system
Route planning	More precise scheduling: managing scale, constraints, and seasonal fluctuations of its operations
Real time information	Streamlining reporting and analysis procedures to achieve real-time inventory information

Enterprise Resource Planning Systems (ERP)

Information flows in ERP

ERP is a business management system made up from a collection of applications that integrates all facets — marketing, finance, human resources, sales, manufacturing, logistics, etc.—of the company into a common database.

Fig.5.1 describes typical modules in ERP systems. The name of software modules may vary, but they all have similar functionality. From an information management point-of-view, the information flows from the upper part of the picture downwards:

● Production master schedule inputs sales orders and forecasts. In case of complex products, the products may be configured prior to taking the sales order in. Order entry and promise system may be connected if all required information is stored in the system.

● MPS generates schedule, whereas materials requirements planning creates purchasing orders for suppliers and production orders for plants based on MPS, capacity, bill-of-materials, and inventory records.

● Inventory statuses are updated based on shipments and receiving of parts, components and finished products.

● Financial control follows the real process. Invoices are sent to customers, employees are paid according to payroll accounting and suppliers are paid with regards to received goods and services. Financial records end up with bookkeeping, which creates the balance sheet as well as profit/loss statement for the fiscal period.

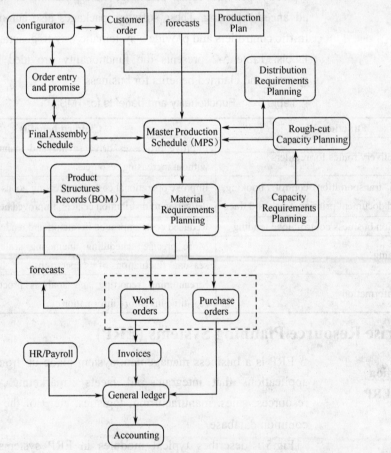

Fig.5.1   General structure of ERP system

Each part of the software is connected to each other and piece of information should be stored in only one place. Duplicate records are avoided

**Main suppliers
of ERP software**

by linking the information in the single database. In many cases these information systems are required to support multiply currencies and languages, specific, industries, and an ability to customize without programming as well. Currently, the leading vendors of ERP software application include SAP, Oracle, BAAN, PeopleSoft and JD Edwards. Table 5-3 summarizes the core functionalities and benefits stemming from ERPs.

Table 5-3   Functionality and benefits for ERP

Functionality	Claimed benefits
Integrated material handing, human resources and finance control	Integration and standardization of processes: improved customer service (?)
Multi-site, multi-languages, multi-user systems	Distributed responsibility, despite information transparency. "bring the organizations' people, systems and processes together"
Integration of data storage	Cost savings: each customer or address is entered only one in the system
Advanced reporting features	Evaluation of customers, products, suppliers etc. Tracking back the habits of doing business and to get more control on the complex system

New Words and Expressions

Tactical ['tæktikəl] *adj.*		战术的，策略的
Schedule ['skedʒjul] *vt.& n.*		安排日程，安排表
Optimize ['ɔptimaiz] *vt.*		使最优化，使尽可能有效
Patter ['pætə] *n.*		节奏，速度
Configurator [kən'figjureitə] *n.*		配置器
Invoice ['invɔis] *n. vt.*		发票，开发票
HR/payroll manager['peirəul] *n.*		人力资源/工资经理
General ledger ['ledʒə] *n.*		总账
Accounting [ə'kauntiŋ] *n.*		财会
Fiscal ['fiskəl] *adj.*		政府财政的
Balance sheet *n.*		资产负债表
Customize [kʌstəmaiz] *vt.*		定制，定做

NOTES

1. From the managers' point-of-view, this means that a WMS enables to optimize transactions to and from warehouse operators, recognize problem areas and major shifts in activity levels and patters, while making it possible continuously determine performance indicators, such as productivity, shipping and inventory accuracy, warehouse order cycle time, and storage density.

从管理者的角度看，WMS 有助于优化与仓库经营者之间的交易、找到问题所在、实现（仓储）活动水平和效率的重大转变，同时又可能不断地确定绩效指标，诸如生产效率、运输和库存的准确性，仓库订货周期和存储密度。

2. Transportation management systems (TMS) are software applications that facilitate the procurement of transportation activities, and the execution of transportation plans with continuous analysis and collaboration.

运输管理系统是便利运输服务的采购、通过持续的分析与协作而实施运输计划的应用软件。

3. Inventory statuses are updated based on shipments and receiving of parts, components and finished products.

根据配件、组件和成品的运输和收货情况对库存状况进行更新。

EXERCISES

I. Phrases translation

warehouse management systems (WMS)	sales orders
Transportation management systems (TMS)	promise system
material flows	purchasing orders
material handling automation	financial records
Enterprise resource planning systems (ERP)	duplicate records

II. Fill in the blanks and put the sentences into Chinese

1. WMS systems are providing real time views on _____, i.e. tracking and keeping note of the movement and storage of material within a warehouse facilitating the optimal use of space, labour, and equipments.

2. Some WMS systems also include a _____ that makes them related with the TMS systems.

3. Transportation management systems (TMS) are software applications that facilitate_____ _____, and the execution of transportation plans with continuous analysis and collaboration.

4. In many cases these information systems are required to support multiply currencies and languages, specific, industries, and an ability _____ as well.

5. In case of complex products, the products may be configured _____. Order entry and promise system may be connected if all required information is stored in the system.

III. Challenging questions for discussion

1. What are the functions of warehouse management systems (WMS)?

2. What are the Transportation management systems (TMS)?

3. What is the definition of Enterprise resource planning systems (ERP)?

4. How does the information flow in the Enterprise resource planning systems?

5. What are the functions of Enterprise resource planning systems?

Part III   Supplementary Reading

Cisco's E-commerce Connection

Starting of Cisco's E-commerce System

Cisco developed the world's largest e-commerce site

In 1997, Cisco sold more than $1 billion of a total $6.4 billion worth of routers, switches, and other network interconnect devices over the Web. Cisco's Web site (www.cisco.com) has developed over several years, beginning with technical support for customers and developing into one of the world's largest e-commerce sites. Today, Cisco offers nearly a dozen Internet-based applications to both end-use customers and reseller partners.

Cisco began providing Internet support in 1991, including software downloads, defect tracking, and technical advice. Customers and reseller partners were logging onto Web site about one million times a month to receive technical assistance, check orders, or download software. The on-line service has been so well received that over 70% of all customer service inquiries are delivered on-line, as are 90% of software updates.

Virtual Order of the System

How does the virtual order system work

Cisco builds virtually all its products to order, so there are very few off-the-shelf products. Before the Cisco Web site, ordering a product was lengthy and complicated. Cisco began deploying e-commerce tools in 1995, and by 1996, the Internet Product Center allowed users to purchase any Cisco product over the Web. In 1999, the same customer's engineer could sit down at a PC, configure a product on-line, immediately detect any errors, and route the order to Cisco's procurement department. Cisco's large customers take advantage of immediate and automatic access to Cisco's on-line ordering, configuration, and technical support tools. But, because of their large purchasing volumes, these large customers sought a faster alternative to Cisco's Web site. Therefore, an alternative program was launched in 1997 that interactively links the customer's and Cisco's computer systems over the Internet and private networks. In this way the configuration of new system and the price is validated at the customer's own PC before the order is placed.

Advantages of the E-commerce System

Advantages for both Cisco and its customers

With on-line pricing and configuration tools, about 98% of the large orders go through Cisco's system, saving time for both CISCO and its customers. Lead times were reduced, down from 4 to 10 days to only 2 to 3 days, and the productivity of customer' order increased an average of 20%. In the first 5 months of the system's operation in 1996, CISCO booked over $100 million in sales on the Internet alone. In 1997, the figure grew more than tenfold. Cisco closed 1998 with $4 billion in on-line sales. On-line sales grew to 85% of total volume during 1999, reaching $37 million per day.

Benefits from the Cisco's E-commerce-connection

The system reduced the cost of operating, technical staff and softwared istribution, but enhanced technical support and customer service

● Reduced operating cost: Cisco estimates that putting its applications on-line saves the company hundreds of millions of dollars per year, or over 17% of the total operating costs.

● Enhanced technical support and customer service: With 70% of its technical support and customer service calls handled on-line, CISCO's technical support productivity has increased by 200% to 300% per year.

● Reduced technical support staff cost: The on-line technical support reduces technical support staff costs by $125 million per year.

● Reduced software distribution cost: Customers download new software releases directly from Cisco's site, saving the company $180 million in distribution, packing, and duplicating costs per year. Having product and pricing information on the Web and Web-based CD-ROMs saves Cisco an additional $5 million per year in printing and distributing catalogs and marketing materials to customers.

New Words and Phrases

End-use customers and reseller partners	最终用户和销售伙伴
Defect tracking	错误追踪
Procurement department [prəˈkjuəmənt]	采购部门
Configuration [kənˌfigjuˈreiʃən] *n.*	结构，形状，配置
Validate [ˈvælideit] *v.*	使有效，证实
Duplicate [ˈdjuːplikeit] *v.*	复写，复制

NOTES

1. Cisco builds virtually all its products to order, so there are very few off-the-shelf products.

思科公司实际上建立了所有产品的订货系统，这样就很少有架下产品。

2. In this way the configuration of new system and the price is validated at the customer's own PC before the order is placed.

照此方法，新系统的结构配置和价格在下订单之前在客户自己的 PC 上就能确定。

EXERCISES

I. Form Phrases

最终用户和销售伙伴
End-_____ partners

替代程序
_____ program

客户服务
_____ service

产品和价格信息
_____ information

网上销售
_____ sales

运营成本
_____cost

软件下载
_____software

前置期
_____time

复印成本
_____ costs

技术支持
Technical support

订单递交
Order_____

II. Fill in the blanks and put the sentences into Chinese

1. Cisco's large customers take advantage of immediate and automatic access to Cisco's_____.

2. Enhanced technical support and customer service: With 70% of its technical support and customer service calls handled on-line, Cisco's _____has increased by 200% to 300% per year.

3. Today, Cisco offers nearly a dozen Internet-based applications to both _____and _____.

4. Customer's _____productivity increased an average of 20%.

5. _____ were reduced, down from 4 to 10 days to only 2 to 3 days, and customer' _____productivity increased an average of 20%.

III. Challenging questions for discussion

1. Describe how Cisco succeeded in selling its products and providing services to its customers on-line.

2. What are the benefits of Cisco's connection on-line to Cisco and its customers?

3. What steps are involved in ordering a Cisco networking product on-line?

Chapter 6 Warehousing

 Chapter Outline

Part I　Warehousing Activities

Overview of warehousing activity

Company-operated warehousing layout

Company-operated warehousing activity:

Receiving	Checking
Put-away	Packing and marking
Storage	Staging & Consolidation
Replenishment	Shipping
Order selection	

Objectives of warehousing activities

Part II　Types of Warehousing

Overview of warehousing

Comparison of private and public warehousing

Types of public warehousing

general merchandise warehouses

refrigerated or cold storage warehouses

bonded warehouse

special commodity warehouses

bulk storage warehouses

Contract warehousing

Part III　Supplementary Reading

Cross-docking

Crossdock

Why Cross-docking is Becoming Popular among Recailers

Criteria for Vsing Cross-docking

Part I   Warehousing Activities

Typical Straight-thru Flow Design of Warehousing

Warehousing activity is an important link between the producer and the customer. To illustrate the activities in a general warehouse, we will first learn its basic layout, which can be classified into four types, according to the activities flow planning: U-shaped, straight-thru, modular-spine, or multistory flow pattern. Fig.6.1 illustrates an example of straight-thru flow design. It works well for operations in which the peak receiving and shipping times coincide.

Lift truck is one of the most frequently used facilities in warehousing.

Despite the name or role, warehouse operations have a fundamental set of activities in common. The following activities are performed to some degree in all warehousing operations. However, one or more of them may not exist in a given warehouse or are combined with other activities.

The Main Activities in a Warehouse

Merchandise and materials arrive at warehouses in large quantity shipments. The first activity is receiving.

Material Receiving   **Material Receiving** is usually the unloading of high volume of similar product.

It involves physically accepting materials, unloading it from the transportation facilities, verifying quantity and condition of the material, and documenting this information as required. Lift trucks can be used for receiving.

General Warehouse Activities

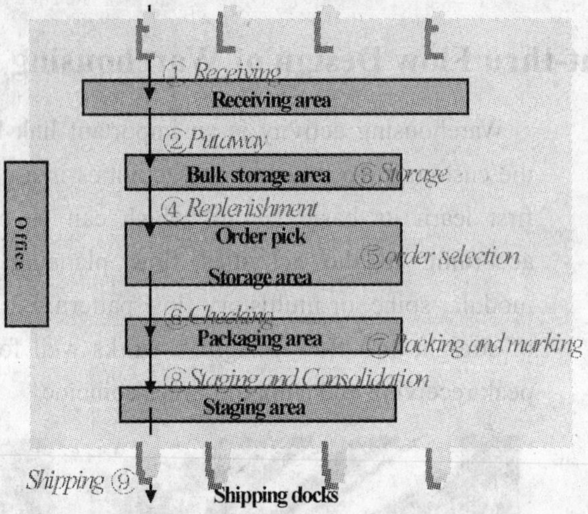

Fig.6.1   Straight-thru warehousing layout and functions

Remove the goods

Put-away means removing the goods from the receiving area, transfer them to a storage area, moving them to a specific location and recording this movement. This movement is mostly handled by a lift truck.

Storage

Storage is the physical containment of merchandise while it is awaiting a demand. The storage method depends on the size and quantity of the items in inventory and the handling characteristics of the product or its container.

Replenishment

Replenishment occurs when material is relocated from storage to a temporary resupply area from which orders are directly filled.

Picking product according to orders

Order Selection is one of the major activities within warehouses. It involves picking the required quantity of specific products for movement to a packing area. For each order, the combination of products must be selected and packaged to meet specific customer order requirements. The typical selection process is coordinated by a warehouse management system.

Check the products selected

Checking means verifying and documenting order selection in terms of product number and quantity.

Product packing and labeling

Packing & marking refers to placing one or more items of an order into an appropriate container and labeling that container with customer shipping destination data as well as other handling information that may be required.

Staging & consolidation means physically moving material from the packing zone to a shipping area based on a prescribed instructions related

Staging & consolidation for shipping	to a particular outbound vehicle or delivery route. It may involves the sortation of batch picked for individual orders and accumulation of distributed picks when an order has more than one item and the accumulation is not done and the picks are made.

Shipping involves loading a transportation vehicle with material from the staging area. Firms may use conveyors or lift trucks to move products. Shipment content checking is typically required when product changes ownership. It often include the following tasks:

Loading on an outbound vehicle

- Packaging merchandise in appropriate shipping containers;
- Preparing shipping documents, including packing lists, address labels and bills of lading;
- Weighing shipments to determine shipping charges;
- Accumulating orders by outbound carrier;
- Loading trucks (in many cases, this is a carrier's responsibility)

Administration

Clerical/Office administration refers to all of the tasks related with keeping track of items as they move into, through, and out of the warehouse.

New Words and Expressions

Warehousing ['wɛəhauziŋ] *n.*		入库，仓储
Layout ['lei,aut] *n.*		布局，设计
Order pick		订单分拣
Package ['pækidʒ] *n.*		包装，包装材料
Staging [steidʒiŋ] *v.*		分批运输
Shipping dock		出货站台
Unload ['ʌn'ləud] *v.*		卸下
Verify ['verifai] *v.*		查验，验证
Lift truck		叉车
Identify [ai'dentifai] *v.*		确定，识别
Modular ['mɔdjulə] *adj.*		模块的
Coincide [ˌkəuin'said] *v.*		一致，符合
Replenish [ə'rɪplenɪʃ] *v.*		补给，补充
Sortation [sɔː'teiʃ ən] *n.*		分类
Accumulation [əkjuːmjuˈleiʃ(ə)n] *n.*		积聚，堆积物
Consolidate [kənˈsɔlideit] *v.*		整合，合并，巩固
Administration [ədminisˈtreiʃ ə] *n.*		管理

NOTES

1. which can be classified into four types, according to the activities flow planning: U-shaped, straight-thru, modular-spine, or multistory flow pattern.

（仓库的布局）可根据仓储活动流程规划分为四类：U 型仓库、直通型仓库、模块型仓库或多层流程仓库。

2. Merchandise and materials arrive at warehouses in large quantity shipments.

商品和物资大批量地运到仓库。

3. It involves physically accepting materials, unloading it from the transportation facilities, verifying quantity and condition of the material, and documenting this information as required.

接收工作涉及接收实物，将实物从运输设施上卸下，查验所到货的数量和质量，按要求将有关信息记载。

4. outbound vehicle or delivery route

外运的运输工具或发运路线

5. piece-by-piece check

逐件检查

EXERCISES

I. Vocabulary Training

1. **Brainstorming**

Ask the students of the whole class to think of as many words or phrases that associates with warehousing activities.

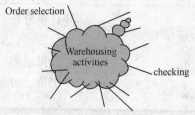

2. **Pair Work—Interpret and write**

Activity Plan Design

● Students work in pairs.

● Students A chooses 5 to 10 words from the above words list of warehousing activities，and write down on his own notebook.

● Students A interprets or describes the activities which he has written on the notebook to Students B who listens and tries to write down the word from the description.

● Then，Student B turn to interpret and student A listen and write.

II. Fill in the blank and put the sentence into Chinese

1. _____ _____ is an important link between the producer and the customer.

2. Order selection means _____ the required quantity of specific products and packaged to meet _____order requirement.

3. Put away means transfer the goods from _____area to_____area.

4. Firms may use_____or_____to move products.

5. _____is typically required when product changes ownership.

6. Marking means labeling the items with_____data and _____.

III. Phrases translation

仓储操作	运送路线
基本布局	标识
按订单分拣	产品编号
储存区	仓库管理系统
大批量运输	订单要求
办公管理	运输目的地
装运检验	运输工具
升降货车	搬运信息

IV. Topics for group discussion

1. What activities does warehousing operate? Describe some of them.

2. Introduction of warehouse layout.

3. Why does the author say warehousing activity is an important link between producers and customers?

Part II   Types of Warehousing

Overview of Warehousing

Different forms of warehouses

Warehousing is an integral part of a logistics system. There are estimated 750,000 warehouse facilities worldwide, including professionally managed warehouses, and company stockrooms, garages and even garden sheds.

Two options of warehousing: public & private warehousing

When a firm decides to store product, it faces two warehousing options: rented facilities, called *public warehousing*, or owned or leased facilities, called *private warehousing*.

Comparing the two options

Firms must examine closely to choose between the two options. For example, the price of a public warehouse is most probably higher because it will be operated at a profit; it may also have selling and advertising cost. However, a firm makes no initial investment in the facilities. For customer service, private warehousing can generally provide higher service levels because of its more specialized facilities and equipment, and its better familiarity with the firm's products, customers and market.

In some instances, innovative public warehouses can provide higher levels of service owning to their expertise and strong competitive drive to serve the customer.

In the following, we will discuss about public warehousing.

Public Warehouses

Types of public warehouses

Public Warehouses. There are many types of public warehouses, including: (1) general merchandise warehouses for manufactured goods, (2) refrigerated storage warehouses, (3) bonded warehouse, (4) special commodity warehouses, and (5) bulk storage warehouses.

Warehouses for general merchandise

General Merchandise Warehouse. The general merchandise warehouse is probably the most common form. It is designed to be used by manufacturers, distributors, and customers for storing almost any kind of product.

Warehouses for refrigerated products

Refrigerated Warehouses. Refrigerated or cold storage warehouses provide a temperature-controlled storage environment. They tend to be used for preserving perishable items such as fruits and vegetables. However, a number of other items (e.g., frozen food products, some pharmaceuticals, photographic paper and film, and furs) require this type of facility.

Warehouses for special commodities

Special Commodity Warehouses. *Special commodity warehouses* are used for particular agricultural products, such as grains, wool, and cotton. Ordinarily each of these warehouses handles one kind of product and offers special services specific to that product.

Warehouses for bonded products

Bonded Warehouses. Some general merchandise or special commodity warehouses are known as bonded warehouses. Goods such as imported tobacco and alcoholic beverages are stored in this type of warehouse, although the government retains control of the goods until they are distributed to the market place. The advantage of the bonded warehouse is that the import duties need not be paid until the merchandise is sold, so that the importer has the funds on hand to pay these fees.

Warehouses for bulk cargoes

Bulk Storage Warehouses. Bulk storage warehouses provide tank storage of liquids and open or sheltered storage of dry products such as coal, sand, and chemicals.

New Words and Phrases

Integral ['ɪntɪgrəl]*adj.*	完整的，必需的组成部分
Facility [fə'sɪlɪti] *n.*	设施，设备，工具
Stockroom ['stɔkrum]	储藏室
Familiarity [fə,mɪli'ærɪti] *n.*	熟悉，了解
Innovative ['ɪnəuveitiv] *adj.*	创新的，革新的
Perishable ['periʃəbl]*adj.*	易腐烂的，易变质的
Pharmaceutical [,fɑːmə'sjuːtikəl] *n..*	药物
Customer service	客户服务
Competitive drive [kəm'petitiv]	竞争驱动力
Specialized facilities	特殊设施，专用设施
Private warehousing	自用仓库
Public warehousing	公共仓库
Bulk [bʌlk] *adj*	大量的；大批的
Bulk cargo	大宗散装货物
Photographic paper [fəutə'græfik]	照相纸
Temperature-controlled ['temprɪtʃə(r)]	温控的
Shelter ['ʃeltə] *n.*	掩蔽处，遮蔽处

NOTES

1.   …including professionally managed warehouses, and company stockrooms, garages and even garden sheds.

包括专业管理的仓库和公司的储藏室、车库，以及甚至庭院货棚。

2. two warehousing options: rented facilities, called *public warehousing*, or owned or leased facilities, called *private warehousing*.

两种仓储选择：租用的仓储设施，叫做公共仓储，和自有的或租赁的仓储设备，叫做（企业）自用仓储。

Public warehouse

公共仓库：对大众提供储存货品服务并收取费用的仓库。并不一定为公众所有，也可能为私有仓库。

Private warehouse

企业自用仓库：公司拥有自己的仓库或长期租赁他人仓库，并只存放本公司自己的物品，根据本身的需求可装设特定的装卸或储存设备。亦称为公司自家仓库

3. general merchandise warehouse

普通商品仓库

4. bonded warehouses

保税仓库

EXERCISES

I. Phrases translation

仓储设施
Warehouse fa_____

公共仓库
Pu_____ warehousing

自用仓库
Pr_____ warehousing

广告成本
Ad_____ cost

首笔投资
Initial in_____

客户服务
C____ service

服务水平
Ser____ level

竞争动力
Co_____ drive

制造商
Manu_____

经销商
Dis_____

温控仓库
_____-controlled warehouse

进口税
Imported du_____

罐装储存
Ta_____ storage

易腐物品
Pe_____ products

农产品
Ag_____ products

大宗散装存储产品
Bu_____ storage products

普通商品仓库
Ge_____ commodity warehouse

冷藏仓库
Re_____ warehouse

特种商品仓库
Sp_____ commodity warehouse

保税仓库
Bo_____ warehouse

II. Fill in the blanks and put the sentences into Chinese

1. The two types of warehouses according to the ownership are_____warehousing and_____ warehousing.

2. Comparing the two types warehousing, the price of _____ tends to be higher, and generally speaking, _____ can provide better customer service.

3. There are many types of public warehouses, including: general merchandise warehouses; _____; bonded warehouse, _____, and_____.

4. _____ is designed to be used for storing almost any kind of product.

5. Goods such as imported tobacco and alcoholic beverages are often stored in_____ warehouse with its imported duties unpaid until they are distributed to the marketplaces.

6. _____ provides tank storage of liquids and open or sheltered storage of dry products such as coal, sand, and chemicals.

7. Perishable products such as fruits and vegetables shall be preserved in_____ warehouses.

III. Challenging questions for discussion

1. Compare the advantages and disadvantages between public and private warehouses.
2. What kinds of products need temperature-controlled warehouse?
3. What's the advantage of bonded warehouses?
4. What kinds of commodities are stored in bulk storage warehouses?

Part III   Supplementary Reading
Cross-docking

Crossdock

Crossdocks are high speed warehouses.

If an arriving item has already been requested by a customer, there is no need to store it as anticipation inventory; instead, the item can move directly from receiving to shipping, without intermediate storage and retrieval. Thus the item can move much more quickly through the facility and the most costly part of warehouse labor can be avoided.

In a high-volume crossdock the turnover times may be measured in hours. To support this velocity of movement, a crossdock may be nothing more than a slab of concrete with a roof and walls punctuated with doors for trailers. Freight is pulled off arriving trailers, sorted and loaded onto departing trailers without intermediate storage.

There is little or no storage provided in a crossdock because items do not stay long enough; but there is generally a lot of material-handling equipment, such as forklifts and pallet jacks, to move freight. Labor is frequently the main cost and it is devoted to unloading incoming trailers, moving the freight to the appropriate outgoing trailers, and loading. Consequently, the issues within a crossdock are those of material-handling and product flow rather than location and retrieval.

Fig.6.2   Crossdocks built in various types

Why Cross-docking is Becoming Popular among Retailers

Because of its impact on costs and customer service, cross-docking is becoming popular, especially among retailers. For example, approximately 75 percent of food distribution involves the cross-docking of products from supplier to retail food stores. The biggest impact of a crossdock is on reducing transportation costs. This can be achieved by consolidating multiple shipments so that full truck loads can be sent.

The Home Depot is a major retailer and the largest user of Less-than-Truck-Load (LTL) shipping in North America. Nowadays, LTL costs about twice the cost of Truck Load (TL) shipping, so there is a strong incentive to fill trailers. The Home Depot has begun doing this by having vendors ship full trailers to its crossdock. (The trailers are full because they hold product for many stores.) At the crossdock the product is sorted out for individual stores and consolidated with product from other vendors bound for the same store. The result is that each store has enough freight or a few close neighbors generate a full truck load from the crossdock. The result can be considerable savings.

Additional benefits include less inventory (because all product flows right through) and less labor (because product does not have to be put away and later retrieved).

Criteria for Using Cross-docking

Cross-docking should be considered as an option by firms meeting two or more of the following criteria:
- Inventory destination is known when received.
- Customer is ready to receive inventory immediately.
- Shipment to fewer than 200 locations daily.
- Daily throughput exceeds 2,000 cartons.
- More than 70 percent of the inventory is conveyable.
- Large quantities of individual items received by firm.
- Inventory arrives at firm's docks prelabeled.
- Some inventory is time sensitive.
- Firm's distribution center is near capacity.
- Some of the inventory is prepriced.

Operations

Most crossdocking freight terminals are laid out as long, narrow warehouses with doors around the perimeter. Fig.6.3 illustrates a typical terminal, where the small shaded rectangles represent incoming trailers with freight to be unloaded, and small clear rectangles represent (empty) outgoing trailers. Terminals range in size from fewer than 10 doors to more than 500 doors. Inside a terminal, a variety of material handling methods is used to transport freight. Forklifts and palletjacks carry heavy or bulky items, and carts transport smaller items. In addition, large terminals may have draglines, which circulate carts around the inside perimeter of the dock.

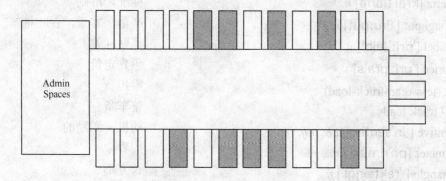

Admin Spaces

Fig.6.3   Typical terminal for crossdocking

There are two types of doors in a terminal: receiving, or strip, doors, where full trailers are parked to be unloaded, and shipping, or stack, doors, where empty trailers are put to collect freight for specific destinations. Once established, the designations of these doors do not change, although the trailers parked at them will. A shipping door always receives freight for the same destination.

A receiving door may be occupied by any incoming trailer, regardless of its origin or contents. Arriving trucks may deliver their trailers directly to an unoccupied receiving door; or, if none is available, they may place them in a queue. After the trailer is backed into a receiving door, a worker unloads the freight. After unloading items of a shipment onto a cart, the worker walks to the destination trailer and loads the items into that trailer; or he places the cart on the dragline, if the terminal is so equipped. To handle pallet loads, the worker uses a palletjack, or hails a forklift driver, or finds a forklift and delivers the load himself, if union rules permit.

After a trailer has been completely stripped, a driver replaces it with another incoming trailer from the queue of trailers waiting to be stripped. After an outgoing trailer has been filled, a driver replaces it with an empty trailer to be filled with freight for the same destination.

New Words and Expressions

Cross-docking [dɔkiŋ]　　　　　　　　　直接换装，越库
Crossdock　　　　　　　　　　　　　　直接换装库，交叉运作库
Retrieval [əri'tri:vəl] v.　　　　　　　再取出来
Turnover ['tə:n,əuvə] n.　　　　　　　周转量
Velocity [vi'lɔsiti] n.　　　　　　　　速度
A slab [slæb]of concrete ['kɔnkri:t]　水泥板
Punctuate ['pʌŋktjueit] v.　　　　　　（不时地）分隔开
Trailer ['treilə] n.　　　　　　　　　　拖车
Freight [freit] n.　　　　　　　　　　货物
Palletjack ['pælit dʒæk] n.　　　　　托盘千斤顶

Approximately [əˈprɔksiˈmətli] *adv.*	近似地，大约
Retailer [riːˈteilə] *n.*	零售商
Criteria [kraiˈtiəriə] *n.*	标准，准则
Throughput [ˈθruːput] *n.*	产量，容量，吞吐量
Prelabel [ˈpriːˈleibl] *v.*	预贴标签
Preprice [ˈpriːˈprais] *v.*	预先定价
LTL (less-than-truck-load)	零担货
TL（truck load）	整车货
Incentive [inˈsentiv] *n.& adj.*	动机，激励的
Perimeter [pəˈrimitə] *n.*	周界
Rectangle [ˈrektæŋgl] *n.*	长方形
Queue [kjuː] *n.& v.*	队列，排队
Cart [kɑːt] *n.*	手推机，大车
Dragline [ˈdræglain] *n.*	牵引索
Hail [heil] *v.*	招呼
Union (of labor)	工会
Strip [strip] *v.*	剥去，卸载

NOTES

1．Cross-docking

直接换装，又叫越库、接驳式或通过型物流，指货物从进货区进货后,直接到出货区至配送货车上出货，没有入库、储存、拣货等作业。

2．…the item can move directly from receiving to shipping, without intermediate storage and retrieval.

产品可以直接从收货区移到发货区，不需要中间的储存阶段和取货阶段。

3．In a high-volume crossdock the turnover times may be measured in hours. To support this velocity of movement, a crossdock may be nothing more than a slab of concrete with a roof and walls punctuated with doors for trailers. Freight is pulled off arriving trailers, sorted and loaded onto departing trailers without intermediate storage.

在大量的直接换装中，周转次数可以小时来衡量。为了支持同转速度，直接换装加可以仅仅是供拖车活动的水泥板，常有屋顶和墙。货物从到达的拖车上卸下，分类并装载到出货拖车上，不需要中间储存。

4．The Home Depot is a major retailer and the largest user of Less-than-Truck-Load (LTL) shipping in North America.

Home Depot 是主要的零售商，也是北美拼车运输最大的客户。

5．Cross-docking should be considered as an option by firms meeting two or more of the following criteria.

如果企业满足下列准则中的两个或两个以上时，就可考虑选择采用直接换装作业。

6. At the crossdock the product is sorted out for individual stores and consolidated with product from other vendors bound for the same store.

在交叉运作仓库，产品按商店分拣开来，并与来自不同供应商、运往同一家商店的产品整合在一起。

7. Fig.6.3 illustrates a typical terminal, where the small shaded rectangles represent incoming trailers with freight to be unloaded, and small clear rectangles represent (empty) outgoing trailers.

图 6.3 显示了典型的（交叉）仓库，图中小的阴影长方形代表进来的拖车，带着需要卸下的货物，小的空白的长方形代表（空的）出去的拖车。

EXERCISES

Questions for Discussion

1. What is cross-docking?

2. What are the fundamental warehouse activities removed by crossdocks, and what enables crossdocks to omit these activities?

3. What are the advantages of cross-docking? And why?

4. How does retailer use cross-docking?

5. When should cross-docking be considered?

6. Where are the most convenient doors in a rectangular crossdock?

Chapter 7 Material Handling

Chapter Outline

Part I   Material Handling System

Overview of material handling system

Classify of material handling systems

Mechanized material handling systems

Semi-automated material handling systems

Automated material handling systems

Information-directed material handling systems

Part II   Mechanized Material Handling Equipment

Overview of material handling equipment

Types of material handling equipment：

    Lift trucks

    Towlines

    Two tractor with trailers

    Conveyors

    Carousels

Part III   Supplementary Reading

Safety in Material Handling

    What Should Workers Know Before Handling Materials

    Potential Hazards for Workers

    Precautions Should Be Taken When Moving Materials Manually

    Precaution Should Be Taken When Moving Materials Mechanically

    Safety Measures Regarding Conveyors

    Safety Measures Regarding Cranes

    Safety Precautions For Operating Powered Industrial Trucks

Part I   Material Handling Systems

Introduction of Material Handling Systems

Material handling systems are a large investment

Material handling equipments and systems often represent a major capital investment for an organization. Like the decisions related to the number, size, and location of warehouses, material handling can affect many aspects of the firms' operation.

The Material Handling Institute, an industry trade association for manufacturers of material handling equipments and systems, has estimated that:

The hardware and software used to move, store, control, contain, and unitize materials in factories and warehouses exceed $50 billion annually.

Much of the growth in size and variety of the market is fueled by major changes in the requirements of warehouse and distribution operations (e.g., reduced order cycle times, reduced inventory levels, reduced order sizes, SKU proliferation).

Types of Material Handling Systems

Material handling system can be classified as mechanized, semi-automated, automated, and information-directed.

Comparison of four material handling systems

A combination of labor and handling equipment is utilized in mechanized systems to facilitate receiving, processing, and/or shipping. Generally, labor constitutes a high percentage of overall cost in mechanized handling.

Automated systems, in contrast, attempt to minimize labor as much as possible by substituting equipment capital investment.

When a combination of mechanical and automated systems is used to handle material，the system is referred to as semi-automated.

An information-directed system applies computerization to sequence mechanized handling equipment and direct work effort. Mechanized handling systems are most common, but the use of semi-automated and automated systems is increasing.

The main drawback to automated handling is lack of flexibility. One factor contributing to low logistical productivity is that information- directed handling has not yet to achieve its full potential. This situation is predicted to be dramatically changed during the first decade of the 21st century.

Mechanized Material Handling Systems

Mechanized system is traditional and will continue to be in use

Mechanized materials handling equipment has been the mainstay of the traditional warehousing and will likely continue to be important even with the move toward automated warehousing. Mechanized materials handling systems employ a wide range of handling equipment. Such equipment can be categorized according to the functions performed that is, storage and order picking, transportation and sorting, and shipping.

Semi-automated Material Handling Systems

Equipments in semi-automated system

Mechanized handling is often supplemented by semiautomatic equipment. Typical equipments utilized in semi-automated handling systems includes automated guided vehicle systems(AGVS), computerized sortation, robotics and various forms of live racks.

Automated Material Handling Systems

For several decades the concept of automated handling has offered great potential. Initial automated handling efforts focused on master carton order selection systems. Recently, emphasis has shifted to automated high-rise storage and retrieval systems.

Advantages of an automated system

The appeal of automation is that it substitutes capital equipment for labor. In addition to requiring less direct labor, an automated system operates faster and more accurately than its mechanized counterpart. Table 7-1 shows the benefits of automated material handling systems.

Table 7-1   Benefits of automated material handling systems

Benefit	Proportion of respondents that "agree" or "strongly agree"
Labor cost reduction	98.8%
Ability to increase output rate	95.2%
Improvement in consistency of service	92.1%
Reduction in material handling	92.1%
Increased accuracy level	89.5%
Service availability	87.0%
Improvement in speed of service	81.0%

Source: Koft Q.Dadzie,and Wesley J. Johnston,"Innovative Automation Technology in

Corporate Warehousing Logistics,"*Journal of Business Logistics*,2,no.1(1991),p.76.

Disadvantages of an automated system

However, automated systems are not without disadvantages. Its shortcomings are the high capital investment, maintenance costs, inflexibility and user training.

Information-directed Material Handling System

Characteristic of information-direct ed system

The concept of information-directed is appealing because it combines the control typical of automated handling with the flexibility of mechanized systems. Information-directed systems use mechanized handling controlled by information technology. Two common examples of information-directed material handling systems are RF-controlled equipment and light-directed operations.

New Words and Expressions

Association [əˌsəusiˈeiʃən] *n.*	协会
Proliferation [prəuˌlifəˈreiʃən] *n.*	增殖，扩散
Automate [ˈɔːtəmeit] *v.*	使自动化,自动操作
Combination [ˌkɔmbiˈneiʃən] *n.*	组合,合并
Sequence [ˈsiːkwəns] *n.*	次序，顺序
Flexibility [ˌfleksəˈbiliti] *n.*	灵活性
Vehicle [ˈviːikl] *n.*	交通工具,车辆
Sortation [sɔːˈteiʃən] *n.*	分类
Robotics [rəuˈbɔtiks] *n.*	机器人学，机器人技术
Initial [iˈniʃəl] *adj.*	最初的，初始的

NOTES

1. SKU

stock-keeping unit 的简写。这是一种采用条形码跟踪库存的方法，通常用于计算机控制的自动化系统的库存再订货或补充。

2. One factor contributing to low logistical productivity is that information-directed handling has yet to achieve its full potential.

造成物流效率低下的一个因素是信息导向处理系统还没有发挥全部潜能。

3. Much of the growth in size and variety of the market is fueled by major changes in the requirements of warehouse and distribution operations.

仓储和配送作业的重要变化极大地刺激了市场的多样性和其规模的增长。

4. Mechanized material handling equipment has been the mainstay of the traditional warehouse and will likely continue to be important even with the move toward automated warehousing.

机械化物资操作系统一直是传统仓储的支柱，且仍将可能继续发挥其重要作用，即使仓储业向自动化发展变化。

5. master carton

马斯特箱。为提高搬运效率，把各种罐状、瓶状或盒状的产品组合进更大的单元，称作马斯特箱。马斯特组合的最常见的单元是托盘，薄衬纸，以及各种类型的集装箱。

6. In addition to requiring less direct labor, an automated system operates faster and more accurately than its mechanized counterpart.

除了需要较少的直接劳力外，与机械化系统相比，自动化系统还可以更快、更精确地作业。

7. Two common examples of information-directed material handling systems are RF-controlled equipment and light-directed operations.

两种常见的信息导向物资操作系统是射频控制设备和光导向操作系统。

EXERCISES

I. Fill in the blank and put the sentence into Chinese

1. A combination of _____ and _____ equipment is utilized in mechanized systems to facilitate receiving, processing, and/or shipping.

2. Information-directed systems apply _____ to sequence mechanized handling equipment and direct work effort.

3. _____ equipment has been the mainstay of the traditional warehouse and will likely continue to be important even with the move toward _____ warehousing.

4. Initial automated handling efforts focused on master carton _____.

5. Information-directed systems use mechanized handling controlled by_____.

II. Phrases translation

物资操作系统	机械化操作系统
自动化操作系统	信息导向操作系统
存储和订单处理设备	运输和分类设备
出货设备	自动导向车辆系统
计算机分类	活动货架
高层自动化存取系统	射频波控制设备
光导向操作	订货拣选系统

III. Discuss the advantages and disadvantages of different types of material handling systems

Types of MHS	Advantage	Disadvantage
Mechanized material handling		
Semi-automatic		
Automated		
Information-directed		

IV. Challenging questions for discussion

1. What are the classifications of material handling systems?

2. Illustrate the differences of the four systems of material handling.

3. How does material handling affect the firm's operations?

4. Discuss the advantages and disadvantages of the automated material handling system.

5. What is the appeal of the information-directed material handling systems?

Part II   Mechanized Materials Handling Equipment

Introduction

The primary mission of materials handling equipment is to facilitate merchandise flow in an orderly and efficient manner from manufacturer to point of sale. In this section the focus of discussion is put on the mechanized materials handling equipment.

The following equipment is commonplace in manual warehousing.

Lift Trucks

Function of lift trucks

Lift trucks also called forklifts can move loads of master cartons both horizontally and vertically but are not limited to unit load handling. Boxes may also be transported depending upon the nature of the product.

Types of lift trucks

Many types of lift trucks are available. High-stacking trucks are capable of up to 40 feet of vertical movement. Palletless side-clamp versions are available for handling bulky product without pallets. Other lift truck variations are available for narrow aisle and side-loading operations. Particular attention to narrow-aisle lift trucks has increased in recent years, as warehouses seek to increase rack density and overall storage capacity.

Disadvantage of lift trucks

The lift truck is not economical for long-distance horizontal movement because of the high ratio of labor per unit of transfer; it is most effectively utilized in shipping and receiving and placing merchandise in high cube storage.

Walkie-rider Pallet Trucks

Characteristic and application

Walkie-rider pallet trucks provide a low-cost, effective method of general material handling utility. Typical applications include loading and unloading of transportation equipment, order selection and accumulation, and shuttling loads over longer transportation distances throughout the warehouse. Walkie-rider pallet trucks are widely used in grocery warehouse.

Towlines

Advantage and application

Towlines consist of either in-floor or overhead-mounted cable or drag devices. They are utilized to provide continuous power to four-wheel trailers. The main advantage of a towline is continuous movement. However, such handling devices have far less flexibility than lift trucks. The most common application of towlines is for order selection. Order selectors place merchandise on four-wheel trailers that are then towed to the shipping dock. A number of automated decoupling devices are available to route trailers from the main towline to the shipping docks.

Tow Tractor with Trailers

Application of tow tractor with trailers

A tow tractor with trailer consists of a driver-guided power unit towing a number of individual four-wheel trailers that hold several unitized loads. The typical size of the trailers is 4*8 feet. The tow tractor with trailer, like the towline, is used to facilitate order selection. The main advantage of a tow tractor with trailers is flexibility. It is not as economical as the towline because it requires more labor.

Conveyors

Application and classification

Conveyors are used widely in shipping and receiving operations and form the basic handling device for a number of order selection systems. Conveyors are classified according to power, gravity, and roller or belt movement. In power systems, the conveyor is powered by a drive chain from either above or below. Considerable conveyor flexibility is offered in such power configuration installations. Gravity and roller or belt systems permit the basic installation to be rearranged with minimum difficulty. Portable gravity-style roller conveyors are often used for loading and unloading and, in some cases, are transported on over-the-road trailers to assist in unloading vehicles. Conveyors are effective in that only the product is moved, eliminating the need for a movement unit to return.

Carousels

Application in order selection

A carousel operates on a different concept than most other mechanized handling equipment. Rather than requiring the order selector to go to the inventory storage location, the carousel moves inventory to the order selector. A carousel consists of a series of bins mounted on an oval track or rack. There may be multiple track levels, allowing for very high-density carousel storage. The entire carousel rotates, moving the selection bin to a stationary operator. The typical carousel application is the selection of packages in pack, repack, and service parts.

The rationale behind carousel systems is to shrink order selection labor requirements by reducing walking length and time. Carousels, particularly modern stackable systems, also significantly reduce storage space requirements. Some carousel systems also utilize computer-generated pick lists and computer-directed carousel rotation to further increase selection productivity. These systems are referred to as paperless picking because no paperwork exists to slow down employee efforts.

Varieties of carousel system

A variation of the carousel system is movable racks. Such racks move horizontally to eliminate the permanent aisle between the racks. This system, often used in libraries, provides more storage density but reduces picking efficiency since the racks must be moved to access specific products.

The mechanized material handling equipment discussed is representative of a wide range of alternatives. Most systems combine different handling devices. For example, lift trucks may be used for vertical movements while tow tractor with trailers and walkie-rider pallet trucks are the primary methods of horizontal transfer.

New Words and Expressions

Facilitate [fə'siliteit] *v.*	推动，使便利
Lift truck	叉车，铲车
Unit load	单元负载
Aisle [ail] *n.*	走廊，过道
Walkie-rider pallet truck	步行码垛车
Application [ˌæpli'keiʃən] *n.*	应用
Accumulation [əkju:mju'leiʃ(ə)n] *n.*	堆积，累积
Towline ['təulain] *n.*	拖缆
Decoupling [di'kʌpliŋ] *n.*	退耦，解耦
Tow tractor with trailers	带挂车的牵引车
Conveyor [kʌn'veiə(r)] *n.*	传送带，输送机
Shipping and receiving operation	发货和收货操作
Configuration [kənˌfigju'reiʃən] *n.*	构造，结构，配置，外形
Carousel [ˌkærə'zel] *n.*	旋转式传送带
Bin [bin] *n.*	储料箱

Oval ['əuvəl] *adj.*   卵形的，椭圆的

Multiple ['mʌltipl] *adj.& v.*   多样的，多重的；成倍增加

Rotate [rəu'teit] *v.*   （使）旋转

Stationary ['steiʃ(ə)nəri] *adj.*   不动的，固定的

Rationale [,ræʃə'nɑːli] *n.*   基本原理

Stackable ['stækəbl] *adj.*   可叠起堆放的

NOTES

1. Lift trucks-also called forklifts-can move loads of master cartons both horizontally and vertically but are not limited to unit load handling.

叉车，又称铲车，可水平和垂直地搬移主箱，但不限于对单元负荷的操作。

2. Particular attention to narrow-aisle lift trucks has increased in recent years, as warehouses seek to increase rack density and overall storage capacity.

因为仓库寻求提高堆垛密度和总体储存容量，近年来窄过道叉车更加受到重视。

3. Towlines consist of either in-floor or overhead-mounted cable or drag devices.

拖缆由安装在地面上或顶部的电缆或拖拉设备组成。

4. A number of automated decoupling devices are available to route trailers from the main towline to the shipping docks.

许多自动化的退耦装置可用于将拖车从主拖缆传送到出运站点。

5. A tow tractor with trailer consists of a driver-guided power unit towing a number of individual four-wheel trailers that hold several unitized loads.

带挂车的曳引车是由司机操纵的有动力的车头拖着多个单体的四轮挂车所组成，每个挂车装载着几个单元化的负荷物。

6. The rationale behind carousel systems is to shrink order selection labor requirements by reducing walking length and time.

旋转输送带系统的基本原理是通过减少步行的距离和时间以降低对订单拣货劳力的需求。

EXERCISES

I. Fill in the blank and put the sentence into Chinese

1. Lift trucks also called _____ can move loads of master cartons both _____ and_____.

2. A tow tractor with trailer consists of a driver-guided power unit towing a number of individual _____that hold several unitized loads.

3. Conveyors are used widely in _____and _____operations and form the basic handling device for a number of _____systems.

4. Lift trucks may be used for _____movements while tow tractor with trailers and Walkie - rider pallet trucks are the primary methods of _____transfer.

5. A carousel consists of a series of _____ mounted on an oval_____.

6. The typical carousel application is the _____ in pack, _____, and service parts.

II. Phrases Translation

叉车	步行码垛车
拖缆	旋转式输送带
单元负载	动力结构装置
高垛叉车	库存存储位置
出运货物和收货入库作业	高密度旋转储存
订单拣货	

III. Challenging questions for discussion

1. Discuss the types of lift trucks.
2. What is the application of walkie-rider pallet truck?
3. Why is carousel a different concept than most other mechanized handling equipment?
4. What is the advantage of the carousel?

IV. Chess game

7. Have a break because your lift truck is not economical for long distance movement	6. How high can a high-stacking truck reach?	5. Fail use the right suitable equipment, sing an English song	4. Where is a carousel most probably used?
8. Two typical applications of Walkie-rider pallet truck			3. Describe a carousel
9. The advantages of Walkie-rider pallet trucks			2. When is lift truck mostly effectively used?
10. It is the right choice to use Walkie-rider pallet trucks in grocery, two steps forward to the victory!	11. The main advantage of towline	Victory!	1. The advantage of a tow tractor with trailer

Part III   Supplementary Reading

Safety in Material Handling

Handling and storing materials involve operations such as lifting up tons of steel with a crane; driving a truck loaded with concrete blocks; carrying bags or materials manually; and stacking pallets or other materials such as drums, barrels, and lumber.

The efficient handling and storing of materials are very important to industry. Unfortunately, the improper handling and storing of materials often result in costly injuries.

To reduce the number of accidents associated with workplace equipment, workers must be trained in the proper use of the equipment they operate, including safely and effectively use equipments such as powered industrial trucks, conveyors, cranes and slings.

What Should Workers Know Before Handling Materials

Applying general safety principles—such as proper work practices, equipment, and controls—can help reduce workplace accidents involving the handling materials. Whether moving materials manually or mechanically, workers should know and understand the potential hazards associated with the task at hand and how to control their workplaces to minimize the danger.

Because numerous injuries can result from improperly handling and storing materials, workers should also be aware of accidents that may result from the unsafe or improper handling of equipment and from improper work

Fig.7.1 Handling material with lift truck

practices. In addition, workers should be able to recognize the methods for eliminating, or minimizing, the occurrence of such accidents. Workers should examine their workplaces to detect any unsafe or unhealthful conditions, practices, or equipment and take corrective action.

Potential Hazards for Workers

Workers frequently mention the weight and bulkiness of objects that they lift as major factors of their injuries. In 1999, for example, more than 420,000 workplace accidents resulted in back injuries. Bending, followed by twisting and turning, were the more commonly mentioned movements that caused back injuries.

Other hazards include falling objects, improperly stacked materials, and various types of equipment.

Precautions Should Be Taken When Moving Materials Manually

When moving materials manually, workers should attach handles or holders to loads. In addition, workers should always wear appropriate personal protective equipment and use proper lifting techniques. To prevent injury from oversize loads, workers should seek help in the following:

● When a load is so bulky that workers cannot properly grasp or lift it,

- When workers cannot see around or over a load, or
- When employees cannot safely handle a load.

Precautions Should Be Taken When Moving Materials Mechanically

Using mechanical equipment to move and store materials increases the potential of injuries. Workers must be aware of safe equipment operating techniques. Employees should avoid overloading equipment when moving materials mechanically by letting the weight, size, and shape of the material being moved dictate the type of equipment used. All material handling equipment has rated capacities that determine the maximum weight the equipment can safely handle and the conditions under which it can handle that weight. Workers must ensure that the equipment capacity is displayed on each piece of equipment and is not exceeded except for load testing.

Although workers may be knowledgeable about powered equipment, they should take precautions when stacking and storing material. When picking up items with a powered industrial truck, workers must do the following:

- Center the load on the forks as close to the mast as possible,
- Avoid overloading a lift truck,
- Adjust the load to the lowest position when traveling,
- Follow the truck manufacturer's operational requirements, and
- Pile and cross-tier all stacked loads correctly when possible.

Safety Measures Regarding Conveyors

When using conveyors, workers may get their hands caught, be struck by material falling off the conveyor, or may get caught in the conveyor and drawn into the conveyor path as a result. To prevent or reduce the severity of an injury, following precautions must be taken to protect workers:

- Install an emergency button or pull cord designed to stop the conveyor at the work station.
- Design the emergency stop switch so that it must be reset before the conveyor can be restarted.
- Prohibit workers from riding on a materials-handling conveyor.
- Provide guards where conveyors pass over work areas or aisles to keep workers from being struck by falling material.

Safety Measures Regarding Cranes

Employers must permit only thoroughly trained and competent workers to operate cranes. Operators should know what they are lifting and what it weighs. For example, the rated capacity of mobile cranes varies with the length of the boom and the boom radius. When a crane has a telescoping boom, a load may be safe to lift at a short boom length or a short boom radius, but may overload the crane when the boom is extended and the radius increases.

To reduce the severity of an injury, the following precautions must be taken:

- Equip all cranes that have adjustable booms with boom angle indicators.
- Provide cranes with telescoping booms with some means to determine boom lengths unless the load rating is independent of the boom length.
- Require workers to always check the crane's load chart to ensure that the crane will not be overloaded by operating conditions.
- Instruct workers to plan lifts before starting them to ensure that they are safe.
- Take additional precautions and exercise extra care when operating around power lines.
- Direct workers to always keep hoisting chains and ropes free of kinks or twists and never wrapped around a load.
- Train workers to attach loads to the load hook by slings, fixtures, and other devices that have the capacity to support the load on the hook.

Safety Precautions for Operating Powered Industrial Trucks

Workers who handle and store materials often use fork trucks, platform lift trucks, motorized hand trucks, and other specialized industrial trucks powered by electrical motors, must be aware of the safety requirements pertaining the design, maintenance, and use of these trucks.

- Fit high-lift rider trucks with an overhead guard if permitted by operating conditions.
- Locate battery-charging installations in designated areas.
- Do not place arms and legs between the mast or outside the running lines of the truck.
- Set brakes and put other adequate protection in place to prevent movement of trucks, trailers, or railroad cars when using powered industrial trucks to load or unload materials onto them.
- Provide sufficient headroom under overhead installations, lights, pipes, and sprinkler systems.
- Handle only stable or safely arranged loads.
- Disconnect batteries before repairing electrical systems on trucks.
- Ensure that replacement parts on industrial trucks are equivalent to the original ones.

New Words and Expressions

Stack pallet		堆叠托盘
Drum [drʌm] n.		鼓形圆桶
Barrel ['bærəl] n.		大桶，一桶的量，（液量单位）桶
Precaution [pri'kɔːʃən] n.		防范，预防
Costly		损失很大
Hazard ['hæzəd] n.		伤害

Powered industrial truck	工业用机动卡车
Bulkiness *n.*	体积大，庞大
Sling [sliŋ]	吊索，吊货网，吊钩
Cross-tier	交叉层
Severity [si'veriti] *n.*	严重性
Crane's load chart	起重机负荷表
Mast [mɑːst]	柱杆，桅杆
Boom radius ['reidjəs]	吊臂幅度

NOTES

1. To reduce the number of accidents associated with workplace equipment, workers must be trained in the proper use of the equipment they operate, including safely and effectively use equipments such as powered industrial trucks, conveyors, cranes and slings.

为了减少与工场设备相关的事故次数，必须培训工人们正确使用他们所操作的设备，包括安全有效地使用工业用机动卡车等设备。

2. Bending, followed by twisting and turning, were the more commonly mentioned movements that caused back injuries.

弯腰，接着扭腰、转身都是经常提到的造成背部受伤的动作。

3. When moving materials manually, workers should attach handles or holders to loads.

当人工搬运物料时，工人应系上把手或固定器装载物品。

4. Design the emergency stop switch so that it must be reset before the conveyor can be restarted.

设计应急终止开关，这样传送带重新开启前必须重新设置。

5. Do not place arms and legs between the mast or outside the running lines of the truck.

不要把手和腿放在柱杆之间或车辆的运行线外。

EXERCISES

Challenging questions for discussion

1. Explain the potential hazards for workers.
2. What precautions should the workers take when moving materials manually?
3. What precautions should be taken when moving materials mechanically
4. Explain the safety measures regarding conveyors.
5. What safety measures should workers take when operating cranes?
6. What is the safety precaution for operating powered industrial trucks?

Chapter 8 Packaging

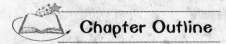

Chapter Outline

Part I   Packaging Perspective

Packaging perspective

Types of packaging

      Consumer package

      Industrial package

Functions of packaging

Containment	Utilization
Protection	Convenience
Apportionment	Communication

Part II   Package Design

Overview of package design

Factors governing good packaging design

Saving Money through Efficient and Effective Packaging

Considerations for package design

Part III   Supplementary Reading

Packaging Materials

    Introduction of Packaging Material

    Traditional Materials

      New Emerging Packaging

      Film-based Packaging

      Blanket-wrapping

      Returnable Containers

      Intermediate Bulk Containers

      Plastic Pallets

      Refrigerated Containers

Part I Packaging Perspective

Overview of Packaging

Packaging is highly appreciated now

Packaging is an important concern for warehousing and materials handling, one that receiving increased attention around the world. For example, under China's previous planned economy, Shanghai's production sector placed major emphasis on the quality of products and paid little attention to packaging. Shanghai commodities on both the domestic and world markets were often said to display "first-class quality, second-class packaging and third-class pricing." Shanghai lagged far behind developed countries and other coastal areas of China in terms of packaged goods. Over the past years, Shanghai has increased the investment for its packaging industry in order to ensure that its packaged products meet the demands of consumers for damage-free goods. Manufacturers have come to realize that the improved packaging of commodities can significantly increase the added value of products.

Packaging story of Shanghai product

Packaging relates with other activities

Packaging is closely tied to warehouse efficiency and effectiveness. The best package increases service, decreases cost, and improves handling. Good packaging can have a positive impact on layout, design, and overall warehouse productivity.

Types of Packaging

Consumer package & industrial package

There are two basic kinds of packages: the consumer package and the industrial package.

The consumer package is also referred to as the interior, or marketing package, because it is what the customer sees when the product is on the shelf. It is designed to appeal to and inform the final customer.

Interior package & exterior package

The industrial package is also known as the exterior package, and is primarily a logistics responsibility. This package is discarded before the products are placed on the shelf, so customer may never even see this material.

Functions of Packaging

Marketing function of packaging

Packaging serves two basic functions: marketing and logistics. In the marketing function, it provides customers with information about the product and promotes the product through the use of color and shape.

This information may be in the form of instructions on how to use, store, and dispose of the product, or it could be guidance on how to handle items during transit.

Logistics function of packaging

A second critical function is from a logistics perspective that of protection. This role may involve protection from damage in the warehouse or on the way of transportation, security from tampering or contamination by other products, or shielding from weather.

Six main function of packaging

More specifically, packaging performs six functions:

1. **Containment.** Products must be contained before they can be moved one place to another. If the package breaks open, the item can be damaged or lost, or even cause environmental pollution.

2. **Protection.** To protect the contents of the package from damage or loss from outside environmental effects.

3．**Apportionment.** To reduce the large output from industrial production to a desirable smaller "consumer" size.

4．**Unitization.** To permit primary packages to be unitized into secondary packages. This reduces the number of times a product must be handled.

5．**Convenience.** To allow products to be used conveniently; that is, with little wasted effort by customers.

6．**Communication.** The use of unambiguous, readily understood symbols such as a UPC (Universal Product Code).

New Words and Expressions

Packaging [ˈpækidʒiŋ] n.   包装
Perspective [pəˈspektiv] n.   远景，前途
Sector [ˈsektə] n.   部分，部门
Lag [læg] vt.   落后，滞后
Coastal [ˈkəustl] adj.   沿海的
Discard [disˈkɑːd] vt.   丢弃，抛弃
Tamper [ˈtæmpə] vi.   损害
Contamination [kən,tæmiˈneiʃən] n.   玷污，污染，污染物
Shield [ʃiːld] vt.(from)   保护，防护
Apportionment [əˈpɔːʃənmənt] n.   分配，分派，分摊
Unambiguous [ˌʌnæmˈbigjuəs] adj.   不含糊的，明确的
Symbol [ˈsimbəl] n.   符号，记号，象征

NOTES

1. Packaging is an important concern for warehousing and materials handling, one that receiving increased attention around the world.

包装对仓储和物资搬运作业至关重要，它在全球日益受到关注。

2. Over the past two years, Shanghai has increased the investment for its packaging industry in order to ensure that its packaged products meet the demands of consumers for damage-free goods.

在过去的两年里，上海增加了它在包装业的投资，以确保它的包装产品满足消费者对无损伤货物的要求.

3. This role may involve protection from damage in the warehouse or on the way of transportation, security from tampering or contamination by other products, or shielding from weather.

这个作用包括防止货物在仓库时或运输途中的损坏，免受其他货物的挤压和污染，或免于天气的影响。

4. UPC

UPC 是 Universal Product Code 的简写，通用产品码：由美国制定的条形码，于 1973 年开始推行。

EXERCISES

I. Fill in the blank and put the sentence into Chinese

1. Shanghai has increased investment for its _____ in order to ensure that its packaged products meet the demands of consumers for _____ goods.

2. Manufacturers have come to realize that the improved packaging of commodities can significantly increase the _____ of products.

3. Good packaging can have a positive impact on_____, design and overall _____.

4. The _____ package, which is designed to appeal and inform the final customer, is also referred to the _____ ,or _____ package.

5. The _____ package is discarded before the products are placed on the shelf, so may never even see this material.

6. In the _____ function, _____ provides customers with information about the product and promotes the product through the use of _____ and_____.

7. More specifically, packaging performs six functions that is protection,_____ , _____ ,apportionment, communication and _____.

II. Phrases translation

商业包装	国内外市场
工业包装	包装工业
产品质量	无损伤货物

包装的功能   通用商品码

III. Do you know the six main functions of packaging from the logistics perspective? Please discuss with your partner and complete the following table

Main function	Detail explanation（详细说明）
1.	
2.	
3.	
4.	
5.	
6.	

IV. Challenging questions for discussion

1. What is it implied by the example of Shanghai?
2. What kinds of the packaging are they?
3. What are the functions of packaging?
4. What information can be provided in the marketing function?
5. What is the logistics function of packaging?

Part II   Packaging Design

Overview of Package Design

Package design is important

The package should be designed to provide the most efficient storage. Good packaging interfaces well with the organization's materials handling equipment and allows efficient utilization of storage space as well as transportation cube and weight constraints.

Nowadays, the master carton and the unitized load become basic handing units for logistical operations.

Concept of master carton

Individual products or parts are typically grouped into cartons, bags, bins, or barrels for handling efficiency. Containers used to group individual products are called *master cartons*.

The weight, cube, and damage potential of the master carton determines transportation and materials handling requirements. If the package is not designed for efficient logistical processing, overall system performance suffers.

Factors Affecting Good Packaging Design

Good package design is influenced by (1) standardization, (2) pricing (cost), (3) product or package adaptability, (4) protective level, (5) handling ability, (6) product packability, and (7) reusability and recyclability.

Saving Money through Efficient and Effective Packaging

Packaging affects costs and customer service level

Packaging impacts both costs and customer service levels. Product packaging in standard configurations and order quantities helps logistical efficiency. Investing in efficient and effective packaging can save a company money in the following ways:

● Lighter packaging may save transportation costs.

● Careful planning of packaging size/cube may allow better space utilization of warehousing and transportation.

● More protective packaging may reduce damage and requirements for special handling.

● More environmentally conscious packaging may save disposal costs and improve the company's image.

● Use of returnable containers provides cost savings as well as environmental benefits through the reduction of waste production.

Two Issues Shall Be Taken into Consideration for Package Design

Good package design can improve cube utilization

Cube Utilization. Cube Utilization can be improved through reduced package size. For example, orange juice can be concentrated by eliminating air inside packages. IKEA, the Swedish retailer of unassembled furniture, emphasizes cube minimization to the point that ships pillows vacuum-packed. IKEA uses a cube minimization strategy to successfully compete in the United States even though the company ships furniture from Sweden. Some experts believe that improving cube utilization is the greatest opportunity of packaging and predict that, in general, packaging cube can be reduced by as much as 50%, which doubles transportation efficiency.

Weight utilization can be achieved with good package design

Weight Utilization. Heavy products, like steel ball or liquid in glass bottles, often meet the weight limitation of a transport vehicle before its cube is filled. The total weight can sometimes be reduced by package changes. For example, using plastic bottles instead of glass increases the number of bottles that can be loaded in a trailer. Even when package design is not changed, heavy products may offer lightweight special opportunities as lightweight product can be top loaded to take advantage of the empty cube without substantially changing total weight or transportation cost.

New Words and Expressions

Constraint [kən'streint] *n*.		约束
Standardization [ˌstændədai'zeiʃ ən] *n*		标准化
Adaptability [ədæptə'biliti] *n*.		适应性
Conscious ['kɔnʃəs] *adj*.		有意识的
Concentrate ['kɔnsentreit] *v*.		集中，浓缩
Unassembled [ˌʌnə'sembld] *adj*.		未装配的
Lightweight *adj*.		轻质的
Substantially [səb'stænʃ(ə)li] *adv*.		实质上地，重大地

NOTES

1. Good packaging interfaces well with the organization's materials handling equipment and allows efficient utilization of storage space as well as transportation cube and weight constraints。

好的包装能很好地与该组织的物资搬移设备相匹配，使得在满足运输容积和重量的约束条件的情况下能有效地利用存储空间。

2. If the package is not designed for efficient logistical processing, overall system performance suffers.

如果包装的设计不是针对高效的物流流程，整个系统的性能就会受到损害。

3. IKEA uses a cube minimization strategy to successfully compete in the United States even though the company ships furniture from Sweden.

IKEA 使用体积最小化战略在美国竞争中很成功，即使该公司是从瑞典运输家具。

4. Even when package design is not changed, heavy products may offer special opportunities as lightweight product can be top loaded to take advantage of the empty cube without substantially changing total weight or transportation cost.

即使在不改变包装设计的情况下，重物品的运输也可有多种选择，因为可利用空余的容积将轻物品装载在顶部以避免大幅度改变总重量或总运输成本。

EXERCISES

I. Fill in the blank and put the sentence into Chinese

1. Good packaging interfaces well with the organization's materials handling equipment and allows efficient utilization of _____ as well as transportation _____ and _____ constraints.

2. Containers used to group individual products are called _____.

3. Good package design is influenced by_____, pricing (cost), product or package adaptability, _____, handling ability, product packability, and reusability and_____.

4. Packaging impacts both _____and _____levels.

5. Careful planning of packaging size/cube may allow better space utilization of _____ and_____.

6. More environmentally conscious packaging may save _____costs and improve the company's_____.

7. Use of returnable containers provides _____as well as environmental benefits through the_____.

8. _____ and _____shall be taken into consideration for package design.

II. Phrases translation

主箱	处理成本
运输容积和重量	可回收使用的容器
标准结构	容积利用率
订货数量	体积最小化
运输成本	运输效率
包装尺寸	真空包装
环保包装	载重率

III. What benefits will efficient and effective packaging bring to a company? Line the specific packaging with its benefits

1. Lighter packaging   a. Reducing of waste production
2. Environment-conscious packaging   b. Saving disposal costs
3. Well-planned packaging   c. Making full use of space in transportation
4. Returnable containers   d. Reducing damage
5. Protective packaging   e. Saving transportation costs

IV. Challenging questions for discussion

1. What is the function of master carton?
2. What are the factors influence good packaging design?
3. How can we save money with packaging?
4. What factors shall be taken into consideration for package design?

Part III   Supplementary Reading
Packaging Materials

Introduction of Packaging Materials

Numerous material types are used for logistics packaging. Traditional alternatives are reviewed first, followed by a discussion of emerging material alternatives.

Traditional Materials

Corrugated materials

Corrugated materials and corrugated cardboard boxes are the general one required by common carriers in the United States since the early 1900s.

Other traditional packaging materials include burlap bags, blankets, steel cans, pails, drums and straps, cages, and multiwall paper bags and drums.

New options include low-density plastic film, shrink-wrap, stretch-wrap, bags and barriers, high-density plastic boxes and totes, plastic strapping, and plastic foam cushioning and dunnage for fragile and irregular shapes.

New Emerging Packaging

Shippers push new emerging package

Technological innovation has improved a logistical packaging renaissance. Shippers are encouraging experimentation with new, less costly, and creative packaging systems.

Emerging packaging includes film-based packaging, blanket-wrapping, returnable containers, intermediate bulk containers, pallet pools, plastic pallets, and alternatives that require special material handling equipment. Although several of these are adaptations of traditional packaging concepts, they are differentiated from traditional methods in two critical respects. First, they are customized for specific logistical systems and products; and second, they are designed to minimize the costs of packaging and solid waste disposal.

Film-based Packaging

Film-based packaging

Film-based packaging utilizes flexible packaging materials rather than rigid packaging. Today they are used to form actual shipping packages for consumer goods such as cans and bottles, furniture, appliances, and small vehicles. The new packages generally are combined with rigid materials. For example, cans are shrink-wrapped into a corrugated fiberboard tray and plastic bottle trays have corner support.

Advantages of Film-based packaging

Film-based flexible packaging provides several advantages. Film-based systems operate automatically, reducing the labor costs. A roll of film fits most product equally well, thus eliminates the need to maintain inventories of various sized boxes. It also minimizes shipment weight and cube and reduces inventory storage space; additionally, less rubbish remains after the product is unpacked. A final advantage is that damage is reduced. Research shows that freight is generally handled more carefully when it is clearly visible rather concealed in a box.

Blanket-wrapping

Application of blanket-wrapping

Blanket-wrapping is a traditional form of packaging provided by household goods movers. It is ideally suited for products like tables or chairs.

Support decking is erected with plywood and bars that lock into trailer walls; products are stacked into the decking and the product surfaces are protected with blankets.

The blanket-wrap has been extended into premium uncartoned transportation service.

Returnable Containers

Application and trend of blanket-wrapping

Most reusable packages are steel or plastic, although some firms reuse corrugated fiberboard boxes. Automobile manufacturers use returnable racks for interplant shipment of body parts, and chemical companies reuse steel drums. There is an increasing trend, however, to reusable packaging applications for many small items and parts such as ingredients, grocery perishables, interplant shipments, and retail warehouse-to-store totes.

Intermediate Bulk Containers

Application of IBCs

Intermediate Bulk Containers (IBCs) are used for granular and liquid product shipment. Typical products include resin pellets, food ingredients, and adhesives. The most frequently used IBCs are bulk bags and boxes.

Plastic Pallets

Characteristic of plastic pallets

Plastic pallets is sanitary, lightweight, and recyclable, and the life cycle costs are comparable to traditional wooden pallets. The grocery industry is testing alternative plastic pallet designs for durability and operational performance.

Refrigerated Containers

Functions of refrigerated

Refrigerated pallets are self-contained refrigerated shipping units. They can be loaded inside a regular dry van, which eliminates dependency on trucks with refrigerated power units. They can also facilitate the efficient and effective flow of a full range of products that depend on controlled temperatures to extend shelf life and marketability, including fresh foods, flowers, chemicals, and frozen foods.

New Words and Expressions

Emerge [i'mə:dʒ] *vi.*   涌现

Premium ['primjəm] *n.*   额外费用

Corrugated ['kɔrəgeɪtɪd] *adj.*   波纹状的，弄皱的

Corrugated cardboard   瓦楞纸板

Ingredient [in'gri:diənt] *n.*   拼料，配料

Granular ['grænjulə] *adj.*   颗粒的，粒状的

Resin ['rezin] *n.*   树脂

Adhesive [əd'hi:siv] *n.*   黏合剂

Sanitary ['sænitəri] *adj.*   清洁的

Fiberboard *n.*   纤维板

Rigid ['ridʒid] *adj.*   硬的，刚性的

Tray [trei] *n.*   盘，碟

Freight [freit] *n.*   货物，运费，货运

Conceal [kən'si:l] *vt.*   隐藏，隐蔽

Decking [dek] *vt.*   装饰，修饰，装甲板

Erect [i'rekt] *vt.*   使竖立，使直立

Fragile ['frædʒail] *adj.*   易碎的，脆的

Irregular [i'regjulə] *adj.*   不规则的，无规律的

Renaissance [rə'neisəns] *n.*   复兴，新生

Differentiate [ˌdifə'renʃieit] *v.*   区别，区分

NOTES

1. Traditional alternatives are reviewed first, followed by a discussion of emerging material alternatives.

先回顾传统的包装材料选择，然后是对正涌现的包装材料选择的讨论。

2. Other traditional packaging materials include burlap bags, blankets, steel cans, pails, drums and straps, cages, and multiwall paper bags and drums.

其他传统包装材料包括粗麻布包、毛毡、钢罐、桶、鼓、绑扎带、笼、多层纸袋和多层纸桶。

3. New options include low-density plastic film, shrink-wrap, stretch-wrap, bags and barriers, high-density plastic boxes and totes, plastic strapping, and plastic foam cushioning and dunnage for fragile and irregular shapes.

包装材料的新选择包括低密度塑料膜、收缩包装、弹性包装、袋子和阻隔物、高密度塑料箱、搬运箱、塑料绑带和用于易碎和不规则形状物品的塑料泡沫垫料和填衬料。

4. Emerging packaging include film-based packaging, blanket-wrapping, returnable containers, intermediate bulk containers, pallet pools, plastic pallets…

新型包装包括薄膜类包装、毡布包裹、可回收容器、中型散货容器、托盘组和塑料托盘……

5. Intermediate Bulk Containers (IBCs) are used for granular and liquid product shipment.

中型散货容器适用于颗粒状和液状物品的运输。

6. Plastic pallets are sanitary, lightweight, and recyclable, and their life cycle costs are comparable to traditional wooden pallets.

塑料托盘卫生、质轻、可循环使用，而且它们的生命周期成本可与传统的木质托盘相比。

7. They can also facilitate the efficient and effective flow of a full range of products that depend on controlled temperatures to extend shelf life and marketability, including fresh foods, flowers, chemicals, and frozen foods.

它们也能够促进包括新鲜食品、花卉、化学制品和冷冻食品在内的，依靠温控来延长保存期和增强销售能力的广大范围产品的高效率和有效果的流通。

EXERCISES

Challenging questions for discussion

1. What is the difference between materials of traditional packaging and new emerging packaging?

2. What is the advantage of the film-based packaging ?

3. Give some examples of new emerging packaging.

4. Please explain the usage of blanket-wrapping and returnable container.

5. Explain the application of the refrigerated container?

Chapter 9 Physical Distribution

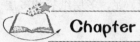

Chapter Outline

Part I   Physical Distribution

　Concept of Physical Distribution

　　What is physical distribution

　　Distribution performance cycle

　　Distribution functionality

　Types of distribution:

　　Intensive distribution

　　Selective distribution

　　Extensive distribution

Part II   Distribution Center

　Introduction of distribution center

　Difference to a warehouse

　Trends of distribution center

Part III   Supplementary Reading

　An Integrated System of DC

　　Designing and Equipping Distribution is a Complex Process

　　The sports Authority's Regional Distribution Center—An Overview

Part I Physical Distribution

Conception of Physical Distribution

What is physical distribution

Physical distribution operations involve processing and delivering customer orders. Physical distribution is integral to marketing and sales performance because it provides timely and economical product availability. The overall process of gaining and maintaining customers can be broadly divided into transaction-creation and physical-fulfillment activities. The transaction-creating activities are advertising and selling. Physical distribution performs the physical-fulfillment activities.

Distribution performance cycle

The typical physical distribution performance cycle involves five related activities. They are order transmission, order processing, order selection, order transportation, and customer delivery. The basic physical distribution performance cycle is illustrated as following:

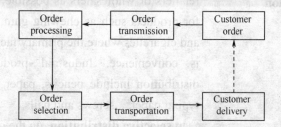

Distribution functionality

From a logistical perspective, physical distribution links a firm with its customers. Physical distribution resolves marketing and manufacturing initiatives into an integrated effort. The interface between marketing and manufacturing can be conflictive. On the one hand, marketing is dedicated to delighting customers. In most firms, minimal limits are imposed by marketing and sales when it comes to accommodation customers. Often, this means that marketing and sales would like to maintain a broad product line with high inventory regardless of each product's actual profit potential. In this way, any customer's requirement, no matter how small or large, would be satisfied. The expectation of physical distribution is that zero defect service will be achieved and customer-focused marketing efforts will be supported.

Importance of related operations in physical distribution

The very fact that physical distribution deals with customer requirements means that related operations will be more erratic than characteristic of manufacturing support and procurement performance cycles. Attention to how customers order products is essential to reduce physical distribution operational variance and simplify transactions. First, every effort should be made to improve forecast accuracy. Second, a program of order management coordination with customers should be initiated to reduce uncertainty as much as possible. Third, and finally, physical distribution performance cycles should be designed to be as flexible and responsive as possible.

The key to understanding physical distribution performance-cycle dynamics is to keep in mind that customers initiate the process by ordering. The logistical response capability of the selling enterprise constitutes one of the most significant competencies in overall marketing strategy.

Types of Distribution

Three types of distribution can be used to make product available to consumers: (1) intensive distribution, (2) selective distribution, and (3) exclusive distribution.

Intensive distribution

In **intensive distribution**, the product is sold to as many appropriate retailers or wholesalers as possible. Intensive distribution is appropriate for products such as chewing gum, candy bar, soft drinks, bread, film, and cigarettes where the primary factor influencing the purchase decision is convenience. Industrial products that may require intensive distribution include pencils, paper clips, transparent tape, file folders, typing paper, screws and nails.

Selective distribution

In **selective distribution**, on the other hand, the number of outlets that may carry a product is limited, but not to the extent of exclusive dealing. By carefully selecting wholesalers or retailers, the manufacturer can concentrate on potentially profitable accounts and develop solid working relationships to ensure that the product is properly merchandised. The producer also may restrict the number of retail outlets if the product requires specialized servicing or sales support. Selective distribution may be used for product categories such as clothing, appliances, televisions, stereo equipment, home furnishings, and sports equipment.

Exclusive distribution

When a single outlet is given an exclusive franchise to sell the product in a geographic area, the arrangement is referred to as **exclusive distribution**. Products such as specialty automobiles, some major appliances, certain brand of furniture, and lines of clothing that enjoy a high degree of brand loyalty are likely to be distributed on an exclusive basis. This is particularly true if the consumer is willing to overcome the inconvenience of traveling some distance to obtain the product. Usually, exclusive distribution is undertaken when the manufacturer desires more aggressive selling on the part of the wholesaler or retailer, or when channel control is important. Exclusive distribution may enhance the product's image and enable the firm to charge higher retail prices.

New Words and Expressions

Physical distribution [ˌdistri'bjuːʃən]	实物配送
Performance [pə'fɔːməns] *n.*	履行，执行，运行，性能
Physical-fulfillment [ful'filmənt]	实物实现
Illustrate ['iləstreit] *v.*	插图，解释说明
Conflictive *adj.*	冲突的
Erratic [i'rætik] *adj.*	反复无常的，不稳定的
Dynamics [dai'næmik] *n.*	动态，动力学
Transparent [træns'pɛərənt] *adj.*	透明的
Outlet ['autlet, -lit] *n.*	市场渠道，批发商店
Franchise ['fræntʃaiz]*n.*	特许（经营）权

NOTES

1. Physical distribution is integral to marketing and sales performance because it provides timely and economical product availability.

实物配送是履行营销和达成销售业绩所必不可少的，因为它提供了及时且经济的获取产品的可能性。

2. They are order transmission, order processing, order selection, order transportation, and customer delivery.

它们是订单传送、订单处理，订单拣货、订货运输以及向客户交货。

3. Attention to how customers order products is essential to reduce physical distribution operational variance and simplify transactions.

注意客户是如何订购产品对降低实物配送操作的不协调性和简化交易至关重要。

4. The logistical response capability of the selling enterprise constitutes one of the most significant competencies in overall marketing strategy.

销售企业的物流响应能力构成总营销战略中最重要的竞争力之一。

EXERCISES

I. Form phrases

实物配送

_____ distribution

订单处理

Order _____

实物履行

Physical _____

客户要求

Customer _____

集约式分销		选择性分销	
_____ distribution		_____ distribution	
独家分销		零售价	
_____ distribution		_____ Price	

II. Fill in the blanks and put the sentences into Chinese

1. The overall process of _____ customers can be broadly divided into _____ and physical-fulfillment activities.

2. They are order transmission, _____ , order selection, _____ , and customer delivery.

3. Often, this means that marketing and sales would like to maintain a broad product line with high inventory _____ each product's actual profit potential.

4. The _____ that physical distribution deals with customer requirements means that related operations will _____ than characteristic of manufacturing support and procurement performance cycles.

5. Physical distribution _____ should be designed to be as _____ as possible.

6. The producer also may _____ the number of retail outlets if the product requires specialized servicing or _____.

III. Please complete the following table to get yourself familiar with the information on types of distribution

Type of distribution	Appropriate customers	Appropriate products

IV. 🎧Listen to the conversation, and answer the question or complete the sentences

1. Darden restaurant successfully manages 4 distinctly different distribution styles for supply chain management _____, _____, _____, _____.

2. What kind of products are central distribution used for ?

3. What are the characteristics of independent supply chain?

4. How does Darden use direct distribution strategy?

5. What is the distribution strategy Darden uses for its US $150 million or more seafood?

118

V. Challenging questions for discussion

1. Please explain the physical distribution performance cycle.

2. Discuss and compare the three approaches of distribution: intensive distribution, selective distribution, and exclusive.

3. Why do we say that physical distribution links a firm with its customers?

Part II   Distribution Center

Introduction of Distribution Center

Concept of distribution center

Distribution center (DC) is a logistics link to fulfill physical distribution as its main function. Generally speaking, it's a large and highly automated center destined to receive goods from various plants and suppliers, take orders, fill them efficiently, and deliver goods to customers as quickly as possible.

Differences to a Warehouse

DC emphases on goods moving

Unlike a warehouse, however, the emphasis of a distribution center is on the moving of goods rather than on long-term storage. Practically, it's a short-term storage center located close to a major to facilitate the rapid processing of orders and shipment of goods to customers.

The difference between Distribution Centers and Warehouses is as follows:

DC differs from warehouse in performance cycle, activities, data collecting, products stored and its focus

Warehouses	Distribution centers
Warehouses (Ws) handle most products in four cycle, e.g., receive, store, ship, and pick.	Distribution centers (DCs) handle most products in two cycle, e.g., receive and ship.
Ws perform a minimum of value-added activities (receive-store-ship generally in original forms).	DCs perform a great deal of value-added activities, e.g., final assembly (applying the postponement strategy).
Ws collect data in batches (generally) (receive and ship goods in batches).	DCs collect data in real time (might deliver less than the batch size. The transfer batch may not, and many times should not, be equal to the process batch-OPT rule).
Ws store all products (slow or fast moving).	DCs hold predominantly high demand items.
Ws focus on minimizing the operating costs to meet shipping requirements.	DCs focus on maximizing the profit impact of fulfilling customer (external customer) delivery requirement.

Trends of Distribution Center

Trends one: demise
Trends two: DC with modified roles

There are some experts in this field that predict the demise of warehouses because in inventory stocking will no longer be needed. They claim that efficient consumer response (ECR) and Just-In-Time (JIT) in combination with point of sales (POS) data will fully synchronize the company's demand chain. Most other experts disagree and believe that integrated logistics will spur DCs to modify their roles, which will be based on speeding the flow of products and providing value-added services. Examples of the changing role of warehouses can be seen in consolidations of shipments, cross-docking, and value-added processes such as packaging, sub-assembly, kitting, labeling, and final custom work such as providing color and style to products based on customer orders. Certainly, e-Commerce has led to warehouse expansion in the USA and Europe and refocus by existing warehousing companies.

New Words and Expressions

Distribution center	配送中心
Logistics link	物流结点
Destine ['destin] vt.	注定
Deliver [di'livə] vt	递送
Point of sales (POS)	销售时点信息系统
Synchronize ['sɪŋkrənaɪz] v	使同步
Minimum ['miniməm] adj. & n.	最小的，最低的；最小值，最小化
Final assembly [ə'sembli]	总装（配）
In batches [bætʃ] adv	分批地，成批地
Spur [spə:] n.& v.	刺激；鞭策，刺激
Predominant [pri'dɔminənt] adj	主要的，突出的，有影响的
Consolidation [kən,sɔli'deiʃən] n.	巩固，合并
Demise [di'maiz] n. & vt .	消失，死亡
Sub-assembly n.	分装
kit n.	成套工具，用具包，工具箱，成套用具
Refocus [ri:'fəukəs] v.	重调重心，新聚集

NOTES

1. Generally speaking, it's a large and highly automated center destined to receive goods from various plants and suppliers, take orders, fill them efficiently, and deliver goods to customers as quickly as possible.

一般而言，配送中心是设计用来从不同工厂和供应者中接收货物，接受订单，高效地履行订单，并将货物尽快地送给客户的一个高度自动化的大型中心，。

2. DCs collect data in real time (might deliver less than the batch size…).

集散控制系统实时收集信息（可能以少于一批的数量发货……）

3. They claim that ECR and JIT in combination with POS data will fully synchronize the company's demand chain.

他们声称有效客户反应（ECR）、准时制（JIT），结合销售时点（POS）信息，将与公司的需求链完全保持同步。

EXERCISES

I. Form phrases

配送中心	物流结点
Distribution c_____	Logistics l_____
总装配	成批地
Final a_____	In b_____
销售时点信息系统	有效顾客反应
p_____ of sales	Efficient consumer r_____
需求链	外部顾客
D_____ chain	ex_____ customer
增值活动	接受订单
Value-_____activity	take o_____

II. Fill in the blanks and put the sentences into Chinese

1. Distribution center is _____ to fulfill physical distribution as its main _____.

2. Practically, it's a _____ center located close to a major to facilitate _____ of orders and shipment of goods to customers.

3. DCs _____ maximizing the profit impact of _____ (external customer) delivery requirement.

4. They claim that _____and Just-In-Time (JIT) in combination with _____ data will fully synchronize the company's demand chain.

5. Examples of the changing role of warehouses can be seen in _____, cross-docking, and _____.

III. Please write a paragraph introducing the performance cycle, activities, data-collecting, product stored and the focus of DC

IV. Questions for discussion

1. What do you think of the major difference between Distribution Centers and Warehouses?

2. Why do some experts predict the demise of warehouses?

3. How do other experts predict the changing of the role of DCs?

Part III Supplementary Reading
An Integrated System of DC

Designing and Equipping Distribution is a Complex Process

Designing and equipping is an integration exercise

Designing and equipping distribution centers is a complex process, and simply integrating all of the different hardware, software and controls required for today's state-of-art distribution systems has become a major logistics exercise in itself.

Distribution center design is a dynamic process that is constantly evolving to meet changing marketplace demands and expectations. An example is illustrated as follows:

Functions of the installation

The installation was designed to integrate the flow of product throughout the following functional areas of the distribution center: receiving, value-added service (VAS) preparation, VAS processing and takeaway, put-to-store location, and shipping.

The Sports Authority's Regional Distribution Center— An Overview

Inbound goods operation process

Inbound goods are moved from receiving areas to VAS (value-added service) processing station. After scanning and tag-generation, totes move on powered takeaway unit to VAS processing area, where they accumulate on EZ-Logic conveyors. After processing, they move up a belt incline to a re-circulation loop. Totes are diverted off the loop to one of five "fingers" in put-to-store location. Operators fill and seal cartons for the appropriate store and then place them on takeaway conveyor for movement to shipment staging. Here they merge with full pallet orders for truckload delivery to the stores.

Equipments used

To achieve that desired integration, the Sports Authority relies on a wide range use of Hytrol equipment. The units include accumulation conveyors, belt inclines and declines, live rollers, sorters and diverts , trash takeaway conveyors , and more.

When operator scans the tote, the terminal displays the quantity of product inside the tote to be put store location specified.

Inbound goods operation

Inbound goods from the vendors are initially handled in a VAS (value-added service) preparation area. The operators here remove the contents from the cartons and place the items in totes. The totes then are scanned and the information is entered into the WMS. Labels that will accompany the items through the order-fulfillment process are generated at this point as well. Trash takeaway conveyors in the processing area help keep the facility clean and free from debris.

Activities in VAS processing area

The totes then are placed on a powered conveyor that carries them to the VAS processing area. Each tote is diverted to one of four lanes, where they accumulate on the EZ-Logic conveyors. Processing personnel retrieve the totes from the main accumulation line by pressing a foot pedal that controls a pneumatic divert. A work surface at bottom of the chute serves as a table for the processor to empty the contents of the tote and apply the labels and tags. Once the VAS processing is done, the totes are placed on an outbound chute, which leads to a takeaway conveyor and up an incline to a re-circulation loop.

Automated diverts send the processed totes from the re-circulation loop down one of "five fingers" in the put-to-store location section of the DC. There's a total of 152 work stations in these five accumulation lanes. Once a tote is diverted from the finger lane into a store location zone, the operator scans the tote. The terminal indicates the quantity of the product within the tote to be put to the store location specified.

Delivery operation

Operators place the appropriate quantity in a shipping carton, drawing from the carton flow racks behind them. Once the sort orders are completed, order is pushed down the carton-flow takeaway lane. These cartons are then palletized and taken to shipment staging areas, where full truckloads of product are built for store delivery. The system is streamlined and efficient. And most importantly, inventory doesn't get a chance to sit still for very long.

New Words and Phrases

Evolving *adj*		进化的，展开的
Installation [ˌinstəˈleiʃən] *n.*		安装，装置
Inbound [ˈinbaund] *adj.*		入内的，进入方向的
Debris [ˈdebriː, ˈdeib-]*n.*		碎片，残骸
Tote [təut] *v. & n.*		手提，拖，拉；装运物
Retrieve [riˈtriːv] *v.*		重新得到，找回
Conveyor *n.*		传送装置
Pneumatic [nju(ː)ˈmætik]*adj.*		装满空气的，气动的,风力的
Re-circulation *n.*		再循环，再流通
Lane [lein] *n.*		狭窄的通道
Divert [diˈvəːt] *v. n.*		转移，转向；转向装置
Chute [ʃuːt] *n.*		斜道

Staging [ˈsteidʒiŋ] *n.*	待出货
Rack [ræk] *n*	架，行李架
Merge [məːdʒ] *v*	合并，并入，结合起来，吞没，融合
Palletize [ˈpæli,taiz] *v*	把……放在货盘上
Pallet [ˈpælit] *n*	货盘
Streamlined [ˈstriːmlaɪnd] *adj.*	精减的，简化的，高效率的
Takeaway *n.*	移走，入库
WMS (warehouse management system)	仓库管理系统

NOTES

1. Receiving, value-added service(VAS)preparation ,VAS processing and takeaway, put-to-store location ,and shipping.

接收，增值服务准备，增值服务操作及外运，储存定位，以及出货。

2. The units include accumulation conveyors, belt inclines and declines, live rollers , sorters and diverts, trash takeaway conveyors, and more.

这些装置包括堆垛传送带，上下皮带斜道，活动滚筒，分拣器和转向装置，废物移走传送带，等等。

3. Labels that will accompany the items through the order-fulfillment process are generated at this point as well.

伴随着物品一起贯穿履行订单的整个过程的标签也在此处生成。

4. Once the VAS processing is done, the totes are placed on an outbound chute, which leads to a takeaway conveyor and up an incline to a re-circulation loop.

一旦增值服务操作完成，载运物就被放置到外输斜道上，通向移走传送带，再向上传送到达再循环环路。

5. The system is streamlined and efficient. And most importantly, inventory doesn't get a chance to sit still for very long.

这一系统是最新型的且富有效率。最重要的是，存货不可能停滞很长时间。

EXERCISES

I. Form phrases

动态过程	功能区域
D____ process	f____ areas
增值服务	整车运送
V_____ service	full _____ delivery
待出货区	进库货物
st_____ area	in_____ goods
仓库操作人员	仓库管理系统
warehouse op____	warehouse ma_____ system

II. Fill in the blanks and put the sentences into Chinese

1. Inbound goods are moved from receiving areas to _____ processing station.

2. Operators _____ cartons for the appropriate store and then place them on takeaway conveyor for movement to _____.

3. Trash takeaway conveyors in the _____ help keep _____ clean and free from debris.

4. The totes then are _____ a powered conveyor that carries them to the _____.

5. Once the VAS processing is done, the totes are placed on _____, which leads to a takeaway conveyor and up an incline to _____ .

6. Operators place the _____ in a shipping carton, _____the carton flow racks behind them.

III. Challenging questions for discussion

1. Why should we say that distribution center design is a dynamic process?

2. Generally speaking, what are the major functional areas of a distribution center?

3. Please explain the processing procedure in this distribution center.

4. What equipment does the Sports Authority rely on?

5. Do you think this system is efficient? Defend your answer.

Chapter 10 Correspondence

 Chapter Outline

Part I   Business Letters

Overview of business letters

Main parts of a business letter

Other parts of a business letter

Layout of a business letter

Envelope addressing

Part II   Electronic Correspondence

Overview of electronic correspondence

Telex

Fax

E-mail

Part III   Supplementary Reading

Specimen Correspondence

Specimen Envelope

Specimen Letter

Specimen Telex

Specimen Fax

Specimen E-mail

Part I   Business Letters

Overview of Business Letters

Principle of 3 C's   Business letter writing is an important part of business activities. Despite the great advances made in the area of telecommunication, the letter still remains one of the most personal, economical and effective methods of written communication. Because a letter and its reply can make a written contract, it is often used to take the place of personal calls and telephone calls even when the two parties are in the same city, and must therefore be written in accordance with the principle of **three C's**, that is, **clearness**, **conciseness**, and **courtesy**.

Main Parts of a Business Letter

A typical English business letter generally consists of the following **eight main parts**.

Heading (Letterhead)   **1. The heading** is printed in the top center or at the top left margin of a letter, containing all the necessary information of the writer's name, address, postcode, telephone number, telex number, fax number and E-mail address.

Date   **2. The date** should be typed all in one line and below the heading. The format of the date line differs from nation to nation. The common ones are M/D/Y (typical American) and D/M/Y (typical British). Because of the different usage in the United States and in the United Kingdom, the month should be spelt out in full without using figures or abbreviations for it in order to avoid any possible confusion. For example, 5,10,2010 means May 10, 2010 in the United States and October 7, 2010 in the United Kingdom.

Inside name and address   **3. Inside name and address** refers to the name and address of the receiver and should be typed two or four lines spaces below the date and above the salutation at the left margin. It usually consists of the receiver's name, and detailed address such as house or building number, the street, the city, the state or the province, the postcode and the country. This part exactly appears on the envelope but cannot be omitted as the letter will be filed later for the completeness of the documents.

Salutation   **4. The salutation** is merely a matter of custom and a polite greeting to the receiver. It is typed at the left margin, two or three lines spaces below the inside name and address. The salutation varies with the writer's relationship with the receiver and the formality level of the letter. The ones customarily used can be "Dear Sir(s)", "Dear Madam", and "Dear Mesdames", followed by a comma.

Subject line

5. The subject line (or: Caption) gives the general content or purpose of the letter. It comes two lines below the salutation and above the body of the letter, underlined and generally preceded by "Re:" or "Subj.".

Body of the letter

6. Body of the letter contains the message of the letter. It extends the writer's idea and what he expects from the receiver of the letter. It is the most important part of a letter, and should be carefully arranged. The "three C's" principle mentioned above shall be achieved.

Complimentary close

7. Complimentary close is a polite ending of the letter, placed two lines spaces below the body of the letter. It is in line with the salutation and the commonly used closings are "Yours faithfully / sincerely / truly" and "Faithfully / Sincerely / Truly yours".

	Salutation	Complimentary Closes
Very formal	My dear Sir	Respectfully
	Sir	Respectfully yours
	My dear Madam	Yours respectfully
	Madam	Very respectfully yours
Formal	Dear Sir or Madam	Yours faithfully
	Dear Madam	Yours truly
	Gentlemen	Very truly yours
	Sir	Yours very truly
Less formal (the trend today is to use these forms in business correspondence rather than the formal form)	Dear Mr. Carpenter	
	My dear Mr. Carpenter	Yours sincerely
	Dear Mrs. Helen	Very sincerely
	My dear Mrs. Helen	Sincerely yours
	Dear Miss Helen	Sincerely
	My dear Miss Helen	
Personal (Imply personal acquaintance or previous friendly correspondence)	Dear Mr. Black	Yours cordially
		Cordially yours
	Dear Mrs. Brown	Cordially
	Dear Miss Helen	Most sincerely
	Dear Richard	Best regards
		Best wishes

Signature

8. Signature is immediately below the complimentary close by typing the company's name of the writer, followed by the writer's handwritten signature, the writer's typed name for legibility, and the writer's job title or position.

Other Parts of a Business Letter

Reference number/code

Attention line

Identification marks

Enclosure

Carbon copy notation

Apart from the above eight main parts, an English letter may include some other parts if necessary. **Reference number or code** is used as a useful indication for filing and marked with "Our Ref:" and "Your Ref:". **Attention line** is used when the letter is addressed direct to a particular person of a company and marked with "For the attention of (name or title)" or "Attention". **Identification marks** comprise capital initials of the writer and small letter initials of the typist as JS/ms or JS:ms, indicating their own responsibilities. The word "**Enclosure**" or its short form "Encl." is used when enclosures are sent with the letter. The abbreviation of **carbon copy notation** "cc", "Cc" or "CC" is typed if a copy is to be sent to a party or parties concerned.

Layout of a Business Letter

Styles of a business letter

Blocked style

Indented style

There are two common layout styles of a business letter, known as the blocked style and the indented style. Style choice depends on the writer's preference.

1. **Blocked style** is very modern, convenient and popular because all lines begin at the left margin, though sometimes the heading is printed or typed at the top center of the page.

2. **Indented style** is a traditional one and features the inside name and address and the salutation typed in blocked style, each paragraph indented six or ten spaces, the date, the complimentary close and the signature near the right margin, and the subject line centered on the page.

Envelope Addressing

Business envelopes generally have the writer's address printed in the upper left corner, the receiver's name and address typed about half way down the envelope, the postmark or stamps put in the up right corner, and the notations as "Confidential" and "Registered" placed in the bottom left corner. It's important to include the postcode on the envelope to facilitate mechanical mail sorting.

New Words and Expressions

Correspondence [ˌkɔrisˈpɔndəns] *n.*　　　　　　通信，信件
Telecommunication [ˌtelikəmjuːniˈkeiʃ ən] *n.*　　电信
Margin [ˈmɑːdʒin] *n.*　　　　　　　　　　　　　页边的空白

Abbreviation [əˌbriːviˈeiʃən] n.　　　　缩写，缩写式

Salutation [sælju(:)ˈteiʃən] n.　　　　致意，寒暄

Customary [ˈkʌstəməri] adj.　　　　合乎风俗或习惯的

Madam, Mesdames [ˈmædəm]　　　　（用在已婚妇女名字前面）夫人

Caption [ˈkæptin] n.　　　　标题，题目

Precede [pri(:)ˈsiːd] v.　　　　在前，居先，优于

Complimentary [ˌkɔmpliˈment(ə)ri] adj.　　　　恭维的，表示赞美的

Signature [ˈsignitʃə] n.　　　　签字

Legibility [ˌledʒəˈbiliti] n.　　　　（手写或印刷文字）清晰可读性

Title [ˈtaitl] n.　　　　头衔，职称

Position [pəˈziʃən] n.　　　　职位；位置

Indication [ˌindiˈkeiʃən] n.　　　　指示，表示

Identification [aiˌdentifiˈkeiʃən] n.　　　　鉴定，（身份）证明

Capital [ˈkæpitəl] adj.　　　　（字母表字母）大写的

Initial [iˈniʃəl] n.　　　　首字母

Responsibility [risˌpɔnsəˈbiliti] n.　　　　责任，职责

Enclosure [inˈkləuʒə] n.　　　　附件

Notation [nəuˈteiʃən] n.　　　　记号，记法，标志

Supplement [ˈsʌplimənt] vt.　　　　增补，补充

Preference [ˈprefərəns] n.　　　　偏爱，优先选择

Feature [ˈfiːtʃə] vt.　　　　以……为特色，特色

Confidential [kɔnfiˈdenʃəl] adj.　　　　机密的，绝密的

Registered [ˈredʒistəd] adj.　　　　（信件）挂号的

Envelope [ˈenviləup] n.　　　　信封

Facilitate [fəˈsiliteit] vt.　　　　促进，促使，使便利

Mechanical [miˈkænikl] adj.　　　　机械的，机器的

Sorting [ˈsɔːtiŋ] n.　　　　分埋，分拣

Blocked style [blɔkt]　　　　平头式，齐头式

Indented style [inˈdentid]　　　　缩进式

NOTES

1. Despite the great advances made in the area of telecommunication

尽管在电信领域已取得了重大进展

2. This part exactly appears on the envelope but cannot be omitted as the letter will be filed later for the completeness of the documents.

虽然这部分完全一样地出现在信封上，但不能被省略，因为以后要对信件归档以求文档的完整性。

3. Immediately below the complimentary close

紧接在结尾敬辞下面

4. A party or parties concerned
有关方或有关各方

5. To facilitate mechanical mail sorting
以便于机械化的邮件分拣

EXERCISES

I. Translate the following Chinese terms into English

信头	正文	附件	缩进式	平头式
结束语	封内地址	客气称呼	发信日期	署名

II. Translate the following English terms into Chinese

Attention line	Postmark	Reference number
Identification marks	Carbon copy notation	Subject line
Written communication	Abbreviation	Postcode

III. Match the following salutations with their appropriate complimentary closes

1. Dear Mrs. Smith
2. My dear Sir
3. Dear Mr. White
4. Gentlemen
5. Dear Sirs
6. Dear Mary
7. Sir
8. Dear Madam

Yours respectfully

Yours faithfully

Very truly yours

Best wishes

Yours sincerely

Yours cordially

IV. Challenging questions for discussion

1. Why do letters often replace personal calls and telephone calls even when the two parties are in the same city?

2. What is the principle of "Three C's" in writing business letters?

3. How many main parts does a business letter consist of? What are they?

4. What are the two common layout styles of letters?

PART II   Electronic Correspondence

Overview of Electronic Correspondence

Electronic correspondence   With the popularization and development of information technology in the late 1990s, **electronic correspondence** is becoming an integral part in international business. The early forms of electronic correspondence are telegram and telex, but now E-mail and fax are being increasingly used. Messages can be transmitted faster with electronic than with traditional ways, though only people with access to the systems can receive messages.

Telex

Being convenient, expeditious and economical

Telex, the short form of "**Teleprinter/Teletypewriter Exchange**", refers to message sent or received ·through a teleprinter/teletypewriter over the telephone network. It is an exchange service like the telephone service but uses teleprinters instead of telephones. Telex is more convenient, expeditious and economical than telephone or telegram. The main advantage over fax is that the appearance of the receiver's answer back code on the sender's copy of the transmitted message is proof that the message has reached the receiver's telex.

Telex operation

With the telex machine installed in office and connected by the telegraph office, the sender only needs to type the message on the machine and end it by direct dialing at any time. For the telex service is available 24 hours a day and the machine at the other end, even if unattended, can print out the messages automatically. In addition, a tape of a message may be prepared for sending to several different receivers at any time required, and views can be exchanged between the sender and the receiver on teleprinters by adding a "+?" signal at the end of a message, thus enabling business negotiation to be carried on until finished.

Drafting rules

Telex message should be in capital letters. Though it may be all in plain word, telex may also be drafted with some abbreviations and simplified words as the charge for a telex is based on the distance the message has to travel and time spent in transmission. For example, "thanks" is simplified as TKS and "urgent" as URG.

Differences between telex and telegram

There are some differences between telex and telegram.

1. Telex is charged by the transmission time, while telegram is charged by the number of words sent.

2. The structure of telex differs from that of telegram.

3. Combinations are seldom used in a telex, while they are commonly used in a telegram to reduce words.

4. Either punctuation marks (more commonly used) or symbols or words can be used in a telex, while no punctuation marks or symbols are used in a telegram.

5. Simplified words are commonly used in a telex, while no simplified

words are used except the most common ones such as PLS, TKU, etc.

6. The simplified word RGDS should be added at the end of a telex message, while no word or phrase of good wish is required at the end of a telegram message.

Ways of abbreviation

The following are some techniques to abbreviate longer words, which may help in drafting and understanding telexes.

1. To leave out vowels

PLS—please   RPL—reply   TKS—thanks

2. To retain the first syllable and the first consonant of the second syllable

CERT—certificate   EXP—export   ANS—answer

3. To use the first and the last letter of a word

FM—from   BK—bank   YR—your

4. To retain the important consonants and last letter of a word

5. Some universally accepted methods to simplify the telex words are regarded as regulations

(1) --ed (verbs)	...D	SHPD (shipped)
(2) --ing (verbs)	...G	OFFERG (offering)
(3) --ment	...MT or T	PAYMT (payment)
(4) --tion	...TN or N	INFN (information)
(5) --able or ible	...BL	POSSBL (possible)
(6) --tive	...TV	COMPTV (competitive)
(7) --ance or ince	...NC	RMTNC (remittance)
(8) --al	...L	TTL (total)

6. To use the first letter of each word of a phrase or expression

A/M (above-mentioned)   YC (your cable)

FYI (for your information)   ASAP (as soon as possible)

7. To use a letter or letters with the same or similar pronunciation instead of a word

N—and   R—are   B—be

U—you   WZ—with   ZS—this

Example of telex

The following is an example of a telex message:

PLS BE KINDLY IFMD TT SUB VSL LOADG NOW IN YR PORT HAS A DESPATCH / DEMURRAGE AGREEMT WZ PARTIES CONCERNED. THE LAST HR FOR HER DESPATCH IS UPTO 2400HRS 21ST MAY. IF THE LAYTIME LASTS TO 22ND, THE SHP WL ENTER INTO DEMURRAGE N WE WUD CERTAINLY SUSTAIN A GREAT LOSS.

HENCE WE WUD LIKE TO ASK U, AS OUR AGENTS, TO TALK

TO THE PORT TO SPEED UP THE LOADG BY MEANS OF MORE GANGS WORKG, N ASK THE SHP'S MASTER TO OFR THE BEST COOPERATNS WZ THE PORT SIDE AND EVEN DO SOMETHING FLEXIBLE IF NECESSARY, ALL FOR THE PURPOSE OF THE SHP BEING DESPATCHED FM YR PORT.

YR KIND EFFORTS WL B HIGHLY APPRECIATED. WAITG FOR YR GD NEWS. PLS CFM ASAP. B.R.

Fax

Using telephone lines

Fax, shortened from **facsimile transmission**, is widely used for business communication. It uses the telephone line or an especially reserved telephone line for sending and receiving messages, and the telephone number is used as the fax number. The fax system operates worldwide.

Fax operation

Fax takes a few seconds to automatically transmit and receive messages for the cost of a telephone call. What is sent at one end is received simultaneously at the other end just like a duplicating machine.

Writing features

Fax messages can be drafted and transmitted in plain language like a letter, which requires good English and skills for business writing. Some businesses have their names, addresses and contract numbers printed in the form of a heading on top center of fax paper, using as fax head.

E-mail

Using computer networks or telephone lines

E-mail is the short form of **electronic mail**. It refers to a system of sending messages between individuals or from individuals to groups from one computer terminal to another, using a computer network or telephone lines. It can be restricted to a local area network or open to a wide area network. Messages are sent to a mailbox and only those with a user identification and password can have access to the messages. Each user has a unique E-mail address.

Being reliable, speedy, effective and cheap

Compared with telegram, telex, fax, postal service and telephone, E-mail is relatively **reliable, speedy, effective and cheap**. The messages can be sent or picked up anywhere in the world, simultaneously appeared on the computer screen at the other end and printed out instantly or kept in the mailbox for filing until retrieved.

Components of an E-mail

An E-mail consists of two parts, the E-mail head and the body. The **E-mail head** comprises four parts. In the column of "To", the receiver's name, title and E-mail address must be accurate. If any subject is needed, place it in the column of "Subject". In the column of "From" and "Date", the writer's E-mail address and the sending time will be shown automatically. The column of "Enclosure" will indicate the enclosure with the E-mail. And the **E-mail body** usually excludes the salutation as it is shown in the column of "To", unless it is the first time for the writer to address the receiver in order to show good order and formality.

New Words and Expressions

Expeditious [ekspɪˈdɪʃəs]*adj.*	迅速的，敏捷的
Teleprinter [ˌteliˈprintə]*n.*	电传打印机
Teletypewriter [ˌteliˈraitə] *n.*	电传打字机
Unattended [ˈʌnəˈtendid] *adj.*	无人值管、无人照看
Transmission [trænzˈmiʃən] *n.*	传送，传播，传输
Facsimile [ˈfæsineit]*n.*	传真
Simultaneously [siməlˈteiniəsli] *adv.*	同时地
Underneath [ʌndəˈni:θ]*adv. & prep.*	在……下面
Retrieve [riˈtri:v] *v.*	恢复
With access to [ˈækses]	能够进入，接近，获得
Answer back code	回应电码
Business negotiation [niˌgəuʃiˈeiʃən]	商务洽谈
Despatch agreement [disˈpætʃ]	速遣费协议
Demurrage agreement [diˈmʌridʒ]	滞期费协议
Duplicating machine [ˈdju:plikeitiŋ]	复印机
Contract number	合同编号
User identification [aiˌdentifiˈkeiʃən]	用户名、用户标识

NOTES

1. With the popularization and development of information technology in the late 1990s, electronic correspondence is becoming an integral part in international business.

随着信息技术在 20 世纪 90 年代后期的普及和发展，电子信函正成为国际商务中不可缺少的部分。

2. Its main advantage over fax is that the appearance of the receiver's answer back code on the sender's copy of the transmitted message is proof that the message has reached the receiver's telex.

其优于传真的主要方面在于接收方的回应电码在发送方的发送文本上的显示就是接收方已收到电传信息的证明。

3. Even if unattended

即使无人照看

4. What is sent at one end is received simultaneously at the other end just like a duplicating machine.

在一端所发送的，同时就在另一端收到了，就像复印机一样。

5. Messages are held in a mailbox and only those with a user identification and password can have access to the messages.

信息被存放在邮箱中，只有那些有用户识别码和口令的人才能得到这些信息。

EXERCISES

I. Translate the following Chinese terms into English

电报　　　　电传　　　　传真　　　　电子邮件　　　　电传打印机
口令　　　　邮箱　　　　商务洽谈　　　电子信函　　　　电传打字机

II. Translate the following English terms into Chinese

User identification　　　Answer back code　　　Duplicating machine
Information technology　　Computer terminal　　　Popularization and development
Transmission distance　　　E-mail address　　　　Combinations and simplified words

III. Translate the following into Chinese

1. FOR THIS SHPMT, BROKER FAILED TO CLEAR CUSTOMS DUE TO PROBLEMS OF DEMTS. SO HV TO POSTPONE TO NEXT VSL.

2. AS CGO IS VERY HOT SO THEY WANT US TO FOLLOW SHPT CLOSELY N ADV IF ANY DELAYS ASAP.

3. PLS FIND COPY OF FCR ON UR FAX MACHINE N PLS NOTE THIS IS TEL RELEASED PER VNDR'S REGUEST. SO U CAN RELEASE CGO WTH THE PRESENTATION OF COPY OF FCR.

IV. Challenging questions for discussion

1. What is telex? How are the telex messages sent?

2. What is fax? What are the main advantages of the fax?

3. What are the differences between telegram and telex?

4. What is E-mail? How many parts does an E-mail comprise?

Part III   Supplementary Reading

Specimen Correspondence

Specimen Envelope

```
CHINA OCEAN SHIPPING AGENCY                    (Stamp)

SHAHANGHAI BRANCH

13 Zhongshan Road (E1)

Shanghai P.C. 200002

China


                          ABC SHIPPING CO.

                          12 Tower Street

                          London, E.C. 8

                          England


Registered
```

Specimen Letter (the blocked form with a centered heading)

SHANGHAI OCEAN SHIPPING CO.   *(Heading)*

378 Dong Daming Road, Shanghai, P.R.C. 200080, China

Tel: 65416620   Telex: 33057 COSCO CN

Fax: 65458984   Cable: COSCO SHNAGHAI

Our Ref: B367   *(Reference Number or Code)*
Your Ref: R208
Date: March 3, 2007   *(Date)*

DIAMOND LOGISTICS LTD   *(Inside Name and Address)*
47 Federal Street, Springfield
Massachusetts 01101
U.S.A.

For the attention of Mr. David Smith   *(Attention Line)*

Dear Mr. Smith,   *(Salutation)*

Re: Chartering a Vessel   *(Subject Line)*

(Body of the Letter)

Thank you for your letter of February 25. We are pleased to inform you that we have been able to secure the vessel you asked for.

She is the M.V. Dong Fang, a bulk carrier, and is docked at present in Ningpo. She has a cargo capacity of ten thousand tons and a speed of 24 knots which will certainly be able to make the number of trips you mentioned.

Please give us an early reply to confirm the charter and we will send you the charter party.

Yours sincerely,   *(Complimentary Close)*
COSCO SHANGHAI   *(Signature)*
(Signed)…
Wu Chen
Manager
Charter Department

WC/yf   *(Identification Marks)*
Encl. Charter Freight   *(Enclosure)*
cc. our Branch Office in Ningpo   *(Carbon Copy Notation)*
P.S. We have just received your letter of February 28.   *(Postscript)*

Specimen Telex

33052 PENAV CN
MAY 1, 2007 –8:45 AM

ATTN: MR. LI

THIS IS TO ADV U THAT MY VSL IS NOW ON THE WAY TO YR PORT. HER ETA YRS IS 1000HRS TMW. W REQST THAT U GIVE MY SHIP A QUICK BERTHING ARNGMT, SO THAT W MAY DO THE OVERHAULG OF THE MAIN ENGINE IMDTLY.

RGDS

23568 KARLOW HK

Specimen Fax

SHANGHAI OCEAN SHIPPING CO.   *(Fax Headings)*

378 Dong Daming Road, Shanghai, P.C.: 200080, China

Tel: 65416620   Telex: 33057 COSCO CN

Fax: 65458984   Cable: COSCO SHANGHAI

Fax Message

To: Messrs. A.H. Brooks &CO   Fax: 45262800   *(Fax Head)*

From: Samlee   Date: March 1, 2007

Re: Reply to Your Enquiry   Pages: 1 OF 1

Dear Sirs,   *(Fax Body)*

Thank you for your enquiry of February 28, 2007.

We wish to inform you that the M.V. Dong Fang will be loading at No. 1 Dock from 18th to 25th March inclusive. Following her is the M.V. Dong Feng, loading at No. 2 Dock from 20th to 29th March inclusive. The voyage to Alexandria usually takes fifteen days and the freight rate for your goods is $149.78 per ton.

We shall be glad to book three cases for either of these vessels and enclose our shipping form. Please complete and return it as soon as possible.

Yours faithfully,

Samlee

Specimen E-mail

To: David Smith   dsmith@hotmail.com   *(E-mail Head)*

Fm: Sam Brown   sambrown@163.com

Dt: March 3, 2007

Subject: Transfer of Containers

Dear Mr. Smith,   *(E-mail Body)*

Our booking dept. just informed me that owing to the customs problems, cntrs could not be loaded on M.V. Zhong He. So they have to be transferred to M.V. Dong Feng. Reason is that the shipper sent export customs docs to the wrong party and did not make a copy, so we cannot help him in any way.

Best regards,

Sam Brown

New Words and Expressions

Specimen ['spesimin, -mən] *n.*	样品，样本，实例
Charter ['tʃɑːtə] *vt.*	包租（船、飞机等）
Secure [si'kjuə] *vt.*	保护，保证
Knot [nɔt] *n.*	节，海里（测船速的单位）
Compulsory [kəm'pʌlsəri] *adj.*	规定的，强制的，义务的
Berth [bəːθ] *vt. & n.*	靠泊；泊位
Overhaul [ˌəuvə'hɔːl] *vt. & n.*	细密检查，检修
Enquiry [in'kwaiəri] *n.*	询价单
Inclusive [in'kluːsiv] *adj.*	包括的，包含的
COSCO (China Ocean Shipping Company)	中国远洋运输公司
Direct steamer ['stiːmə]	直达轮船
Shipping form	订舱单
Cntrs (containers)	集装箱
Export customs docs	出口海关单据

NOTES

1. a cargo capacity of ten thousand tons and a speed of 24 knots.
   载货能力为 1 万吨，航速为 24 节。

2. Paraphrase of the specimen telegram:

As direct steamer is unavailable, transshipment at Rotterdam is therefore compulsory. We request you to amend the L/C allowing transshipment and extending the date of shipment and validity to July 10 and 20 respectively.

该电报实例释义：因无直达船，故须在鹿特丹转运。要求你方修改信用证，允许转运并将装运日期和有效期分别延至 7 月 10 日和 20 日。

3．Paraphrase of the specimen telex:

This is to advise you that my vessel is now on the way to your port. Her estimated time of arrival at your port is 10:00 hours tomorrow. We request that you give my ship a quick berthing arrangement so that we may do the overhauling of the main engine immediately.

该电传实例释义：谨此通知贵方，我船正在驶往贵港途中，预计到港时间为明天 10:00。现要求贵方做好迅速靠泊安排，以便我方可立即进行主机大修。

4．33052 is the receiver's telex code, PENAV is answer back, and CN is the abbreviation of China; while 23568 is the sender's telex code, KARLOW is the name of a ship, and HK stands for Hong Kong.

33052 是接收方的电传码，PENAV 是应答码，CN 是 China（中国）的缩写；而 23568 是发送方的电传码，KARLOW 是一船名，HK 表示 Hong Kong（香港）。

EXERCISES

I. Arrange the following in indented letter style

1. Sender's name: Shanghai Ocean Shipping Company

2. Sender's address: 378 Dong Daming Road, Shanghai, P.C.: 200080, China

3. Sender's telephone number: 65416620

4. Sender's telex number: 33057 COSCO CN

5. Sender's fax number: 65458984

6. Sender's cable address: COSCO SHNAGHAI

7. Date: March 3, 2007

8. Receiver's name: Diamond Logistics Ltd.

9. Receiver's address: 47 Federal Street, Springfield, Massachusetts 01101, U.S.A.

10. Attention line: Mr. David Smith

11. Salutation: Dear Mr. Smith

12. Subject line: Chartering a Vessel

13. The message: Thank you for your letter of February 25. We are pleased to inform you that we have been able to secure the vessel you asked for. She is the M.V. Dong Fang, a bulk carrier, and is docked at present in Ningbo. She has a cargo capacity of ten thousand tons and a speed of 24 knots which will certainly be able to make the number of trips you mentioned. Please give us an early reply to confirm the charter and we will send you the charter party.

14．Complimentary close: Yours sincerely

15．Signature: COSCO SHANGHAI, Wu Chen, Manager, Charter Department

II. Address an envelope for the above letter

Chapter 11 Logistics Documents 1

 Chapter Outline

Part I   Government Documents
Overview of logistics documents
Types of government documents
Import license
Export license
Certificate of Origin
Generalized System of Preferences Certificate of Origin Form A
Inspection certificate
Inspection certificate of weight/quantity
Inspection certificate of quality
Veterinary inspection certificate

Part II   Commercial Documents (1)

Overview of commercial documents   Bill of exchange
Invoice (commercial invoice)   Packing list
Insurance policy/ insurance certificate   Weight list

Part III   Supplementary Reading
Commercial Documents (2)
Letter of Credit
Shipper's Export Declaration
Specimen Irrevocable Documentary Credit Application
Specimen Letter of Credit

PART I   Government Documents

Overview of Logistics Documents

A large number of documents are needed in the global transport. **Logistics documents** are indispensable in the logistics services, which have the main features of accuracy, completeness, conciseness, and promptness.

Four main features of logistics documents

1. Accuracy refers to the details in logistics documents must be in strict compliance with those in the sales contract, and no vague words or expressions should be used.

2. Completeness means every necessary detail should be included in each logistics document.

3. Conciseness denotes no redundant words or expressions should be used, and no correction should be made on the logistics documents.

4. Promptness means the logistics documents should be ready when they are needed, and unnecessary delay or confusion should be avoided.

Types of logistics documents

There are three kinds of commonly used logistics documents, that is, **government documents**, **commercial documents** and **transport documents**, which are classified roughly according to the document source.

Types of Government Documents

Government documents are issued by government bodies concerned, and include import licence, export licence, inspection certificate, certificate of origin, and generalized system of preferences certificate of origin Form A, etc.

Import Licence

Definition of import licence

Import licence is a permit issued by a national government allowing an importer to bring a specific quantity of certain goods into a country. Each license specifies the volume of imports allowed, and the total volume allowed should not exceed the quota. The main functions of import licences are as follows:

Functions of import licence

1. It functions as a means of exchange control, the licence both permitting importation and allowing the importer to purchase the required foreign currency. Many countries use import license and foreign exchange authorization system to restrict imports.

2. Import licenses are considered to be non-tariff barriers to trade when used as a way to discriminate against another country's goods in order to protect a domestic industry from foreign competition.

3. It is used to control entry of dangerous goods.

Application of import licence

Importers have to present pro forma invoices to their licensing authorities or to their central banks, or sometimes to both to apply for the licence. Licenses can be sold to importing companies at a competitive price, or simply a fee. If the planned importation is legal and meets current requirements, the licence will be issued. Therefore, exporters should not ship the goods to the importers who need licences until the licenses are actually in hand.

Export Licence

Definition of export licence

Export licence is an export control document issued by a national government required before goods can be exported from a country. Export licence is most often used to monitor the export of sensitive technologies, prohibited goods, dangerous goods, strategy goods, or goods in short supply in the home market.

Generalized System of Preferences Certificate of Origin Form A

GSP system

GSP's objectives

Generalized System of Preferences Certificate of Origin Form A issued by the inspection agency in the export trade is an important part of the official documents. Generalized system of preferences is referred to as GSP. **GSP** is a system of general, non-discriminatory and non-reciprocal tariff preferences, under which developing countries enjoy preferential tariffs on the exports of finished and semi finished products (including some primary products) to developed countries. **GSP's objectives** are to increase the export earnings of developing countries, realize the industrialization and accelerate economic growth in developing countries. Generalized System of Preferences Certificate of Origin Form A is used to certify the country of origin of export goods enjoying the GSP tariff preferences.

Certificate of Origin

Definition of certificate of origin

Certificate of origin is a document issued by a certifying authority such as a chamber of commerce or other authorized body in the

Elements of certificate of origin

exporter's country stating the country of origin of the goods. It is usually required by countries which do not use customs invoice or consular invoice to set the proper duties for the imports.Certificate of origin usually includes the following elements: key details (typically consignor, consignee, and description of goods) regarding the shipment and such details to be in accordance with other documents such as documentary credit and commercial invoice; a statement of origin of the goods; the name, signature and/or seal of the certifying authority, etc.

Inspection Certificate

Definition of inspection certificate

Types of inspection certificate

Inspection certificate is a document issued by an authority to indicate that the goods have been inspected prior to shipment and a statement of the results of the inspection. It is generally issued by a neutral, independent third-party inspection service or a government agency. Inspection certificate takes many forms, such as inspection certificate of quality, inspection certificate of weight, inspection certificate of quantity, veterinary inspection certificate, inspection certificate of sanitary, disinfection inspection certificate, inspection certificate of origin, inspection certificate of value, inspection certificate on damaged cargo, inspection certificate of packing, and inspection certificate of fumigation.

Inspection Certificate of Weight/Quantity

Definition of inspection certificate of weight/ quantity

Inspection certificate of weight/quantity confirms that the goods are in line with the weight/quantity specified on the bill of lading, commercial invoice, insurance policy/certificate or other specified documents. In so doing, it confirms to the importer, the exporter, the insurance company or other specified parties that the goods were at a specified weight/quantity at the time of shipment. Inspection certificate of weight/quantity is usually requested by the importer to confirm that the weight/quantity of the goods is in conformity with the export sales contract at the time of shipment.

Inspection Certificate of Quality

Definition of inspection certificate of quality

Inspection certificate of quality confirms that the quality and specification of a particular consignment of goods is in conformity with the sales contract at the time of shipment. It may be issued by the exporter or a relevant government department as required under the letter of credit or sales contract terms. It is essential that cargo description in the quality certificate conform to its terms found in other relevant documents, such as commercial invoice, L/C, insurance policy, etc.

Veterinary Inspection Certificate

Definition of veterinary inspection certificate
Veterinary inspection certificate certifies that a shipment of live animals, fresh, chilled and frozen meats (and sometimes even canned meats) has been inspected for disease. This certificate is generally issued by a third-party independent testing company or government authority.

New Words and Expressions

Indispensable [ˌindis'pensəbl] *adj.*	不可缺少的，不能避免的
Vague [veig] *adj.*	含糊的，不清楚的
Conciseness [kən'sais] *n.*	简明，简洁
Redundant [ri'dʌndənt] *adj.*	多余的，过多的，冗长的
Promptness [prɔmpt] *n.*	迅捷，敏捷，机敏
Quota *n.*	配额，限额，定额
Be in strict compliance with ['kɔmplains]	与……完全一致/相符
Be in conformity with [kən'fɔːmiti]	与……一致/符合
Government bodies	政府部门
Certificate of origin [sə'tifikit]	原产地证书
Generalized system of preferences certificate of origin Form A	普惠制产地证格式 A
Exchange control	外汇管制
Non-tariff barriers to trade ['tærif]	非关税壁垒
Pro forma invoice	形式发票
Tariff preferences	关税优惠
Country of origin	原产国
Certifying authority [ɔː'θɔriti]	认证机构
Chamber of commerce	商会
Customs invoice	海关发票
Consular invoice ['kɔnsjulə]	领事发票
Documentary credit [ˌdɔkju'mentəri]	押汇信用证
Inspection certificate of quality	品质检验证书
Inspection certificate of weight	重量检验证书
Inspection certificate of quantity	数量检验证书
Veterinary inspection certificate ['vetərinəri]	兽医检验证书
Inspection certificate of sanitary ['sæniteri]	卫生检验证书

146

Disinfection inspection certificate [,disin'fekʃən]	消毒检验证书
Inspection certificate of origin	产地检验证书
Inspection certificate of value	价值检验证书
Inspection certificate on damaged cargo	验残检验证书
Inspection certificate of packing	包装检验证书
Inspection certificate of fumigation ['fju:migeiʃən]	熏蒸检验证书
Bill of lading	提货单
Insurance policy	保险单（大保单）
Insurance certificate	保险凭证（小保单）
Letter of credit	信用证

NOTES

1. GSP is a system of general, non-discriminatory and non-reciprocal tariff preferences, under which developing countries enjoy preferential tariffs on the exports of finished and semi finished products (including some primary products) to developed countries.

普惠制是一种普遍的、非歧视的、非互惠的关税优惠制度，给予发展中国家出口到发达国家的制成品、半制成品（包括某些农产品）优惠的关税待遇。

2. GSP's objectives are to increase the export earnings of developing countries, realize the industrialization and accelerate economic growth in developing countries.

普惠制旨在增加发展中国家的出口收入，实现发展中国家的工业化，促进发展中国家的经济发展。

3. A document issued by a certifying authority such as a chamber of commerce or other authorized body in the exporter's country stating the country of origin of the goods.

由认证机关诸如出口国的商会或其他被授权机构所出具的说明货物原产国的单证。

EXERCISES

I. Translate the following Chinese terms into English

官方单证	商业单证	出口许可证	产地检验证书
外汇管制	形式发票	原产国	数量检验证书
领事发票	检验证书	信用证	价值检验证书
政府部门	海运提单	保险单	兽医检验证书
相关单证	国内工业	外国竞争	普惠制产地证格式 A

II. Translate the following English terms into Chinese

Logistics document	Transport document
Import licence	Certificate of origin

Foreign currency	Non-tariff barriers to trade
Tariff preferences	Ccertifying authority
Chamber of commerce	Customs invoice
Documentary credit	Commercial invoice
Inspection certificate of weight	Inspection certificate of quantity
Inspection certificate of sanitary	Disinfection inspection certificate
Inspection certificate on damaged cargo	Inspection certificate of packing
Inspection certificate of fumigation	Insurance certificate

III. Challenging questions for discussion

1. What are the main types of logistics documents?
2. What are the main types of government documents?
3. What are the objectives of GSP?
4. What are the main functions of import licence?

IV. Be familiar with each column of the following government documents

一般原产地证书

ORIGINAL

1. Exporter（full name and address） 2. Consignee（full name, address, country）	CERTIFICATE NO. **CERTIFICATE OF ORIGIN** **OF** **THE PEOPLE'S REPUBLIC OF CHINA**			
3. Means of transport and route 4. Country / region of destination	5. For certifying authority use only			
6. Marks and numbers	7. Number and kind of packages description of goods	8. H.S.Code	9. Quantity	10. Number and date of invoices
11. Declaration by the exporter The undersigned hereby declares that the above details and statement are correct; that all the goods were produced in China and that they comply with the Rules of Origin of the People's Republic of China.	12. Certification It is hereby certified that the declaration by the exporter is correct.			
Place and date, signature and stamp of authorized signatory	Place and date, signature and stamp of certifying authority			

中华人民共和国出口许可证
EXPORT LICENCE OF THE PEOPLE'S REPUBLIC OF CHINA

1. 出口商： Exporter		3. 出口许可证号： Exporter licence No.
2. 发货人： Consigner		4. 出口许可证有效截止日期： Export licence expiry date 年　月　日
5. 贸易方式： Forms of trade		8. 进口国（地区）： Country/Region of purchase
6. 合同号： Contract No.		9. 付款方式： Payment
7. 报关口岸： Place of clearance		10. 运输方式： Mode of transport

11.唛头—包装件数 Marks & numbers—number of packages

12. 商品名称：　　　　　　商品编码： 　　　　　　　　　　　Code of goods

13. 规格、等级 Specification	14. 单位 Unit	15. 数量 Quantity	16. 单价（USD） Unit Price	17. 总值（USD） Amount	18. 总值折美元 Amount in USD
19. 总计 Total					

20. 备注 　Supplementary details	21. 发证机关签章 　Issuing authority's stamp & signature 22. 发证日期 　Licence date　　年　　月　　日

商务部监制　　　　　　　　　　　　　　　　　　　　本证不得涂改，不得转让

普惠制原产地证书
ORIGINAL

1. Goods consigned from (Exporter's business name, address, country)	Reference No: **GENERALIZED SYSTEM OF PREFERENCES** **CERTIFICATE OF ORIGIN** **(Combined declaration and certificate)** **FORM A** **Issued in THE PEOPLE'S REPUBLIC OF CHINA** （country）
2. Goods consigned to(Consignee's name, address, country)	See Notes, overleaf
3. Means of transport and route(as far as known)	4.For official use

5. Item number	6. Marks and numbers of packages	7. Nunber and kind of packages; description of goods	8. Orign criterion（see Notes verleaf）	9. Gross weight or other quantity	10.Number and date of invoices

11. Certification It is hereby certified, on the basis of control carried out, that the declaration by the exporter is correct.	12. Declaration by the exporter The undersigned hereby declares that the above details and statements are correct; that all the goods were produced in _____**CHINA**_____ （country） and that they comply with the origin requirements specified for those goods in the Generalized System of Preferences for goods exported to （importing country）
Place and date, signature and stamp of certifying authority	Place and date, signature of authorized signatory

中华人民共和国上海进出口商品检验局

SHANGHAI IMPORT & EXPORT COMMODITY INSPECTION
BUREAU
OF THE PEOPLE'S REPUBLIC OF CHINA

地址：上海市中山东一路 13 号
Address:13,Zhongshan Road
（E.1），Shanghai

No.

检 验 证 书
INSPECTION CERTIFICATE

日期
Date

电话：
Tel:86-21-32155296

收 货 人：
Consignee:
发 货 人：
Consignor:
品 名：
Commodity:
报验数量/重量：
Quantity/Weight
Declared:
运 输：
Transportation:
进口日期：
Date of Arrival:
卸毕日期：
Date of Completion
of Discharge:
发 票 号：
Invoice No.:
合 同 号：
Contract No.:
标记及号码：
Mark & No.:

注意：本证书译文如有任何异点，概以中文为准。
（N.B. In case if divergence, the Chinese text shall be regarded as authentic）

中华人民共和国上海进出口商品检验局

SHANGHAI IMPORT & EXPORT COMMODITY INSPECTION
BUREAU
OF THE PEOPLE'S REPUBLIC OF CHINA

地址：上海市中山东一路13号

Address:13,Zhongshan Road

（E.1），Shanghai

检 验 证 书

INSPECTION CERTIFICATE

No.

日期

Date

电话：

Tel:86-21-32155296

发 货 人：

Consignor...

收 货 人：

Consignee:...:..................................

品　名：　　　　　　标记及号码：

Commodity...Mark & No.

报验数量/重量：

Quantlty/Weight

Declared...

官方兽医证明如下：

1. The undersigned Official Veterinarian, certify that ....

主 任 兽 医

Chief Veterinarian

PART II   Commercial Documents (1)

Overview of Commercial Documents

Types of commercial documents

Commercial documents are issued by various businesses such as the exporter, the importer, the insurance company, the shipping company, and the bank to define the business relations between the parties concerned and provide an accounting record of individual transaction. **Commercial documents** take many forms including bill of exchange or draft, insurance policy/insurance certificate, pro forma invoice, commercial invoice, consular invoice, customs invoice, packing list, weight list, measurement list, beneficiary certificate, credit note, debit note, letter of credit, etc.

Bill of Exchange

Types of draft

Bill of exchange, also known as **draft,** is an unconditional order in writing, signed by a person (drawer) such as an exporter, and addressed to another person (drawee), typically a bank, ordering the drawee to pay a stated sum of money to yet another person (payee), often the exporter, on demand or at a fixed or determinable future time. The most common types of drafts are **sight drafts** which are payable when presented, and **time drafts** (also called usance drafts) which are payable at a future fixed (specific) date or determinable (e.g. 30, 60, 90 days) date.

Invoices

Types of invoices

Invoice is a document offered by the exporter to the importer regarding the sold goods. There are four invoices mainly used in international trade: pro forma invoice, commercial invoice, consular invoice and customs invoice.

Pro forma invoice

Pro forma invoice is a preliminary invoice made out by an exporter at the importer's request before a sale or shipment of the goods, informing the importer of the kinds and quantities of goods to be sent, their value, shipping costs, and important specifications such as weight, size, and similar characteristics. Pro forma invoice is used by the importer to see what the purchaser will cost, obtain any necessary import licenses and foreign exchange approval, and apply for a letter of credit.

Commercial invoice

Commercial invoice, issued by the exporter to the importer, provides details of a transaction and forms the basis of the transaction between the importer and the exporter. It is one of the most important documents used in international trade. It primarily functions as a check for the importer against charges and delivery and as the determination of value of goods for the assessment of customs duties, preparation for consular documentation, insurance claims and packing purposes. In some cases, it may form a sales contract if it is in writing and contains all the material terms. The main parts on a commercial invoice usually include the issue date, the importer, the exporter, the invoice number, shipping marks, descriptions and quantities of the goods, prices, delivery terms and other important information concerning the transaction. **Commercial invoice** has different meanings to different parties involved. For example, it is a sales invoice for the exporter, a purchase invoice for the importer, and a document required by customs to determine true transaction value of goods for the assessment of customs duties, to prepare customs declaration, to record trade statistics, and to exercise import control.

Consular invoice

Consular invoice is an export invoice covering a shipment of goods certified in the exporting country by the consul of the importing country. This invoice is required by customs of certain importing countries to verify the value, quantity, and nature of the goods imported and to enable them to charge the correct import duties. A certificate of origin may also be required. The invoice must be purchased from the consulate of the importing country to which the goods are being shipped and usually is prepared in the language of that country.

Customs invoice

Customs invoice is an invoice made out on a special form stipulated by the customs authorities of the importing country to allow imports to enter the country. This invoice includes information that the country desires and is not found on the ordinary commercial invoice. It is only used in a few countries. Customs invoice is required by the importing country in order to clear the customs, to verify country of origin for import duty and tax purpose, to compare export price and domestic price, and to fix antidumping duty, etc.

Packing List

Definition of packing list

Packing list, also known as **packing slip,** is a document prepared by the shipper, i.e. the exporter at the time the goods are dispatched, giving details of the invoice, the shipper, the consignee, country of origin, vessel or flight details, port or airport of loading and discharge, place of delivery, shipping marks, container number, weight and/or volume (cubic) of goods, etc., but it does not contain prices. Its prime purpose is to give an inventory of the shipped goods, and it is usually required by the customs for clearance purposes.

Use of packing list

Packing list accompanies the goods and the carrier's documents throughout the transit. A copy of the packing list is often attached to the shipment itself and another copy sent directly to the consignee to assist in checking the shipment when received. Today, the provision of a packing list document is mandatory for customs and banks under documentary credit systems. Packing list may be used by different parties in different aspects. For example, it is used by the shipper to evidence the detailed weight, volume, size, packing and packaging of the cargo delivered; it is used by the freight forwarder to determine the total shipment weight and volume and whether the correct cargo is being shipped; and it is used by the carrier to calculate freight or carriage.

Weight List

Definition of weight list

Weight list, sometimes known as **weight note**, **weight memo**, or **weight certificate**, is usually issued by the exporter describing the weight of each piece of goods, and also a shipping document that accompanies delivery packages. Weight list may be used by different parties in different aspects. For example, it is used by the shipper to evidence the gross weight and the net weight of each unit of package, and the total weight of the cargo delivered; it is used by the freight forwarder to determine the total shipment weight; and it is used by the carrier to calculate freight or carriage.

Insurance Policy / Insurance Certificate

Definition of insurance policy

Insurance policy is a document confirming insurance of cargo and indicating the type and amount of insurance coverage in force on a particular shipment. It is used to assure the insured that insurance is provided to cover loss of or damage to cargo while in transit. This document is normally issued to the party buying the insurance by an insurance company or its agent, which may include a carrier, freight forwarder, customs broker or logistics firm.

Elements of an insurance policy

Insurance policy usually includes the name, address and signature of the insurer; policy number; the name and the endorsement of the assured; points of origin and destination of the shipment; conditions of coverage, exclusions, and deductible, if appliable; a description of the risks covered and the insured time; a description of the consignment; the sum or sums insured and premium, etc.

Definition of insurance Certificate

Insurance certificate, a simplified insurance policy, usually contains similar data as an insurance policy, but it excludes the detailed rights and obligations of both sides at the back of the document.

New Words and Expressions

Drawer [ˈdrɔːə]n.	出票人
Drawee [drɔːˈiː] n.	收票人
Payee [peiˈiː]n.	收款人
Preliminary [priˈliminəri]adj.	初步的，开始的，预备的
Specification [ˌspesifiˈkeiʃən] n.	规格，详述，详细说明书
Verify [ˈverifai] vt.	查证，证实，检验
Consulate [ˈkɔnsjulit]n.	领事，领事馆
Clear vt.	清关，清除，扫清
Clearance [ˈkliərəns] n.	清关
Mandatory [ˈmændətəri]adj.	命令的，托管的，强制性的
Aspect [ˈæspekt] n.	外观，方面，方向，容貌
Carriage [ˈkæridʒ] n.	运费，运输
Deductible [diˈdʌktəbl] a.	可扣除的
Bill of exchange / draft	汇票
Packing list / slip	装箱单
Beneficiary certificate [beniˈfiʃəri]	受益人证明
Credit note	贷项通知书
Debit note [ˈdebit]	借项通知书
Sight draft	即期汇票
Time draft / usance draft [ˈjuːzəns]	定期汇票/远期汇票
Customs duties	关税
Consular documentation [ˈkɔnsjulə]	领事单证
Insurance claims	保险索赔
Shipping marks	装运标志，唛头
Delivery terms	交付条件
Customs declaration	报关
Antidumping duty [ˌæntiˈdʌmpiŋ]	反倾销税
Freight forwarder	货运代理
Weight note/ memo/ certificate	重量单/备忘录/单据
Gross weight	毛重

Net weight	净重
Insurance coverage	保险责任范围
The insured	被保险人
Customs broker ['brəukə]	报关经纪人，报关代理
The insurer	保险人
The sum or sums insured	投保金额

NOTES

1．Bill of exchange is an unconditional order in writing, signed by a person (drawer) such as an exporter, and addressed to another person (drawee), typically a bank, ordering the drawee to pay a stated sum of money to yet another person (payee), often the exporter, on demand or at a fixed or determinable future time. 汇票是一种无条件的书面支付命令，由一人，如出口商（出票人）签发给另一人（付款人），通常为银行，要求其见票即付或在未来某一确定的时间支付一定数额的款项给受款人（通常是出口商）。

2．Its prime purpose is to give an inventory of the shipped goods, and it is usually required by the customs for clearance purposes.

其首要目的是给出所运货物的一份清单，并且出于清关的需要，海关常常要求（出示）此单据。

3．A copy of the packing list is often attached to the shipment itself and another copy sent directly to the consignee to assist in checking the shipment when received.

所运货物本身通常附有一份装箱单，另一份装箱单直接寄送给收货人以便收货时核对货物。

4．Today, the provision of a packing list document is mandatory for customs and banks under documentary credit systems.

如今，海关和银行都要求跟单信用系统下（的货物交易）必须提供装箱单。

5．It primarily functions as a check for the importer against charges and delivery and as the determination of value of goods for the assessment of customs duties, preparation for consular documentation, insurance claims and packing purposes.

它主要作为进口商核对费用和所发运货物的依据，用以确定征收海关关税的商品的价值，以及准备领事单据、保险索赔和包装事项。

6．charge the correct import duties
课以正确的进口税

7．against the stipulated documents
凭规定的单据

8．indicating the type and amount of insurance coverage in force on a particular shipment
表明对某批运输货物生效的保险的类别与金额的单据

EXERCISES

I．Translate the following Chinese terms into English

汇票　　　　　即期汇票　　　　　贷项通知书　　　　　装运标志

报关	装箱单	受益人证明	保险公司
毛重	海运费	货运代理	业务关系

II. Translate the following English terms into Chinese

Weight list	Measurement list
Debit note	Time draft
Customs duties	Consular documentation
Insurance claims	Descriptions of the goods
Delivery terms	Trade statistics
Import control	Antidumping duty
Weight note	Net weight
Insurance coverage	The insured
In transit	Customs broker
The insurer	The sum or sums insured

III. Challenging questions for discussion

1. What are the main types of invoices?

2. What are the main parts on a commercial invoice?

3. What are the functions of the packing list?

4. What's the difference between insurance policy and insurance certificate?

5. What's the main difference between the weight certificate and the quality certificate?

6. What main elements must be included in a certificate of origin?

IV. Be familiar with each column of the following commercial documents

BILL OF EXCHANGE

凭   信用证

Drawn under..L/C NO. ....

日期

Dated............................支取   Payable with interest @__%__按__息__付款

号码   汇票金额   上海

NO............. Exchange for   Shanghai.................20.................

见票...................................日后（本汇票之正本未付）付交

At................ sight of this **SECOND** of Exchange（First of Exchange being unpaid）Pay to the order of

金额

The   sum

of

此致：

To...

  ....

上海市纺织品进出口公司
SHANGHAI TEXTILES IMPORT & EXPORT CORPORATION
27 CHUNGSHAN ROAD E .1 .
SHANGHAI, CHINA
TEL：86-21-65342517   FAX：86-21-65724743

COMMERCIAL INVOICE

TO: M/S.

号码
No:_____

售货合约号码
Sales Confirmation No._____

日　期
Date_____

装船口岸
From_____

目的地
To_____

信用证号数
Letter of Credit No._____

开证银行
Issued by_____

唛号　Marks & Nos	货名数量　Quantities & Descriptions	总值　Amount

We certify that the goods
are of Chinese origin.

上海市纺织品进出口公司
Shanghai Textiles Import & Export Corporation
SHANGHAI, CHINA
_____

Revenue Canada　　　Revenu Canada
Customs and Excise　　Douanes et Accise

CANADA CUSTOMS INVOICE
FACTURE DES DOU ANES CANADIENNE

| 1 Vendor(Name and Address) /Verdeur (Name et adresse). | 2 Date of Direct Shipment to Canada/Date d'expedition directe vers le Canada |
| | 3 Other References (Inchlde Purchaser's Order No.) Autres refer ences (Inchrre le n de commande de l' acheteur) |

4 Consignee (Name and Address) /Destinataire (Nom et adresse)	5 Purchaser's Name and Address (if other than Consigree) Nom et adresse de l'acheteur (S'il differe du destinataire)
	6 Country of Trans hipment/Pays de transbordement
	7 Country of Origin of Goods Pays d'origine des marchandises	IF SHIP MENT INCLUDS GOODS OF DIFFERENT ORIGINS ENTER ORIGINS AGAINST ITEMS IN 12.

| 8 Transportation Give Mode and Place of Direct Shipment to Canada Transport Preciser mode et point d'expedition directe Vers le Canada | 9 Conditions of Sale and Terms of Payment (i.e. Sale, Consigrment Shipment. Leased Goods, etc.) Conditions de vent et modalites de paiement (p.ex.vente, expedition en consignation, location de marchan-dises.etc.) |
| | 10 Currency of Settlement/Devises du paiement |

| 11 No of Pkgs ND'e De colis | 12 Specificadion of Commo dities (Kind of Packages, Marks and Numbers, General Description and Char acteristics, ie. Grade, Quality | 13 Quantity (State Unit) (Preciser I' unite) | Selling Price/Prix de vente | |
| | | | 14 Unit Price Prix unitaire | 15 Total |

| 18 If any offields 1 to 17 are incbuded on an attached comm ercial invoice. Check this box Cammercial Invoice No._____ ☐ | 16 Total Weight/Paids Total | | 17 Invoice Total |
| | Net | Gross/Bru | |

| 19 Exporter's Name and Address (If other than Vendor) Nom et adresse de l' exportatur (S'il deffere du vendeur) | 20 Originaotor (Name and Address) /Expediteur d' origine (Nom et adresse) |

| 21 Departmendal Pouhing (If applicable) /Decision du Ministere (S'il ya lieu) | 22 If fields 23 to 25 are not applicable, check this box Siles zones 23 a 25 sont sans object, cocher cette boite　☐ |

| 23 If included in field 17 indicate amount Si compris dans le total a la zone 17. Preciser (i)Transportation charges, expenses and insurance from the place of direct shipment to $_____ (ii)Costs for construction, erection and assembly incured afer importation into Canada. $_____ (iii)Export packing $_____ | 24 If not incbuded in field 17 indicate amount Sinon copris dans le total a la zone 17 preciser (i)Transportation charges, Expenses and insurance to the place of direct shipment to Canada. $_____ (ii)Amounts for commissionsother than buying commissions. $_____ (iii)Export packing $_____ | 25 Check (If applicable): Cocher (S'ily a; ieu): (i)Royalty payments or subsequent proceeds are paid or payable by the purchaser.　☐ (ii)The purchaser has supplied goods or services for use in the production of these goods.　☐ |

DEPARTMENT OF NATIONAL REVENUE CUSTOMS AND EXCISE　MINISTERE DU REVENU NATIONAL　DOUANES ET ACCISE

160

中 国 人 民 保 险 公 司

THE PEOPLE'S INSURANCE COMPANY OF CHINA

总公司设于北京   一九四九年创立

Head Office:BEIJING   Established in 1949

保 险 单   号次

INSURANCE POLICY   No.SH02/304246

中 国 人 民 保 险 公 司 (以 下 简 称 本 公 司)

This Policy of Insurance witnesses that The People's Insurance Company of China（hereinafter called

根 据

"the Company"),at the request of ---

（以下简称被保险人）的 要 求，由 被 保 险 人 向 本 公 司 缴 付 约 定

（ hereinafter called "the Insured"） and in consideration of the agreed premium paid to the Company by the

的 保 险 费，按 照 本 保 险 单 承 保 险 别 和 背 面 所 载 条 款 与 下 列

Insured, undertakes to insure the undermentioned goods in transportation subject to the conditions of this Policy

条 款 承 保 下 述 货 物 运 输 保 险，特 立 本 保 险 单。

as per the Clause printed overleaf and other special clauses attached hereon.

标 记 Marks & Nos.	包装及数量 Quantity	保险货物项目 Description of Goods	保险金额 Amount Insured
As per Invoice No.			

总保险金额:

Total Amount Insured: ---

保 费   费率   装载运输工具

Premium: as arranged   Rate as arranged   Per conveyance S.S.-------------------

开行日期   自   至

Slg.on or abt.   As Per B/L   From _____ to _____

承保险别

Conditions

所保货物，如遇出险，本公司凭本保险单及其他有关证件给付赔款。

Claims, if any, payable on surrender of this Policy together with other relevant documents.

所保货物，如发生本保险单项下负责赔偿的损失或事故，

In the event of accident whereby loss or damage may result in a claim under this Policy immediate notice applying

应立即通知本公司下述代理人查勘。

For survey must be given to the Company's Agent as mentioned hereunder:

赔款偿付地点

Claim payable at _____

日期   上海   中国人民保险公司上海分公司

Date _____Shanghai   THE PEOPLE'S INSURANCE CO. OF CHINA

地址：中国上海中山东一路 23 号。   SHANGHAI BRANCH

Address: 23 Zhongshan Dong Yi Lu Shanghai, China.

Cables: 42001 Shanghai.   ------------------------------------

Telex: 33128 PICCS CN   *General Manager*

PART III   Supplenentary Reading
Commercial Documents (2)

Letter of Credit

Definition of L/C

Letter of credit (L/C) is a written promise which is issued to the exporter (i.e. the beneficiary) by the opening or issuing bank upon the request of the importer (i.e. the applicant), promising to pay a certain sum of money within a certain period of time against the stipulated documents. The documents the importer requires in the credit may vary, but at a minimum include a commercial invoice and a bill of lading. Other documents the importer may specify are certificate of origin, consular invoice, insurance policy/certificate, inspection certificate and **Documentary L/C** others.

Ls/C are the most common method of making international payments because the transaction risks are shared by the importer and exporter, and they are more formally called documentary Ls/C because the banks handling the transaction deal in documents instead of in goods.

Types of L/C

There are a number of different kinds of Ls/C, such as irrevocable L/C, documentary L/C, clean L/C, confirmed L/C, unconfirmed L/C, transferable L/C, acceptance L/C, sight L/C, usance L/C, deferred payment L/C, back-to-back L/C, revolving L/C, red clause L/C, standby L/C. Each type of L/C has its own advantages and disadvantages for the importer and for the exporter.

Two basic forms of L/C

Of all the types, two basic forms of Ls/C are the revocable L/C and irrevocable L/C. There are also two types of irrevocable L/C: the irrevocable L/C not confirmed, and the irrevocable confirmed L/C.

Shipper's Export Declaration (SED)

Definition of SED

Shipper's export declaration is a document prepared by the shipper and presented to a government authority specifying goods exported along with their quantities, weight, value and destination.

The SED is used by a nation's customs authority to control exports and compile trade statistics. Some countries such as the United States are in the course of instituting new procedures that will require exporters to submit their SEDs electronically, which involves using a computer with a modem and specially designed forms software.

Specimen Irrevocable Documentary Credit Application

IRREVOCABLE DOCUMENTARY CREDIT APPLICATION

TO: BANK OF CHINA   **Place/date:**

Beneficiary(full name and address)	L/C NO.
	Ex-Card No.
	Contract No.
	Date and place of expiry of credit

| Partial shipments
□allowed □not allowed | Transshipment
□allowed □not allowed | □Issue by airmail
□With brief advice by teletransmission
□Issue by express delivery
□Issue by teletransmission(which shall be the operative instrument)
Amount(both in figures and words) |
| Loading on board/dispatch/taking in charge at/from
Not later than
_____ for transportation
to | | |

| Description of goods: | Credit available with
□by sight payment □by acceptance □by negotiation
□by deferred payment at against the documents detailed herein
□and beneficiary's draft for of the invoice value |
| Packing: □ | □C&F   ☒CIF
□or other terms |

Documents required:(marked with ×)

1.( ) Signed commercial invoice in   copies indicating L/C No. and contract No.

2.( ) Full set of clean on board ocean bills of lading made out to order and blank endorsed, marked "freight [ ]to collect/[ ]prepaid[ ]showing freight amount" notifying

3.( ) Air way bills showing "freight [ ]to collect/[ ]prepaid[ ]indicating freight amount" and consigned to

4.( ) Memorandum issued by   consigned to

5.( ) Insurance policy/certificate in   copies for   of the invoice value showing claims payable in destination in currency of the draft. Blank endorsed, covering([ ]ocean marine transportation) all risks, war risks

6.( ) Packing List/Weight Memo in   copies indicating quantity/gross and net weight of each package and packing condition as called for by the L/C

7.( ) Certificate of quantity /weight in copies issued by an independent surveyor at the loading port, indicating the actual surveyed quantity /weight of shipped goods as well as the packing condition.

8.( ) Certificate of quality in   copies issued by [ ]manufacture / [ ] public recognized surveyor /[ ]

9.( ) Beneficiary's certified copy of cable/telex dispatched to the accountees within 24 hours after shipment advising[×] name of vessel/[ ]No./[ ]wagon No., date, quantity, weight and value of shipment.

10.( ) Beneficiary's certificate certifying that extra copies of the documents have been dispatched according to the contract terms.

11.( ) Shipping Co's Certificate attesting that the carrying vessel is charted or booked by accountee or their shipping agents:

12.( ) Other documents, if any:

Additional instructions:

1.( ) All banking charges outside the opening bank are for beneficiary's account.

2.( ) Documents must be presented within 15 days after the date of issuance of the transport documents but within the validity this credit.

3.( ) Third party as shipper is not acceptable. Short form/Blank Back B/L is not acceptable.

4.( ) Both quantity and amount   % more or less are allowed.

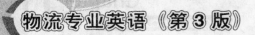

物流专业英语（第3版）

续表

5.(　) Prepaid freight drawn in excess of L/C amount is acceptable against presentation of original charges voucher issued by shipping Co./Air Line/or it's agent.

6.(　) All documents to be forwarded in one cover, unless otherwise stated above.

7.(　) Other terms, if any:

You correspondents to advise beneficiary □adding their confirmation □without adding their confirmation payments to be debited to our _____ account No.

Signature: _____

Specimen Letter of Credit

NATIONAL PARIS BANK

24 MARSHAL AVE DONCASTER MONTREAL, CANADA

WE ISSUE OUR IRREVOCABLE DOCUMENTARY CREDIT NUMBER:QQ2009 IN FAVOUR OF: SHANGHAI KNITWEAR AND MANUFACTURE GOODS IMPORT AND EXPORT TRADE CORPORATION.

321, CHONGSHAN ROAD SHANGHAI, CHINA

BY ORDER OF: YI YANG TRADING CORPORATION

88 MARSHALL AVE

DONCASTER VIC 3108

CANADA

FOR AN AMOUNT OF USD89 705.00

DATE AND PLACE OF ISSUE: SEP.18th, 2009 MONTREAL

DATE OF EXPIRY: NOV 15, 2009

PLACE: IN BENEFICARY'S COUNTRY

BY NEGOTIATION OF BENEFICIARY'S DRAFT DRAWN ON US AT SIGHT IN MONTREAL

THIS CREDIT IS TRANSFERABLE AGAINST DELIVERY OF THE FOLLOWING DOCUMENTS

+ COMMERCIAL INVOICES IN 3 COPIES

+ CANADA CUSTOMS INVOICES IN 3 COPIES

+ ORIGINAL CERTIFICATE IN 3 COPIES

+ FULL SET OF NEGOTIABLE INSURANCE POLICY OR CERTIFICATE BLANK ENDORSED FOR 110 PERCENT OF INVOICE VALUE COVERING ALL RISKS.

+ FULL SET OF ORIGINAL MARINE BILLS OF LADING CLEAN ON BOARD PLUS 2 NON-NEGOTIABLE COPIES MADE OUT OR ENDORSED TO ORDER OF NATIONAL PARIS BANK 24 MARSHALL AVE DONCASTER MONTREAL, CANADA.

164

+ SPECIFICATION LIST OF WEIGHTS AND MEASURES IN 4 COPIES COVERING SHIPMENT OF COTTON TEA TOWELS.

AS PER S/C MN808

FOR 1-300 SIZE 10 INCHES*10 INCHES 16000 DOZ AT USD 1.31/DOZ.

301-600 SIZE 20 INCHES*20 INCHES 6000 DOZ AT USD 2.51/DOZ.

AND 601-900 SIZE 30 INCHES*30 INCHES 11350 DOZ AT USD 4.73/DOZ.

CIF MONTREAL

FROM SHANGHAI TO MONTREAL

NOT LATER THAN OCT.31TH, 2009

PARTIAL SHIPMENTS: ALLOWED

SPECIAL INSTRUCTIONS:

+ ALL CHARGES IF ANY RELATED TO SETTLEMENTS ARE FOR ACCOUNT OF BENEFICIARY.

+ IN CASE OF PRESENTATION OF DOCUMENTS WITH DISCREPANCY (IES) A CHARGE OF USD 55.00 WILL BE DEDUCTED.

THIS CREDIT IS SUBJECT TO UCP DOCUMENTARY CREDITS(2007 REVISION) ICC PUBLICATION 600.

New Words and Expressions

Compile [kəm'pail] vt.	汇集，编辑，编制；搜集(资料)
Institute ['institju:t] vt.	着手，实行，开始；制定
Submit vt.	提交；委托，提出，提供
Modem ['məudəm] n.	【无线电】调制解调器
Written promise	书面承诺
Opening / issuing bank	开证行
Upon the request of	经……的要求
Revocable L/C ['revəkəbl]	可撤销信用证
Irrevocable L/C [i'revəkəbl]	不可撤销信用证
Clean L/C	光票信用证
Confirmed L/C [kən'fə:md]	保兑信用证
Unconfirmed L/C	不可保兑信用证
Transferable L/C [træns'fɜ:rəb(ə)l]	可转让信用证
Acceptance L/C [ək'septəns]	承兑信用证
Sight L/C	即期信用证
Usance L/C ['ju:zəns]	远期信用证
Deferred payment L/C [di'fɜ:d]	延期支付信用证
Back-to-back L/C	背对背信用证
Revolving L/C	循环信用证

Red clause L/C	红条款信用证
Standby L/C	备用信用证
Irrevocable L/C not confirmed	不保兑的不可撤销信用证
Irrevocable confirmed L/C	保兑的不可撤销信用证
Shipper's export declaration [,deklə'reiʃən]	托运人出口报关单

NOTES

1. and they are more formally called documentary Ls/C because the banks handling the transaction deal in documents instead of in goods.

由于银行是根据单据而不是根据商品来处理交易的，所以信用证较正式地被称为跟单信用证。

2. Some countries such as the United States are in the course of instituting new procedures that will require exporters to submit their SEDs electronically, which involves using a computer with a modem and specially designed forms software.

一些国家如美国正在开始实行新程序，要求出口商以电子方式提交托运人出口报送单，这涉及使用带有调制解调器的计算机和专门设计的格式的软件。

EXERCISES

I. Translate the following Chinese terms into English

托运人出口报关单	保兑的不可撤销信用证	可转让信用证
远期信用证	光票信用证	不可保兑信用证
可撤销信用证	保兑信用证	不可撤销信用证
即期信用证	承兑信用证	被授权机构

II. Translate the following English terms into Chinese

Written promise	Issuing bank	Irrevocable L/C not confirmed
Transaction risks	Standby L/C	Deferred payment L/C
Back-to-back L/C	Red clause L/C	Revolving L/C

III. Challenging questions for discussion

1. What is a letter of credit? Please list some main Ls/C.

2. What is the most commonly used L/C?

3. What is the shipper's export declaration? What does it function as?

4. What's the difference between credit note and debit note?

IV. Answer the questions according to the given letter of credit

FROM: INDUSTRIAL BANK OF JAPAN, LIMITED, TOKYO

TO: BANK OF CHINA, SHANGHAI

SQUENCE OF TOTAL: 27: 1/1

FORM OF DOC. CREDIT: 40A: IRREVOCABLE

DOCU. CREDIT NO.: 20: ILC136107800

DATE OF ISSUE: 31C: 101015

DATE N PLACE OF EXP.: 31D: 101215 IN THE COUNTRY OF BENEFICIARY

APPLICANT: 50: ABC COMPANY, 1-3 MACHI KU STREET, OSAKA, JAPAN

BENEFICIARY: 59: SHANGHAI DA SHENG CO., LTD. UNIT C 2/F JINGMAO TOWER, SHANGHAI ,CHINA.

CURRENCY CODE, AMOUNT:32B: USD21240.00

AVAILABLE WITH /.BY ... 41D: BANK OF CHINA BY NEGOTIATION

DRAFTS AT...: 42C: SIGHT FOR 100PCT INVOICE VALUE

DRAWEE: 42D: THE INDUSTRIAL BANK OF JAPAN,HEAD OFFICE

PARTIAL SHIPMENT: 43P: ALLOWED

TRANSSHIPMENT: 43T: NOT ALLOWED

LOAD/DISPATCH/TAKING :44A: SHANGHAI

TRANSPORTATION TO...: 44B: OSAKA/TOKYO

LATEST DATE OF SHIPMET: 44C: 101130

DESCRIP GOODS/SERVICE: 45A: 4,000 PCS "DIAMOND" BRAND CLOCK ART NO. 791 AT USD5.31 PER PIECE CIF OSAKA/TOKYO PACKED IN NEW CARTONS

DOCUMENTS REQUIRED: 46A: IN 3 FOLD UNLESS OTHERWISE STIPULATED:

1. SIGNED COMMERCIAL INVOICE.

2. SIGNED PACKING LIST.

3. CERTIFICATE OF CHINESE ORIGIN.

4. BENEFICIARY'S CERTIFICATE STATING THAT ONE SET OF ORIGINAL SHIPPING DOCUMENTS INCLUDING ORIGINAL "FORM A" HAS BEEN SENT DIRECTLY TO THE APPLICANT.

5. *COPY OF TELEX FROM APPLICANT TO SUPPLIERS APPROVING THE SHIPPING SAMPLE.

6. INSURANCE POLICY OR CERTIFICATE ENDORSED IN BLANK FOR 110 PCT OF CIF VALUE, COVERING W.P.A RISKS AND WAR RISKS.

7. 2/3 PLUS ONE COPY OF CLEAN "ON BOARD" OCEAN BILLS OF LADING, MADE OUT TO ORDER AND BLANK ENDORSED MARKED "FREIGHT PREPAID" AND NOTIFY APPLICANT.

ADDITIONAL CONDITION:47A:

ALL DRAFTS DRAWN HEREUNDER MUST BE MARKED "DRAWN UNDER INDUSTRIAL BANK OF JAPAN, LTD., HEAD OFFICE, CREDIT NO. ILC136107800 DATED OCT.15, 2005" AND THE AMOUNT OF SUCH DRAFTS MUST BE ENDORSED ON THE REVERSE OF THIS CREDIT.

T/T REIMBURSEMENT IS NOT ACCEPTABLE

DETAILS OF CHARGES 71 B: ALL BANKING CHARGES OUTSIDE JANPAN ARE FOR BENEFICIARY'S ACCOUNT

PRESENTAION PERIOD 48: DOCUMENTS MUST BE PRESENTED WITHIN 15 DAYS AFTER THE DATE OF ISSUANCE OF THE SHIPPING DOCUMENTS BUT WITHIN THE VALIDITY OF THE CREDIT.

CONFIRMATION 49: WITHOUT

SPECIAL INSTRUCTION TO THE ADVISING BANK: ALL DOCUMENTS INCLUDING BENEFICIARY'S DRAFTS MUST BE SENT BY COURIER SERVICE DIRECTLY TO OUR HEAD OFFICE. MARUNOUCHI, CHIYODA-U, TOKYO, JAPAN 100, ATTN. INTERNATIOANL BUSINESS DEPT. IMPORT SECTION, IN ONE LOT. UPON OUR RECEIPT OF THE DRAFTS AND DOCUMENTS, WE SHALL MAKE PAYMENT AS INSTRUCTED BY YOU.

SEND. TO REC, INFO. 72: ACKNOWLEDGE RECEIPT

TRAILER ORDER IS

IT IS SUBJECT TO THE UNIFORM CUSTOMS AND PRACTICE FOR DOCUMENTARY CREDITS (2007 REVISION), INTERNATIONAL CHAMBER OF COMMERCE PUBLICATION NO.600.

根据上述信用证内容，回答下列问题：

1. 本信用证的种类为（至少四种）_____。
2. 该信用证的有效期、交单期分别为_____。
3. 如果已装船提单的签发日为 11 月 15 日，则受益人最迟应在几月几日向银行交单？
4. 该信用证项下，汇票的种类是谁？汇票的付款人是_____。
5. 受益人应提交的单据种类及其份数为_____。
6. 根据《跟单信用证统一惯例》（UCP600）的有关规定对标有"*"符号的部分内容进行分析，并指出这种条款对受益人的影响。

Chapter **12** Logistics Documents 2

 Chapter Outline

Part I   Transport Documents (1)

Overview of transport documents

Parties involved in shipping documents

Types of shipping documents

Circulation of shipping documents

Booking note   Shipping order

Stowage plan   Tally sheet

Part II   Transport Documents (2)

Mate's receipt   Bill of lading

Functions of B/L   Types of B/L

Export manifest   Delivery order

Part III   Supplementary Reading

Transport Documents (3)

   Sea waybill   Air Waybill

   Multimodal Transport Document   Rail Waybill

   Road Waybill   Dock Receipt

   Post Parcel Receipt and Courier Receipt

   Comparative Table for the Functions of Transport Documents

PART I   Transport Documents (1)

Overview of Transport Documents

Main types of transport documents

The carriage of the goods in international trade is an intricate matter. Interests of all parties concerned must be matched and considered carefully. These interests are best looked after by the proper administration that comprises the use of many documents. **Transport documents** include shipper's letter of instruction, booking note, shipping order, mate's receipt, dock receipt, container load plan, bill of lading, delivery order, equipment interchange receipt, sea waybill, air waybill, railway bill, road waybill, cargo manifest, forwarders' certificate of receipt, forwarders' certificate of transport, etc.

Parties Involved in Shipping Documents

As far as maritime transport is concerned, the main **parties involved in the shipping documents** are the shipper or the consignor, the shipping company (the carrier), the shipping agent, the freight forwarder, the tally company, the stevedoring company, the consignee and the banks.

Types of Shipping Documents

Main types of shipping documents

Shipping documents take many forms, and usually are worked out and applied for various purposes in the whole process of maritime transport of goods. The shipping documents chiefly refer to such documents as booking note, shipping order, stowage plan, tally sheet, mate's receipt, cargo manifest, freight manifest, outturn report, bill of lading, and delivery order, etc. These documents serve as written evidence of handing and taking over cargo in each link of the chain of sea transport, and also as the necessary certificate for business connections of the parties concerned and demarcation of their respective responsibilities.

Circulation of Shipping Documents

Booking note

The circulation of the relevant shipping documents is as follows:

(1) The shipper (or consignor) makes an application to a shipping company or its agent for the shipment of goods by filling in a **booking note (B/N)**.

Shipping order

(2) After the acceptance of the booking note, the shipping company issues a **shipping order (S/O)** to the shipper, advising him of when and where to deliver the goods alongside the named ship.

(3) The shipper, on the strength of the S/O, goes through the customs declaration formalities for outward goods and gets the goods ready for shipment.

Loading list

(4) The agent prepares a **loading list** for the ship according to the S/O.

Stowage plan

(5) The chief officer works out a **stowage plan**. A number of copies are sent to the tally company and stevedoring company through the agent for the arrangement of loading and discharge.

Tally sheets

(6) The chief tallyman checks all goods loaded on board against the **tally sheets** and signs the S/O.

Mate's receipt

(7) The chief officer, by reference to the tally, endorses the S/O, which then automatically becomes the **mate's receipt (M/R)** to be issued to the shipper after loading.

Bill of lading

(8) After paying for the freight (prepaid), the shipper turns over the M/R to the shipping company or agent in exchange for the **bill of lading**.

(9) The shipper sends the B/L and other relevant documents to the bank for negotiation of payment.

Export manifest

Freight manifest

(10) The agent makes out for the ship a suitable number of copies of the **export manifest (M/F)** and **freight manifest (F/M)**, which are required by the customs at the local port as well as other ports of call.

(11) The consignee secures the B/L from the bank by effecting the payment for goods.

Delivery order

(12) The consignee presents the B/L to the shipping company or agent in exchange for the **delivery order (D/O)**, by which he takes delivery of goods at the warehouse.

Booking Note

Definition of booking note

Booking note is prepared by a shipper and countersigned by the carrier or his agent as a contract for the reservation of shipping space on the carrier's vessel for the transport of the shipper's cargo to a particular destination. Booking note contains the detailed terms and conditions of the carriage contract including freight chargeable, description and dimensions of the goods to be carried, the name of the vessel to carry the goods, the mode of transport, the locality where the goods should be sent for loading, the time when the vessel is ready to receive the goods, the last date when the goods may be received by the vessel for loading, the

Main elements on a booking note

port of destination of the goods, the type of transport document to be issued and, where applicable, the name of the consignee. The booking note is a contract document which imposes legal obligations and confers legal rights on the parties according to its terms. If the shipper fails to tender the stipulated goods for shipment at the designated place and time, he may forfeit any prepaid freight or be liable for damages. Similarly, if the shipper fulfills its obligations under the contract and the carrier defaults, the shipper may claim damages against the carrier.

Shipping Order

Definition of S/O

Main elements on a shipping order

Shipping order is issued by the shipping line to a shipper with a confirmed space booking, authorizing the receiving clerk (cargo checker) at the container terminal or dock to receive a specified amount of goods from the named shipper. The shipping order typically contains the space booking number, names and addresses of the shipper and customs broker or freight forwarder, vessel and voyage number, sailing time, delivery date and location, customs closing date, and number and type of packages. The customs broker or freight forwarder usually requires the packing list of a consignment in order to book the shipping space and to obtain the shipping order and/or to prepare the dock receipt. The shipping order accompanies the dock receipt and the deliverer of the goods presents these two and other documents that may be required in the delivery to the receiving clerk at the closing location. In certain countries, only the space booking number is needed instead of a formal shipping order, since the information in an shipping order is found in the dock receipt.

Stowage Plan

Definition of stowage plan

Stowage plan is a completed diagram of a ship's cargo space showing what cargo has been loaded and its exact stowage location in each hold, tweendeck, or other space in a ship, including deck space. Each port of discharge is indicated by a particular color or other symbol; deck and tweendeck cargo is shown in perspective (top view), cargo stowed in the lower hold is shown in profile (side view), but vehicles are shown in perspective (top view), regardless of stowage. A good stowage plan has to consider many different factors including ship stability, cargo movement handling cost, cargo types and their port of destinations, etc. All cargo is shown on the stowage plan in metric tons and measurement tons (CBM). The stowage plan helps organize loading so that the cargo is accessible for unloading and quickly identifies the location and type of cargo for any given port.

Tally Sheet

Definition of tally sheet

Tally sheet is issued by the tally company after its counting the quantity of the goods in the course of loading and discharging the cargoes. Tally can be divided into tally on shore and tally on board ships. The tally company tallies cargoes on behalf of the cargo owner to check or keep record of all cargo loaded into and discharged from a vessel. This is an essential part of cargo work in order to prevent claims on the ship for so-called short discharge, i.e. when some of the cargo is missing. The crew of the ship can sometimes tally cargoes for the shipping company, and it is sometimes customary for the shipper or consignee to provide his own tally clerks.

New Words and Expressions

Intricate ['intrikit] *adj.*	复杂的，错综的
Demarcation [ˌdiːmɑːˈkeiʃən] *n.*	划界，划定界限，限界
Circulation [ˌsəːkjuˈleiʃən] *n.*	流通，循环，发行量
Endorse [inˈdɔːs] *vt.*	在（支票等）背面签名，背签
Countersign [ˈkauntəsain] *vt.*	副署，会签，连署，确认
Forfeit [ˈfɔːfit] *vt.*	没收，丧失
Default [diˈfɔːlt] *vi.*	疏怠职责，违约
Hold *n.*	货舱，船舱
Tweendeck *n.*	甲板间舱，二层舱
Shipper's letter of instruction	国际货物托运委托书；托运人托运声明书（简称托运书）
Booking note	订舱单
Shipping order	装货单
Mate's receipt [riˈsiːt]	收货单（大副收据）
Dock receipt	集装箱场站收据
Container load plan	集装箱装箱单
Delivery order	提货单
Equipment interchange receipt	设备交接单
Sea waybill [ˈweibil]	海运单
Air waybill	航空运单
Railway bill	铁路运单
Road waybill	公路运单

Cargo manifest ['mænifest]	货物舱单
Forwarders' certificate of receipt	货代收货证明
Forwarders' certificate of transport	贷代运输证明
Tally company ['tæli]	理货公司
Stevedoring company [,sti:vi'dɔriŋ]	装卸公司
Stowage plan ['stəuidʒ]	积载图
Tally sheet	理货单
Freight manifest ['mænifest]	运费舱单
Outturn report	卸货报告
Written evidence	书面证明
Handing and taking over cargo	交接货物
Business connections	业务关系，业务联系
Customs declaration formalities	海关报关手续
Outward goods	出港货物
Get the goods ready for shipment	货物备妥待运
Loading list	装货清单
Chief officer / mate	大副
Chief tallyman	理货组长
Negotiation of payment	议付
Shipping line	航运公司
Short discharge	短卸

NOTES

Each port of discharge is indicated by a particular color or other symbol; deck and tweendeck cargo is shown in perspective (top view), cargo stowed in the lower hold is shown in profile (side view), but vehicles are shown in perspective (top view), regardless of stowage.

每个卸货港均用特定的颜色或其他标志标明；甲板货和二层甲板货用正视图标明，下舱（底舱）的货物用侧视图标明，但车辆不管装在何处，均用正视图标明。

EXERCISES

I. Translate the following Chinese terms into English

订舱单	收货单	集装箱装箱单	航空运单
提货单	短卸	海运单证	海上运输
装卸公司	理货单	卸货报告	业务关系
装货清单	议付	运输方式	公路运单

II. Translate the following English terms into Chinese

shipper's letter of instruction   order   dock receipt equipment interchange receipt

forwarders' certificate of receipt

forwarders' certificate of transport

handing and taking over cargo

customs declaration formalities

get the goods ready for shipment

railway bill

tally company

stowage plan

outward goods

chief mate

shipping space

cargo manifest

freight manifest

written evidence

chief tallyman

shipping line

container terminal

III. Challenging questions for discussion

1. What are the main types of transport documents?

2. What are the main types of shipping documents?

3. How do the relevant shipping documents circulate?

4. Is a shipping order the necessary document used to go through the customs formalities?

IV. Be familiar with each column of the shipping documents given below

THE NAME AND ADDRESS OF BENEFIC ARY

托运单 BOOKING NOTE

（1）收货人：Consignee

（2）通知人：Notify

（17）提单号：B/L No.：

（18）船名VSL：

（19）编号NO：

（20）日期Date：

（21）起运地Loading Port：

（22）装运地Destination：

（3）标记　　　（4）件数　　（5）货名　　　　（6）净重　毛重　（7）尺码

Shipping Marks:　Quantity:　Description of Goods:　N/W　G/W　Measur ement:

（23）特殊条款pecial Coditions:

（8）可否分批

（9）可否转船

（10）装船期限

（11）结汇期限

（13）正本

（14）副本

（15）货存地点

（16）运费缴付方式

（12）运费吨：　　　　　运费吨：　　　　　运费金额：

NAME OF BENEFICIARY AND SIGNA TURE

中国外轮代理公司

CHINA OCEAN SHIPPING AGENCY

装货单

SHIPPING ORDER

托运人
Shipper_____

编号   船名
No._____ S/S_____

目的港
For_____

兹将下列完好状况之货物装船后希签署收货单
Receive on board the undermentioned goods apparent in good order and condition and sign the accompanying receipt for the same

标记及号码 Marks & Nos	件 数 Quantity	货 名 Description of Goods	重量（千克） Weight Kilos	
			净重 Net	毛重 Gross

共 计 件 数（大 写）
Total Number of Package in Writing

日期   时间
Date_____ Time_____

装入何舱
Stowed_____

实 收
Received_____

理货员签名   经 办 员
Tallied by_____ Approved by_____

176

中 国 外 轮 代 理 公 司

CHINA OCEAN SHIPPING AGENCY

收 货 单

MATE'S RECEIPT

托运人
Shipper_____

编号   船名
No._____   S/S_____

目的港
For_____

兹将下列完好状况之货物装船后希签署收货单
Receive on board the undermentioned goods apparent in good order and condition and sign the accompanying receipt for the same

标 记 及 号 码 Marks & Nos	件　数 Quantity	货　名 Description of Goods	重　量（千克） Weight Kilos	
			净　重 Net	毛　重 Gross

共 计 件 数（大 写）
Total Number of Package in Writing
_____

–

日期   时间
Date_____   Time

装入何舱
Stowed_____

实　收
Received_____

理货员签名   大副
Tallied by_____   Chief Officer_____

177

PART II   Transport Documents (2)

Mate's Receipt

Definition of M/R

Mate's receipt is a document issued by the first mate (i.e. the chief officer) of a vessel, who is responsible for cargo, in the name of the shipping company evidencing receipt of a shipment onboard the vessel and stating the quantity, identifying marks and the apparent condition of the goods. If there are any damages to the goods before loading, this will be recorded on the receipt, and it is no longer "clean". It is not a document of title and is issued as an interim measure until a proper bill of lading can be issued. That is, mate's receipt will be issued by the first mate after the goods is tallied into the ship by tally clerks. The shipper or his representative will then take the mate's receipt to the master or the agent to exchange it for a bill of lading, which will incorporate any conditions inserted into the mate's receipt. Nowadays, Mate's receipt is not often signed by the mate of the ship but by some person in the shore office of the shipping company or its agents, although the name of the document remains the same.

Bill of Lading

Definition of B/L

Bill of lading (B/L) is a transport document issued by the carrier or its agent to the shipper, admitting that goods have been received for shipment to a particular destination and stating the terms on which the goods are to be carried. With a B/L, the consignor can come to the bank for negotiation, and the holder of which can get the goods at the port of destination from the carrier. The B/L, together with the insurance policy and commercial invoices, constitutes the chief documents indispensable to international trade and logistics activities. A B/L is usually negotiable and widely used in maritime transport.

Elements of B/L

A B/L mainly contains the following parts: the name of the shipping company (the carrier), the name of the shipper who is usually the exporter or its agent, the name of the consignee, the notify party, the name of the carrying vessel and the voyage No., the two ports (i.e. the port of loading and the port of discharge), marks and numbers, description of goods, kinds of packages, gross weight, measurement, freight and charges (freight prepaid or freight collect), number of original B/L, the signature of the carrier, and the B/L issuing place and date.

Functions of B/L

Receipt of goods

Evidence of contract of carriage

Title document

When the goods are transported by vessel, the **marine or ocean B/L** is one of the most important shipping documents. A bill of lading functions as **a receipt of goods** by the carrier evidencing receipt of the goods from the consignor, **evidence of a contract of carriage** between the shipper and the carrier containing the conditions on which transport is made, and **a document of title to the goods** in the sense that the lawful holder/owner of the B/L is the lawful owner of the goods and the carrier will only release the goods at the stipulated port of destination against the presentation of the original B/L.

Types of B/L

Bills of lading (Bs/L) are of many kinds, and can be classified into the following categories in accordance with different criteria.

(1) In terms of whether or not the goods are on board

Shipped B/L

Shipped B/L (or On Board B/L) is issued by the carrier or its agent when all the goods are loaded on board the ship, and must bear the name of the ship and the date of shipment.

Received for shipment B/L

Received for Shipment B/L is issued by the carrier or its agent when he goods are under his control before loaded on board the ship. The importer does not favor it, and usually the L/C will require the exporter to present shipped B/L for negotiation at the bank. However, with the development of container transport, received for shipment Bs/L are being increasingly applied.

(2) On the basis of the apparent condition of goods noted

Clean B/L

When the shipping company writes on the B/L "The goods loaded are in apparent good order", this B/L is a **Clean B/L** or an **Unclaused B/L**.

Unclean B/L

When the shipping line gives such an indication as "The goods loaded are not in apparent good order" or "The packing is broken or ... is polluted, etc.", this B/L is an **Unclean B/L** or a **foul B/L** or a **claused B/L**, and non-negotiable at the bank.

(3) In the light of different characteristics of consignees

Straight B/L

Straight B/L has a specified name in the column of consignee, which means that the goods can only be received by the specified person and the B/L cannot be transferred to a third person. So it is also called non-negotiable B/L, and thus it is not commonly used in international trade and normally applies to high-value shipments or goods for special purposes.

Order B/L	**Order B/L** does not have a specified name but the phraseology of "To order", or "To the order of …" in the column of consignee. This kind of B/L can be transferred to others by endorsement, thus called negotiable B/L, and widely used in international trade.
Open B/L	**Open B/L** has neither the consignee's name nor the phraseology of "To order" fill in the column of consignee. This type of B/L is also called negotiable B/L, and can be negotiable without endorsement, and ownership of the goods passes when the B/L is handed over to anyone. Owing to the exceedingly high risk involved, this B/L is rarely used.

(4) In accordance with modes of transport

Direct B/L	Under **Direct B/L**, the goods will be directly carried to the port of destination without transshipment.
Transshipment	Under **Transshipment B/L**, the goods will be transshipped in transit.
Through B/L	**Through B/L** is a development of these two Bs/L. Under Through B/L, the goods will at least be carried by two different modes of transport as sea-land or land-sea and taken charge of by different carriers during transport before arriving at the port of destination.
Combined Transport B/L	A multimodal transport operator responsible for the whole voyage issues **Combined Transport B/L**, involving two or more different kinds of transport. This kind of B/L is usually used in container transport and may be a Received for Shipment B/L, but a Through B/L must be a Clean Shipped B/L.

(5) In conformity with the detailed or simplified clauses

Long form B/L	**Long Form B/L** has detailed clauses printed on its back concerning the transport of goods so as to solve any possible transport disputes.
Short form B/L	**Short Form B/L** does not have such clauses on its back. However, if such wording as "all transport clauses are based on the long form B/L of our company" is stamped on the back of a short form B/L, this B/L is equal to a long form one and will be accepted by the bank for negotiation.

(6) In compliance with the types of vessel

Liner B/L	**Liner B/L** is issued by the carrier when the goods are shipped on a regular liner vessel with scheduled route and reserved berth at destination. Its obvious advantage is that the carrier can advise the shipper, before or shortly after the sea voyage, of the estimated time of departure (ETD) and the estimated time of arrival (ETA) so that the importer will also be informed that the goods are dispatched and will arrive on a set date. The majority of B/L is liner B/L.
Charter party B/L	**Charter party B/L** is issued by a charterer of a ship to the exporter.

The terms of the B/L are subject to the charter party between the shipowner and the charterer. A charter B/L usually contains such wordings "subject to the charter party". Banks normally will not accept a charter B/L unless stated otherwise in the credit. This type of B/L is not very popular in international trade.

Export Manifest

Definition of export manifest

Export manifest is a document containing the lists of goods to be loaded onboard a ship and giving the description of a ship's cargo. It gives the details of each consignment such as the maritime transport document reference, e.g. the bill of lading number; the container identification number; the number, kinds, marks and numbers of the packages; the description and gross weight/volume of the goods; the port or place where the goods were loaded on to the ship; the original port or place of shipment for goods on a maritime transportation document.

Delivery Order

Definition of D/O

Delivery order is an order from a shipping line to the terminal superintendent for the release of goods to a consignee following payment of freight charges. It is the necessary document to go through the importing country's customs formalities and the evidence of taking delivery of the goods.

New Words and Expressions

Interim ['intərim] adj.	中间的，暂时的，临时的
Representative n.	代表，代理人
Incorporate vt.	合并，使组成公司，具体表现
Phraseology [ˌfreizi'ɔlədʒi] n.	表达方式，用语，措词，术语
Endorsement [in'dɔ:smənt] n.	背书，保证，签注
Simplify vt.	简化，使简易
Superintendent [ˌsju:pərin'tendənt] n.	监督人，主管，负责人
Original B/L	正本提单
Marine or ocean B/L	海运提单，远洋提单
Receipt of goods	货物收据
Document of title to the goods	货物所有权凭证，物权凭证
Lawful holder	合法持有人
Shipped B/L	已装船提单

Received for shipment B/L [rɪˈsiːvd]	备运提单
Clean B/L	清洁提单
Unclean B/L (foul B/L)	不清洁提单
Non-negotiable B/L [nɪˈɡəʊʃəbl]	不可转让提单，不可流通提单
Claused B/L	不法提单，不清洁提单
Straight B/L	记名提单
Order B/L	指示提单
Negotiable B/L	可转让提单，可流通提单
Open B/L	不记名提单
Direct B/L	直达提单，直运提单
Transshipment B/L	转船提单
Through B/L	联运提单
Combined transport B/L	多式联运提单
Long form B/L	全式提单，繁式提单，详式提单
Short form B/L	简式提单，略式提单
Liner B/L	班轮提单
Scheduled route	预定路线，预定航线
Estimated time of departure (ETD)	预计离开时间
Estimated time of arrival (ETA)	预计抵达时间
Charter party B/L	租船提单
Charter party	租船契约
Export manifest	出口舱单
Container identification number	集装箱识别码，集装箱号码
Terminal superintendent	码头监管人员

NOTES

1. And usually the L/C will require the seller to present shipped B/L for negotiation at the bank.
且通常，信用证要求卖方到银行议付时提交已装船提单。

2. On the basis of the apparent condition of goods noted
根据所批注的货物外观状况

3. In apparent good order
外观状况良好

4. A multi-modal operator responsible for the whole voyage issues combined Transport B/L
由负责全程运输的联运人签发联运提单

5. To solve any possible transport disputes
解决任何可能的运输纠纷

6. Its obvious advantage is that the carrier can advise the shipper, before or shortly after the sea voyage, of the estimated date of departure (ETD) and the estimated time of arrival (ETA) so

that the importer will also be informed that the goods are dispatched and will arrive on a set date.

其明显的一个优势就是承运人能够在航行之前或之后立即联系托运人，告知预计开船日和预计到港日，这样进口商也可以获知货物已经发出并将于固定日抵达。

EXERCISES

I. Translate the following Chinese terms into English

海运提单	货物收据	已装船提单	直达提单
清洁提单	指示提单	不记名提单	联运提单
全式提单	预定航线	多式联运人	班轮提单
租船契约	运费	海运单证	预计抵达时间

II. Translate the following English terms into Chinese

Evidence of contract of carriage	B/L	Lawful holder
Container identification number	Claused B/L	Short form B/L
Document of title to the goods	Straight B/L	Transshipment B/L
Received for shipment B/L	Negotiable B/L	Non-negotiable B/L
Combined transport B/L	Charter party B/L	Export manifest
Estimated time of departure	Terminal superintendent	B/L

III. Judge whether the following statements are true or false

1. A B/L is a contract of carriage in which the shipping company promises to transport the goods received to the destination required.

2. An Order B/L may be negotiable after being endorsed.

3. On the back of short form B/L, there are rights and obligations of the consignor and the carrier.

4. A Through B/L means that the goods will at least be carried by two different modes of transport.

5. Received for Shipment B/L is generally favored by the buyer.

IV. Challenging questions for discussion

1. Which of the following document is used to exchange the bill of lading, the shipping order, the mate's receipt or the tally sheet?

2. What is a bill of lading?

3. What functions does the marine B/L perform?

4. How many types of marine B/L are mentioned in this part? How should they be distinguished from each other?

5. Why is a Straight B/L not negotiable?

V. Make out the B/L according to the L/C given below

Irrevocable documentary credit

Number: LC123-258866

Date: August 24, 2009

Date and place of expiry: October 30, 2009, Shanghai, China

Advising bank: Bank of China

Beneficiary: China xyz import and export corp.

Applicant: UVW corporation

Total amount: USD9 000 (SAY US DOLLARS NINE THOUSAND ONLY)

Shipment from: Shanghai China

To: Osaka Japan

At the latest: October 15, 2009

Description of goods: 100% Cotton Towel as per S/C No. CH200

Total quantity:8, 000pieces

Packing:800 Cartons

Total gross weight: 20, 000kgs

Total measurement: 30CBM

Price term: CIF Osaka

Following documents required:

+Signed commercial invoice in three copies.

+Full set of clean on board ocean bill of lading made out to order and endorsed in blank and marked "freight prepaid" and notify applicant.

+Insurance policy for 110 PCT of the invoice value covering the Institute Cargo Clauses (A), the Institute War Clauses.

Ocean Vessel: "Golden star" Voy. No.: 018E

Container No.: GSTU3156712/20'

Marks & Nos.: ITOCHU OSAKA NO.1-800

LADEN ON BOARD THE VESSEL: October 14, 2009

B/L date: October 15, 2009

B/L signed by BBB shipping agency

Carrier: AAA Shipping Co.

海运提单

托运人 Shipper		SINOTRANS B/L No.
收货人或指示 Consigner or order		中国对外贸易运输总公司 北京BEIJING 联 运 提 单 COMBINED TRANSPORT BILL OF LADING
通知地址 Notify Address		RECEIVED the foods in apparent good order and condition as specified below unless otherwise stated herein. THE Canier, in accordance with the provisions contained in this document:
前段运输 Pre-caniage by	收货地点 Place of Receipt	1）undertakes to perform or to procure the performance of the entire transport form the place at which the goods are taken in charge to the place designated for delivery in this document, and 2）assumes liability as prescnbed in this document for such transport One of the bills of lading must be sumendered duty indorsed in exchange for the goods or delivery order
海运船只 Ocean Vessel	装货港 Port of Loading	

卸货港 Port of Discharge	交货地点 Place of Delivery	运费支付地 Freight payable at	正本提单份数 Number of original Bs/L

标志和号码 Marks and Nos.	件数和包装种类 Number and kind of packages	货 名 Description of goods	毛重（公斤） Gross weight（kgs.）	尺码（立方米） Measurement（m³）

以上细目由托运人提供

ABOVE PARTICULARS FURNISHED BY SHIPPER

运费和费用 Freight and charges	IN WITNESS where of the number of original bills of Lading stated above have been signed, one of which being accomplished, the other(s) to be void.
	签单地点和日期 Place and date of issue
	代表承运人签字 Signed for or on behalf of the carrier
	代 理 as Agents

中国外轮代理公司

CHINA OCEAN SHIPPING AGENCY

装 货 单

SHIPPING ORDER

托运人
Shipper_____

编号   船名
No._____   S/S_____

目的港
For_____

兹将下列完好状况之货物装船后希签署收货单

Receive on board the undermentioned goods apparent in good order and condition and sign the accompanying receipt for the same

标 记 及 号 码 Marks & Nos	件 数 Quantity	货 名 Description of Goods	重 量 公 斤 Weight Kilos	
			净 重 Net	毛 重 Gross

共 计 件 数（大 写）
Total Number of Package in Writing

_____

日期   时间
Date_____   Time

装入何舱
Stowed_____

实 收
Received_____

理货员签名   经办员
Tallied by_____   Approved by_____

中国外轮代理公司

CHINA OCEAN SHIPPING AGENCY

收 货 单

MATE'S RECEIPT

托运人
Shipper_____

—
编号   船名
No._____   S/S_____

-
目的港
For_____
兹将下列完好状况之货物装船后希签署收货单
Receive on board the undermentioned goods apparent in good order and condition and sign the accompanying
receipt for the same

标 记 及 号 码 Marks & Nos	件　数 Quantity	货　名 Description of Goods	重量公斤 Weight Kilos	
			净 重 Net	毛 重 Gross

共 计 件 数（大 写）
Total Number of Package in Writing

_____

日期   时间
Date_____   Time
装入何舱
Stowed_____
实　收
Received_____
理货员签名   大副
Tallied by_____   Chief Officer_____

场站收据

	D/R No.（编号）
Shipper （发货人）	**场站收据**
Consignee （收货人）	Received by the Canier the Total number of containers or other packages or units stated below to be transported subject to the terms and conditions of the canier's regular form of Bill of Loadıng(for Comb illed Transport or port to Port Shipment) which shall be deemed to be incorporated herein.
Notify Party （通知人）	
Pre carriage by（前程运输）　Place of Receipt（收货地点）	Date（日期）:
Ocean vessel（船名）　Voy No.（船航次）　Port of Loading（装货港）	**场站章**
Port of Discharge（卸货港）　Place of delivery（交货地点）	Final Destination for Merchant's References （目的地）

particulars Furrdshed by Merchants	Container No. （集装箱号）	Seel No. （封志号） Mark & Nos. （标记与号码）	No. of Containers or Pkgs. （箱数或件数）	Kind of Packages; Description of Goods （包装种类与货名）	Gross Weight 毛重（公斤）	Measurement 尺码（立方米）
		TOTAL NUMBER OF CONTAINERS OF PACKAGES(IN WORDS)集装箱数或件数合计（大写）				

Container No.（箱号）　Seal No.（封志号）　Pkgs.（件数）　Container No.（箱号）　Seal No.（封志号）　Pkgs.（件数）

Received（实收）　By Terminal clerk（场站员签字）

FREIGHT & CHARGES	Prepaid at（预付地点）	Payable at（到付地点）	Place of Issue（签发地点）	
	Total Prepaid（预付总额）	No. of Original B(S)/L （正本提单份数）	BOOKING（订舱确认） APPROVED BY	

Service Type on Receiving □-CY,□-CFS,□-DOOR	Service Type on delivery □-CY,□-CFS,□-DOOR	Reefer Temperature Required. （冷藏温度）		℉	℃
FYPE OF GOODS （种类）	□Ordinary,□Reefer,□Dangerous,□Auto. （普通）　（冷藏）　（危险品）　（裸装车辆）		危险品	Class: Property: IMDG Code Page: UN NO.	
	□Liquid,□Live Animal,□Bulk,□_____ （液体）　（活动物）　（散货）				

PART III Supplementary Reading
Transport Documents (3)

Sea Waybill

Receipt of goods and contract of carriage

A **sea waybill** is a transport document issued by a shipping company as an alternative to a B/L. It only performs two functions of a B/L, that is, as a receipt of goods and a contract of carriage. In other words, unlike the bill of lading, a sea waybill is not a document of title to the goods or a negotiable document, and thus can only be made out to a named consignee, i.e. the seaway bill obliges the carrier to deliver the goods to the consignee named in the document. Hence there is no need for the consignee to present any transport document at the port of discharge, as long as he can identify himself as the party named as consignee in the seaway bill, the carrier's only responsibility in this connection is to exercise due diligence when confirming the identity of the person claiming to be the consignee, which can speed up processing at the port of discharge. The sea waybill is suitable for short traffics, because the traditional bill of lading would arrive after the goods have reached their destination. Most of the goods shipped on the Atlantic route is done under the sea waybill.

Air Waybill

Definition of an AWB

An **air waybill (AWB)** is a transport document issued by an airline used for the air transport of goods. That is, it is an air consignment note used for the carriage of goods by air.

Difference between AWB and marine B/L

The air waybill is approximately equivalent to the ocean B/L, but it is not a document of title to goods or a negotiable instrument in the same way as is an ocean B/L because the cargo would arrive at the destination airport days or sometimes weeks before the air waybill's arrival via the banking system. Therefore, the consignee is allowed to take delivery of the goods before receiving the air waybill.

Functions of an AWB

Each air waybill has three originals and at least 6 copies. The air waybill must be accurately completed, and clear and complete forwarding instructions must be given to the airline or agent for efficient service. The air waybill mainly functions as a receipt of the goods for dispatch, evidence of the contract of carriage between the carrier and the consignor, a freight bill specifying the charges respectively borne by the consignor and the agent, and a source document for clearance.

Common use of standard AWB

The airline industry has adopted a standard formatted air waybill that accommodates both domestic and international traffic. The standard document was designed to enhance the application of modern computerized systems to air freight processing for both the carrier and the shipper.

Multimodal (or Combined)Transport Document (MTD or CTD)

Definition of MTD

A **multimodal transport document** evidences the contract of carriage of goods by at least two modes of transport, such as shipping by rail and by sea, issued by a multimodal transport operator under a multimodal transport contract.

Difference between MTD and through B/L

Multimodal transport document is quite similar to through B/L and combined transport B/L used for ocean transport, but is broader than them. Though B/L and combined transport B/L are always connected with sea, used for any transport combined with sea, while multimodal transport document may be applied to any kind of combined transport，not necessarily connected with sea transport. Several carriers are involved in through B/L, while multimodal transport document is issued by only one carrier, that is, multimodal transport operator. Multimodal transport document can be either negotiable or non-negotiable, and usually non-negotiable.

Rail Waybill

Definition of railway bill

A **rail waybill,** also called **consignment note for rail transport** or **railway cargo receipt**, serves as the contract of carriage between the railway and consignor, evidencing the receipt of the goods and the date of acceptance for carriage by the carrier. The rail waybill will be delivered with the cargo from the departure station to the consignee at the destination station against payment of the amounts by the consignee. A duplicate is given to the shipper as a receipt for acceptance of the goods. Unlike B/L, it is not a document of title and is not negotiable. The rail waybill is subject to the International Convention for the Transport of Goods by Rail (CIM).

Road Waybill

Definition of road waybill

A **road waybill**, also called **consignment note for road transport** or **CMR consignment note,** which is similar to rail waybill in form and contents, stands for the contract for the carriage of goods by road in vehicles, completed by the sender and the carrier with the appropriate signatures and/or stamp. Like rail waybill, it evidences the place and date of taking over the goods and the place designated for delivery. It is not a transferable document or document of title either, and is subject to the Convention on Contract for the International Carriage for Goods by Road (CMR).

Post Parcel Receipt and Courier Receipt

Definition of post parcel receipt

The **post parcel receipt** is issued by the post office for goods sent by post. It is both a receipt and evidence of dispatch, but it is not a document of title and goods should be consigned to the party specified in the credit.

Definition of courier receipt

When the goods are sent by a courier or an express delivery service, a **courier receipt** will be issued. The worldwide famous express services are EMS, DHL, UPS and Federal Express. This mode of transport will be chosen when the goods are of the greatest concern. Courier service, especially the express delivery services，provide desk to desk service.

Dock Receipt

Definition of dock receipt

Dock receipt is a receipt issued by a port officer or warehouse supervisor to confirm receipt of the goods on the quay or warehouse before shipment from the domestic carrier or the consignor. The dock receipt is used to transfer responsibility when the export goods is moved by the domestic carrier to the port of shipment and left with the international carrier for movement to its final destination.

Comparative Table for the Functions of Transport Documents

Types of modes of transport

In international trade, there are many kinds of modes of transport, such as marine transport, air transport, rail transport, and road transport. Different transport documents are applicable to different modes of transport, and they may be a receipt of goods or a contract of carriage or the document of title to goods. The following is a comparative table for the functions of some transport documents.

Comparative Table for the Functions of Transport Documents

Type of Document	Mode of Transport	Receipt	Contract of Carriage	Document of Title
Marine/Ocean B/L Port to Port	Marine transport	Yes	Yes	Yes
Non-negotiable Sea Waybill	Marine transport	Yes	Yes	No
Chartered B/L	Marine transport	Yes	Subject to Charter Party	Subject to Charter Party
Multimodal Transport Document	At least two modes of transport used	Yes	Yes	Yes or No
Air Waybill	Air transport	Yes	Yes	No
Railway Bill	Rail transport	Yes	Yes	No
Road Waybill Truck Waybill	Road transport	Yes	Yes	No
Post Parcel Receipt	Post service	Yes	Yes	No
Courier Receipt	Courier service and express delivery service	Yes	Yes	No

New Words and Expressions

Name vt.	指定，说出，提名，任命
Identify [ai'dentifai] vt.	识别，认明，鉴定
Identity [ai'dentiti] n.	身分
Instrument ['instrument] n.	文件，证券，契约，票据
Dispatch [di'spætʃ] n.	发送，发运
Accommodate [ə'kɔmədeit] vt.	适应，顺应，装载（乘客），照应，招待
Wagon ['wægən] n.	（铁路的）无盖货车
Duplicate ['dju:plikeit] n.	复本，抄件，副本，副件
Courier ['kuriə] n.	快递员
Quay n.	码头，埠头
Triplicate copy ['triplikit]	三份副本
Exercise due diligence ['dilidʒəns]	恪尽职责
Short traffics	短途运输
Atlantic route	大西洋航线

Consignment note	发货通知书；托运单
Carriage of goods by air	航空运输
Forwarding instructions	货运说明，货运指示
Freight bill	运费单（据）
Source of document for clearance	用于清关的源单据
Document for clearance	结关单据
Post parcel receipt	邮政收据，邮包收据
Express delivery service	快递服务，快件服务
Courier receipt ['kuriə]	专递收据
Dock receipt	码头收据，码头收货单

NOTES

1. The air waybill is approximately equivalent to the ocean B/L, but it is not a document of title to goods or a negotiable document in the same way as is an ocean B/L.

空运单近似地等同于海运提单，但它不像海运提单一样是货物所有权凭证或是可议付票据。

2. The airline industry has adopted a standard formatted air waybill that accommodates both domestic and international traffic. The standard document was designed to enhance the application of modern computerized systems to air freight processing for both the carrier and the shipper.

目前各航空公司已经普遍采用了一种适应国内国际运输的标准的格式化空运提单。这种标准化单证旨在提高承运人和托运人对空运货物的现代化计算机系统的应用水平。

3. issued by a multimode transport operator under a multimode transport contract.

由多式联运人根据多式联运合同签发。

4. The rail waybill will be delivered with the cargo from the departure station to the consignee at the destination station against payment of the amounts by the consignee.

收货人付款后，铁路运单将连同货物从始发站运送到目的站的收货人。

5. International Convention for the Transport of Goods by Rail (CIM)

《国际铁路货物运输公约》

6. A road waybill which is similar to railway bill in form and contents, stands for the contract for the carriage of goods by road in vehicles, completed by the sender and the carrier with the appropriate signatures and/or stamp.

形式和内容都与铁路运单相似的公路运单代表发货人与承运人之间签订的，并有正确的签字和/或盖章的公路车辆运输合同。

7. Convention on Contract for the International Carriage for Goods by Road (CMR)

《国际公路货物运输公约》

8. EMS, DHL, UPS and Federal Express

这是四大快递公司的名称，其中：EMS(Express Mail Service)是指邮政特快专递服务；

DHL（dhl worldwide express）敦豪速递公司，是由三位美国人 Adrian Dalsey，Larry Hillblom 及 Robert Lynn（姓氏之首个英文字母 D,H 及 L）首创的空运速递业，提供户对户空运速递服务；UPS（United Parcel Service of America）联合包裹服务公司；FEDEX（Federal Express）是指联邦快递。

9. Dock receipt is a receipt maybe issued by a Port Authority to confirm receipt of the goods on the quay or warehouse before shipment.

码头收据是一种可由港务机关签发的、确认在码头或码头仓库收到了待装运的货物的收据。

10. The dock receipt is used to transfer responsibility when an exported commodity is moved by the domestic carrier to the port of shipment and left with the international carrier for movement to its final destination.

当出口货物被国内承运人送到装货港，并交给国际承运人运往最终目的地时，码头收据被用来转移责任。

EXERCISES

I. Translate the following Chinese terms into English

多式联运	发货通知书	多式联运合同	快递服务
专递收据	码头收据	（多式）联运单据	提货
港务局	结关单据	大西洋航线	短途运输

II. Translate the following English terms into Chinese

Carriage of goods by air	Exercise due diligence
Forwarding instructions	Source of document for clearance
Express Mail Service	DHL worldwide express
Federal Express	United Parcel Service of America

Consignment note for rail transport

Convention on Contract for the International Carriage for Goods by Road

International Convention for the Transport of Goods by Rail international traffic

III. Challenging questions for discussion

1. In what way is a B/L different from an air waybill?

2. What is the multimode transport document?

3. In what way is an MTD different from a through B/L?

4. What's the function of a dock receipt?

IV. Be familiar with each column of the transport documents given below

中 国 民 用 航 空 局
THE CIVIL AVIATION ADMINISTRATION OF CHINA
国 际 货 物 托 运 书
SHIPPER'S LETTER OF INSTRUCTION

托运人姓名及地址 SHIPPER'S NAME AND ADDRESS 1	托运空账号 SHIPPER'S ACCOUNT NUMBER	供承运人用 FOR CARRIAGE USE ONLY	
		班期/日期 FLIGHT/DATE	航期/日期 FLIGHT/DATE
		6	
收货人姓名及地址 CONSIGNEE'S NAME AND ADDRESS 2	收货人账号 CONSIGNEE'S ACCOUNT NUMBER	已预留吨位 BOOKED	
		运费　　CHARGES	
代理人的名称和城市 ISSUING CARRIERS AGENT NAME AND CITY 3		ALSO NOTIFY	
始发站 AIRPORT OF DEPARTURE 4			
到达站 AIRPORT OF DESTIN ATION 5			
托运人声明价值 SHIPPERS DECLARED VALUE		保险金额 AMOUNT OF INSURANCE XXX	所附文件 DOCUMENT　TO　ACCOMANY AIRWAY BILL 7
运输费用 FOR CARRIAGE NVD	供海关用 FOR CUSTOMS NCV		

处理情况（包括包装方式、货物标志及号码） HANDLING INFORMATION (INCL METHOD OF PACKING IDENTIFING AND NUMBERS) 11

件数 NO.OF PACKAGES	实际毛重 ACTUAL G.W.(KG.)	运价种类 RATE CLASS	收费重量 CHARGEABLE WEIGHT	费率 RATE CHARGE	货物品名及数量（量包括体积或尺寸） NATURE AND QUANTITY OF GOODS (INCL DIMENSION OF VOLUME)
8	9				10

(1) Shipper's Name and Address	Shipper's Account Number	Not Negotiable Air Waybill ISSUED BY	中国国际航空公司 *AIR CHINA* BEIJING CHINA
(2)		Copies 1,2 and 3 of this Air Waybill are originals and have the same validity.	
Consignee's Name and Address (3)	Consignee's Account Number	It is agreed that the goods descnbed here in are accepted in apparent good order and condition (except as noted) for carriage SUBJECT TO THE CONDITTONS OF CONTRACT ON THE REVERSE HEREOF. ALL GOODS MAY BE CARRIED BY ANY OTHER MEANS INCLUDING ROAD OR ANY OTHER CARRIER UNLESS SPECIFIC CONTRARY INSTRUCTIONS ARE GIVEN HERFON BY THE SHIPPER. AND SHIPPER AGREES THAT THE SHIP MENY MAY BE CARRIED VLA INTERYEDLATE STOPPING PLACES WHICH THE CARRIER DEEMS APPROPRLATE. THE SHIPPER'S ATTENTTON IS DRAWN TO THE NOTTCE CONCERNING CARRIER'S LIMITATION OF LLABILITY. Shipper may increase such limitation of liability by declaring a higher vahie for carriage and paying a supplemertal charge ifrequire.	

Issuing Carrier's Agent Name and City (4)		Accounting Infonmation	
Agent's IATA Code	Account No.		

| Airport of Dep arture(Addr. Of First Carrier) and Requested Routing
(5) | Reference Number | Optional Shipping Infonmation |

TO	By First Carrier	Routing and Destination	to	by	to	by	Currency	CHGS	WT/VAL OTHER				Declared Vahie for Carriage NCD	Declare Vahie for Customs NVV
									PPD	COLL	PPD	COLL		

Airport of Destination (6)	Flight/date	for Carriage Use Only (7)	Flight/date	Amount of insurance	INSURANCE-If carrier offers insurance and such insurance is required in accordance with the conditions conditions there of, indicate amourt to be insured in figures in box marked "amount of insurance".

Handling Information
(8)

No. of pieces RCP (9)	Gross Weight (10)	kg lb k	Rate class Commodity Item No.	Changeable Weight	Rate / Charge	Total	Nature and Quantity of Goods (incl. Dimensions or Volume) (12)

Prepaid	Weight Charge	Collect	Other Charges
	Valuation Charge		
	Tax		
	Total Other Charges Due Agent		
	Total Other Charges Due Carrier 50		Shipper certifies that the partioulars on the face here of are correct and thaat in so far as any part of the consignment contains dangerous goods, such part is properly descnled by name and is in proper condition for carriage by air according to the applicable dangerous goods Regulations. Signature of shipper or his Agent
Total Prepaid	Total Collect		(11)
Currency Conversion Rates	C C Charges in Dest Currency		Executed on (date) at (place) Signature of Issuing carrier or its Agent
For Carrier's use only at Destiation	Charges at Destination	Total Collect Charges	

ORIGINAL   3   (FOR SHIPPER)   A

场站收据

Shipper　　　　　（发货人）	D/R No.（编号）
	场站收据
Consignee　　　　（收货人）	Received by the Canier the Total number of containers or other packages or units stated below to be transported subject to the terms and conditions of the canier's regular form of Bill of Loading(for Comb illed Transport or port to Port Shipment) which shall be deemed to be incorporated herein.
Notify Party　　　（通知人）	
	Date（日期）：
Pre carriage by（前程运输）　Place of Receipt（收货地点）	
	场站章
Ocean vessel（船名）　Voy No.（船航次）　Port of Loading（装货港）	
Port of Discharge（卸货港）　Place of delivery（交货地点）	Final Destination for Merchant's References（目的地）

particulars Furrdshed by Merchants	Container No.（集装箱号）	Seel No.（封志号）Mark & Nos.（标记与号码）	No. of Containers or Pkgs.（箱数或件数）	Kind of Packages; Description of Goods（包装种类与货名）	Gross Weight 毛重（公斤）	Measurement 尺码（立方米）
		TOTAL NUMBER OF CONTAINERS OF PACKAGES(IN WORDS)集装箱数或件数合计（大写）				

Container No.（箱号）　Seal No.（封志号）　Pkgs.（件数）　Container No.（箱号）　Seal No.（封志号）　Pkgs.（件数）

Received（实收）　By Terminal clerk（场站员签字）

FREIGHT & CHARGES	Prepaid at（预付地点）	Payable at（到付地点）	Place of lssue（签发地点）	
	Total Prepaid（预付总额）	No. of Original B(S)/L（正本提单份数）	BOOKING（订舱确认）APPROVED BY	

Service Type on Receiving ☐-CY,☐-CFS,☐-DOOR	Service Type on delivery ☐-CY,☐-CFS,☐-DOOR	Reefer Temperature Required.（冷藏温度）		℉	℃
FYPE OF GOODS（种类）	☐Ordinary,☐Reefer,☐Dangerous,☐Auto.（普通）　（冷藏）　（危险品）　（裸装车辆）		危险品	Class:Property:	
	☐Liquid,☐Live Animal,☐Bulk,☐＿＿（液体）　（活动物）　（散货）			IMDG Code Page:UN NO.	

Appendix I　Logistics Terms

A

ABC classification ABC 分类管理

Activity based costing (ABC)作业基础成本法

Access control 存取控制

Accounting cost 会计成本

Advanced label imaging system (ALIS)先进标签影像系统

Advanced Planning and Scheduling (APS)先进规划与排程

Aggregate shipments 合并出货

Article reserves 物品储备

Aisle management 信道管理

Automatic warehouse 自动化仓库

Automatic guided vehicle (AGV)自动导引车

Automated storage and retrieval system(ASRS)自动仓储与检索系统

B

Back order 迟延订单，延期交货

Bar code 条形码

Bar code scanner 条形码扫描机

Basing point pricing 基准点订价法

Batch processing 批处理

Bill of materials (BOM)物料用量清单

Bonded warehouse 保税仓库

Box car 箱式车

Buffer stock 缓冲存货

Bullwhip effect 牛鞭效应

Business process reengineering (BPR)企业流程再造

Business process improvement (BPI)企业流程改进

C

Capacity requirements planning (CRP)能力需求规划

Cargo under custom's supervision 海关监管货物

Cargo tracking 货物追踪

CFS (container freight station)集装箱货运站

Chill space 冷藏区

Combined transport 联合运输

Containerized transport 集装运输

Container transport 集装箱运输

Containerization 集装箱化

Continuous replenishment program (CRP)连续库存补充计划

Computer assisted ordering (CAO)计算机辅助订货系统

Conveyor 输送机

Cross docking 直接换装，越库

Customized logistics 定制物流

Customs broker 报关行

Customs declaration 报关

Cycle stock 经常库存

D

De-containcrization 散装化

Distribution center 配送中心

Distribution logistics 销售物流

Distribution processing 流通加工

Distribution requirements planning (DRP)分销需求计划，配送需要计划

Distribution resource planning (DRP II)配送资源计划

Door-to-door 门到门

Drop and pull transport 甩挂运输

E

Economic order quantity (EOQ)经济订货批量

Efficient customer response(ECR)有效客户反映

Electronic data interchange (EDI)电子数据交换

Electronic order system (EOS)电子订货系统

Enterprise resource planning (ERP)企业资源计划

Environmental logistics 绿色物流

Export supervised warehouse 出口监管仓库

External logistics 社会物流

F

Fixed inteval inventory model 定期存货模式

Fixed-quantity system (FQS)定量订货方式

Fixed-quantity system (FS)定期订货方式

Fork lift truck 叉车

Freeze space 冷冻区

Full container load (FCL)整箱货

G

Global positioning system (GPS)全球定位系统

Goods collection 集货

Goods shed 料棚

Goods shelf 货架

Goods yard 货场

H

Handing/carrying 搬运

Humidity controlled space 控湿储存区

I

Intangible loss 无形消耗

Internal logistics 企业物流

International logistics 国际物流

International freight forwarding agent 国际货运代理

International transportation cargo insurance 国际货物运输保险

Inventory 库存

Inventory control 库存控制

Inventroy count sheet 存货盘点表

Inventory cycle time 库存周期

J

Just in time (JIT)准时制

Just-in-time logistics 准时制物流

L

Land bridge transport 大陆桥运输

Last-in first-out (LIFO)后进先出

Lead time 前置期（或提前期）

Less than container load (LCL)拼箱货

Less than truckload (LTL)零担货运

Logistics activity 物流活动

Logistics alliance 物流联盟

Logistics center 物流中心

Logistics cost 物流成本

Logistics cost control 物流成本管理

Logistics document 物流单证

Logistics information 物流信息

Logistics management 物流管理

Logistics network 物流网络
Logistics operation 物流作业
Logistics technology 物流技术
Logistics resource planning (LRP)物流资源计划
Logistics strategy 物流战略
Logistics strategy management 物流战略管理

M
Material requirements planning (MRP)物料需求计划
Manufacturing resource planning (MRP II)制造资源计划
Military logistics 军事物流

N
Neutral packing 中性包装

O
Order cycle time 订货处理周期
Order picking 拣选
Outsourcing 业务外包

P
Package/packaging 包装
Packing of nominated brand 定牌包装
Pallet 托盘
Production logistics 生产物流

Q
Quick response (QR)快速反应

R
Receiving 收货区
Returned logistics 回收物流

S
Safety stock 安全库存
Sales package 销售包装
Shipping space 发货区
Shipping agency 租船代理
Shipping by chartering 租船运输
Sorting 分拣
Stacking 堆码

Stereoscopic warehouse 立体仓库

Storage 保管

Storing 储存

Supply chain management (SCM)供应链管理

Supply logistics 供应物流

T

Tangible loss 有形消耗

Tally 理货

Temperature controlled space 温度可控区

TEU (twenty-feet equivalent unit)换算箱，标准箱

Third-party logistics(TPL)第三方物流

Through transport 直达运输

Transfer transport 中转运输

Transport package 运输包装

Transportation 运输

U

Unit loading and unloading 单元装卸

V

Value-added logistics service 增值物流服务

Vendor managed inventory (VMI)供应商管理库存

Virtual logistics 虚拟物流

Virtual warehouse 虚拟仓库

W

Warehouse management 仓库管理

Warehouse layout 仓库布局

Waste material logistics 废弃物物流

Weight utilization factor 重量利用系数

Weight tolerance 重量公差

Weight-bulk ratio 重量-体积比

Z

Zero stock 零库存

Zero-inventory logistics 零库存技术

Zone of rate freedom 运费自由区

Zone picking 区域拣货

Appendix II   World Famous Logistics Companies

1. C. H. Robinson Worldwide Inc.

C. H. Robinson Worldwide got its start in 1905 as a produce company. Today, they're one of the North America's largest third party logistics (3PL) companies, with operations in the United States, Canada, Mexico, South America, Europe, and Asia. Most of their revenues come from providing truck, rail, ocean, and air transportation throughout the world. Sourcing and information services are also important components of their business mix.

Over the 98-year history, they've developed strong relationships with customers and carriers across the globe. Their strength lives in all of the staff, who have extended the tradition of service and integrity to companies in every location and situation, and who take pride in making them one of the most resilient resources in the transportation industry.

CHRW is on *Fortune* magazine's list of America's Most Admired Companies, and is the only non-asset-based transportation company listed on the 2002 Fortune 500.

2. KONIKE Transportation Co., Ltd

KONIKE Transportation Co., Ltd is also called "borderless" worldwide logistics company. It has been developing a worldwide network of integrated intermodal transport which enables shippers fast, reliable and flexible services to domestic and overseas markets by sophisticated computerized information system and experienced staff deployed at respective key areas.

3. NYK Company (nippon yusen kabushiki kaisha)

NYK is a company where people are keenly aware of their role in the global community. It began fulfilling that role more than a century ago, when it inaugurated Japan's first international liner service. Today, the company operates the world's largest cargo fleet, serves customers around the world with inland transport and related intermodal logistics services. In addition, the company also operates luxury cruise ships and various leisure and recreational vessels. Continuing growth and diversification, in fact, are the central themes in NYK 21 long-range business vision.

4. The Miebach Logistics Group

The Miebach Logistics Group was founded in Frankfurt in 1973 to provide logistics consultancy and engineering services for large and medium-sized companies. Today the Group has an international network of offices worldwide, providing effective support to clients throughout the world, in Europe, North and South America and India.

In the last five years alone more than 100 systems and plants designed by Miebach Logistics have gone on-line throughout the world. 200 highly skilled consultants and engineers are employed in developing and realizing concepts and ideas to help the clients achieve supply chain excellence and competitive success.

5. Redford Distributors, Inc. Redford

Redford Distributors, Inc. is a warehousing and distribution center specializing in small business and internet business order fulfillment and warehousing. They receive and warehouse your products and ship orders to your customers with 24-hour turnaround time! The aims of Redford is to reduce the shipping cost of the customers.

6. Mitsubishi Warehouse California Corporation ("MWC")

Mitsubishi Warehouse California Corporation provides outstanding warehousing and distribution services to the clients. The company endeavors to seamlessly integrate the services with the operations of the clients. The staff are personally involved with each shipment, using every skills and the latest tools and technologies to ship accurately, on time every time. Above all, the good communication with the customers at every step of the way is the highest priority of MWC.

Through the state-of-the-art MWC Electronics Service Center, Reverse Logistics repair services are provided for electronics such as computers, monitors, projectors and printers. With the combination of warehousing and logistics services, Electronics Service Center offers the customers a complete service solution unrivalled in the industry.

7. Hanjin Shipping Co., Ltd.

Hanjin Shipping Co., Ltd. was born through the 1988 merger bettheyen Hanjin Container Lines (HJCL) and the most reputable and longest standing shipping company in Korea, Korea Shipping Corporation (KSC), which was established in 1950.

Since then, Hanjin has broadened and expanded its operation and service offerings to virtually all aspects of global marine transport. Hanjin has steadily diversified its business by introducing new container and bulk vessels and developing logistics operations in key service areas.

8. Exel Company

Exel is the global leader in supplying chain management, providing customer-focused solutions to a wide range of manufacturing, retail and consumer industries. Exel's comprehensive range of innovative logistics solutions encompasses the entire supply chain from design and consulting through freight forwarding, warehousing and distribution services to integrated information management and e-commerce support.

Exel, a UK listed, FTSE 100 companies, with turnover of £5.1 billion (US$8.3 billion/ €7.4 billion), employs over 74,000 people in 1,600 locations in more than 120 countries worldwide. Exel's customers include over 70% of the world's largest, quoted non-financial companies.

9. TNT Express Company

TNT Express is the world's leading provider of express business. TNT provides on-demand, time-definite and day-certain delivery of documents, parcels and freight. Global Express offers delivery before the end of local business hours on the next business day to almost every destination worldwide for both documents and non-documents. Consignments can weigh up to 500 kilos. Customs clearance is included. Goods in transit insurance, prioritised handling and confirmation of delivery are also available on request. The Global Express service is available for both export and import shipments.

10. UPS Companies

UPS Air Cargo provides freight forwarders direct, airport-to-airport deliveries to over 150 strategically located airports around the world. While it is one of the largest all-cargo airlines in the world, UPS Air Cargo is also versatile. It can accommodate virtually any type of freight, from perishables to aircraft engines. The customers can count on UPS Air Cargo for fast, reliable, airport-to-airport cargo service.

UPS Supply Chain Solutions is the new way to access UPS's extensive portfolio of services designed to meet customers' supply chain needs around the world. The supply chain solutions group includes UPS Logistics, UPS Capital, UPS Freight Services and UPS Mail Innovations.

11. FedEx

FedEx has long been a leader in the global economy. FedEx began building its international network early on with FedEx Express and today that network is unsurpassed, covering more than 210 countries with on-time, reliable transportation solutions.

Yet today's FedEx is even better. With more service choices to more places through its family of companies, FedEx customers can extend their reach further than ever before. FedEx operates hubs all over the world to ensure the certainty of global reach that FedEx customers have come to rely on.

12. DHL Company

DHL was formed in 1969, pioneering the air express industry with its first route from San Francisco to Honolulu. The success of the company was founded in its innovative idea of sending out documentation in advance of cargo arriving, thereby speeding up the process of importing goods.

The DHL Network grew incredibly quickly. By 1977, it had extended its range of services and started to deliver small packages as they'll as documents. 1982 saw the first serious spurt of growth, with an additional 30 countries and territories added in this one year alone. The year after, it opened offices in Eastern Europe, the first air express company to do so, and in 1986 it started operations in China, again the first air express company to do so.

13. Sears' Distribution Center

Sears Roebuck & Co., headquartered in Chicago, Ill., provided its first catalog to U.S. consumers in 1888. Today, Sears operates 863 mall-based retail stores offering home-related products.

The company utilizes innovative supply-chain techniques, such as a high-speed scanner sorter systems to move merchandise quickly to the consumer and reduce overall costs of the supply chain. Sears has more than three million SKUs, 5,000 ship points and 13 distribution centers; handles more than 35 million boxes; has more than 4,000 trading partners; and issues about 30 million purchase orders annually.

14. WR Systems, Ltd. WR 系统公司

WR Systems is a strategic business consulting services and solution provider with a focus in supply chain management (planning and execution), enterprise asset management, e-Commerce, and Enterprise Application integration. WR Systems is comprised of highly experienced technical and business operations professionals. These professionals are actively involved with the day-to-day execution of project work and deliverables. The team is experienced in solving the technical and business related challenges confronting organizations today and providing the proper positioning to meet tomorrow's challenges.

15. Colonial Export, Inc.

Colonial Export, Inc. (CEI) is a global logistics company. CEI has a 10,000 square foot warehouse with all of the material handling equipment necessary to load, package, MIL-SPEC crate, and ship to any destination worldwide.

Its primary customers have been the Foreign Agents of U.S. Department of Defense Contractors (ex: General Dynamics, McDonnel Douglas, Hughes Aircraft Co., United Defense/FMC).

16. Evans Distribution Systems

Evans Distribution Systems is a full-service third-party logistics provider of public and contract warehousing, transportation, distribution, packaging, assembly, inspection and fulfillment solutions. Located in Melvindale (Detroit), Michigan, they offer customized programs to meet unique and ever changing logistics needs.

Evans Distribution Systems' for transportation companies provide a variety of freight distribution services throughout Detroit, Michigan and across the United States. It has three asset based carriers and one non-asset based transportation management company to handle all of truckload and LTL needs, including HAZMAT and customs bonded.

17. AMERICAN SHIPPING CO., INC

AMERICAN SHIPPING CO., INC has brought high quality, cost-effective, flexible services to the Import and Export Community for over 100 years. As a Nationally Permitted US Customs Broker & Export Foreign Freight Forwarder, it participates in all phases of the Automated Broker Interface (RLF, ACH, AES, AMS, and all other programs), enabling the company to Customs clear merchandise or export cargo as fast and efficiently as possible. All the locations are staffed by licensed Customs Brokers with years of expertise to professionally represent the customers and meet all regulatory requirements.

18. AMERICAN INTERNATIONAL CARGO SERVICE INC

American International Cargo Service Inc. transports both ocean and airborne cargo originating in over 40 countries from the Far East, throughout Europe, and most of South America under our own contracts. It provides weekly consolidations and services from virtually all port/airport pairs. Access to multiple carrier selections in all modes of transportation ensures that cargo moves rapidly year-round, at the required price point.

19. Coastal Carriers, Inc.

Coastal Carriers, Inc. is a third party logistics provider based near St. Louis, MO. Through extensive network the company provides customers the most dedicated, responsive, creative, and innovative service in the transportation and logistics field. Through logistics program, customers enjoy the benefits of the following comprehensive services all with a single point of contact: premier over-the-road service, LTL consolidation, warehousing and distribution, dedicated fleet or truck service, air freight, intermodal, and international shipping. Along with current fleet *Coastal* has over 17, 000 carriers on contract serving the contiguous United States, Mexico, and Canada.

20. Wal-Mart Inc.

Wal-Mart became an international company in 1991 when a SAM'S CLUB opened near Mexico City. Just two years later, the Wal-Mart International Division was created to oversee growing opportunities worldwide. The division currently operates stores and clubs employing more than 300,000 associates in the following countries:

Wal-Mart is the first to use retail information system and bar code, EDI, wireless scan gun in its operation and carry out produce and supply cooperation with the big suppliers such as Proctcr&Gamble.Now it is almost the most strongest commerce company on the world, and also the biggest logistics company in the world in the commercial industry.

Appendix III   Global Sea Ports

A

Aalborg 奥尔堡（丹麦）

Aalesund 奥勒松（挪威）

Aarhus 奥胡斯（丹麦）

Abadan 阿巴丹（伊朗）

Abidjan 阿比让（科特迪瓦）

Abu Dhabi 阿不扎比（阿联酋）

Acajutla 阿卡胡特拉（萨尔瓦多）

Acapulco 阿卡普尔科（墨西哥）

Accra 阿克拉（加纳）

Adelaide 阿德莱德（澳大利亚）

Aden 亚丁（也门）

Agana 阿加尼亚（关岛）

Alexandria 亚历山大（埃及）

Algiers 阿尔及尔（阿尔及利亚）

Amsterdam 阿姆斯特丹（荷兰）

Ancona 安科纳（意大利）

Annaba 安纳巴（阿尔及利亚）

Antofagasta 安托法加斯塔（智利）

Antwerp 安特卫普（比利时）

Aomen[Macao] 澳门（中国）

Apapa 阿帕帕（尼日利亚）

Apia 阿皮亚（西萨摩亚）

Aqaba[Akaba] 亚喀巴（约旦）

Arica 阿里卡（智利）

Arkhangelsk 阿尔汉格尔斯克（俄罗斯）

Aseb[Assab] 阿萨布（埃塞俄比亚）

Athens 雅典（希腊）

Aukland 奥克兰（新西兰）

Avenmouth 阿芬默斯（英国）

B

Bahia Blanka 布兰卡（阿根廷）

Baltimore 巴尔的摩（美国）

Bandar Abbas 阿巴斯港（伊朗）

Bandar Khomeini 霍梅尼港（伊朗）

Bandar Seri Begawan 斯里巴加湾市（文来）

Bangkok 曼谷（泰国）

Banjarmaisn 马辰（印尼）

Banjul 班珠尔（冈比亚）

Bar 巴尔（南斯拉夫）

Barcelona 巴萨罗那（西班牙）

Barranquilla 巴兰基亚（哥伦比亚）

Basra 巴士拉（伊拉克）

Bassein 勃生（缅甸）

Bata 把塔（赤道几内亚）

Beihai 北海（中国）

Beira 贝拉（莫桑比克）

Beirut 贝鲁特（黎巴嫩）

Belawan 勿拉湾（印尼）

Belfast 贝尔法斯特（英国）

Belize 伯利兹（伯利兹）

Belmopan 贝尔莫潘（伯利兹）

Benghazi 班加西（利比亚）

Berbera 柏培拉（索马里）

Bergen 卑尔根（挪威）

Berne 伯尔尼（瑞士）

Bilbao 毕尔巴鄂（西班牙）

Birkenhead 伯肯赫德（英国）

Bissau 比绍（几内亚比绍）

Bizerta 比塞大（突尼斯）

Boma 博马（扎伊尔）

Bombay 孟买（印度）

Bordeaux 波尔多（法国）

Boston 波斯顿（美国）

Bourgas 布尔加斯（保加利亚）

Bremen 不来梅（德国）

Bremerhaven 不来梅港（法国）

Brest 布雷斯特（法国）

Brisbane 布里斯班（澳大利亚）

Bristol 布里斯托尔（英国）

Buenaventura 布埃纳文图拉（哥伦比亚）

Buenos Aires 布宜诺斯艾利斯（阿根廷）

C

Cagliari 卡利亚里（意大利）

Calcutta 加尔各答（印度）

Callao 卡亚俄（秘鲁）

Cape Town 开普敦（南非）

Caracas 加拉加斯（委瑞内拉）

Cardiff 加地夫（英国）

Cartagena 卡赫纳（哥伦比亚）

Casablanca[Dar el Beida] 卡萨布兰卡（摩洛哥）

Cebu 宿务（菲律宾）

Charleston 查尔斯顿（美国）

Cheribon 井里文（印尼）

Chiba 千叶（日本）

Chicago 芝家哥（美国）

Chimbote 钦博特（秘鲁）

Chittagong 吉大港（孟加拉国）

Chongjin 清津（朝鲜）

Coatzacoalcos 夸察夸尔科斯（墨西哥）

Colombo 科伦坡（斯里兰卡）

Colon 科隆（巴拿马）

Conakry 科纳克里（几内亚）

Coonstantza 康斯坦萨（罗马尼亚）

Copenhagen 哥本哈根（丹麦）

Corinto 科林托（尼加拉瓜）

Cork 科克（爱尔兰）

Cotonou 科托努（贝宁）

christ Church 克莱斯特切奇（新西兰）

Crotone 克努托内（意大利）

Cumana 库马纳（委内瑞拉）

D

Dacca 达卡（孟加拉国）

Dakar 达喀尔（塞内加尔）

Dalian 大连（中国）

Damman 达曼（沙特阿拉伯）

Da Nang 岘港（越南）

Dar el-Beida[Casablanca] 卡萨布兰卡（摩洛哥）

Darwin 达尔文（澳大利亚）

Dar-es-Salaam 达累斯萨拉姆（坦桑尼亚）

Djakarta 雅加达（印尼）

Djibouti 吉布提（吉布提）

Doha 多哈（卡塔尔）

Dordrecht 多德雷赫特（荷兰）

Douala 杜阿拉（喀麦隆）

Dubai 迪拜（阿联酋）

Dublin 都柏林（爱尔兰）

Dunedin 打尼丁（新西兰）

Dunkirk 敦刻尔克（英国）

Durresi 都拉斯（阿尔巴尼亚）

E

East London 东伦敦（南非）

F

Fredericia 腓特烈西亚（丹麦）

Fredrikstad 腓特烈斯塔（挪威）

Free Town 弗里敦（塞拉利昂）

Freemantle 弗里曼特尔（澳大利亚）

Fuzhou 福州（中国）

G

Gaoxiong 高雄（中国台湾）

Gdansk 格但斯克（波兰）

Gdynia 格丁尼亚（波兰）

Geelong 吉朗（澳大利亚）

Genoa 热那亚（意大利）

Georgetown[Penang] 乔治市[槟城]（马来西亚）

Georgetown 乔治敦（圭亚那，加拿大）

Gibraltar 直布罗陀（西班牙）

Gijon 希洪（西班牙）

Glasgow 格拉斯哥（英国）

Godthab 戈特霍布（格陵兰）

Goteborg 哥德堡（瑞典）

Guangzhou 广州（中国）

Guayaquil 瓜亚基尔（厄瓜多尔）

Guaymas 瓜伊马斯（墨西哥）

H

Haifa 海法（以色列）

Hai-Phong 海防（越南）

Hakodate 函馆（日本）

Halifax 哈里法克斯（加拿大）

Halmstad 哈尔姆斯塔德（瑞典）

Hamburg 汉堡（德国）

Hanoi 河内（越南）

Havana 哈瓦那（古巴）

Helsinki 赫尔辛基（芬兰）

Hiroshima 广岛（日本）

Hongay 鸿基（越南）

Hongkong 香港（中国）

Honolulu 火奴鲁鲁（美国）

Houston 休斯敦（美国）

Hudaydak Al 荷台达（也门）

Hull 赫尔（英国）

Hungnam 兴南（朝鲜）

I

Iloilo 伊洛伊洛[怡朗]（菲律宾）

Iquique 伊基克（智利）

Istanbul 伊斯坦布尔（土耳其）

Izmir[Smyrna] 伊兹密尔（土耳其）

J

Jakarta 雅加达（印尼）

Jidda 吉达（沙特阿拉伯）

Jilong 基隆（中国台湾）

K

Kagoshima 鹿儿岛（日本）

Kakinada 卡基纳达（印度）

Kampong Saon 磅逊（柬埔寨）

Karachi 卡拉奇（巴基斯坦）

Khulna 库尔纳（孟加拉国）

Kiel 基尔（德国）

Kingston 金斯敦（牙买加，加拿大）

Kismayu 基斯马尤（索马里）

Kobe 神户（日本）

Kuala Lumpur 吉隆坡（马来西亚）

Kuching 吉晋（马来西亚）

Kuwait 科威特（科威特）

L

Lagos 拉各斯（尼日利亚）

La Conuna 拉科鲁尼亚（西班牙）

La Guaina 拉瓜伊拉（委内瑞拉）

La Rouchelle 拉罗歇尔（法国）

La Spezia 拉斯佩齐亚（意大利）

La Plata 拉普拉塔（阿根廷）

Latakia 拉塔基亚（叙利亚）

Le Havre 勒阿佛尔（法国）

Leghorn[Livorno] 莱戈恩（意大利）

Leninggrad 列宁格勒（俄罗斯）

Lianyungang 连云港（中国）

Libreville 利伯维尔（加蓬）

Limassol 利马索尔（塞浦路斯）

Limon 里蒙（哥斯达黎加）

Lisboa[Lisbon] 里斯本（葡萄牙）

Liverpool 利物浦（英国）

Lome 洛美（多哥）

London 伦敦（英国）

Long Beach 长滩（美国）

Los Angeles 洛杉矶（美国）

Luanda 罗安达（安哥拉）

Lubeck 卢贝克（德国）
Lyttelton 利特尔顿（新西兰）

M

Macao 澳门（中国）
Majunga 马任加（马达加斯加）
Murmansk 莫尔曼斯克（俄罗斯）
Muscat 马斯喀特（阿曼）
Makasa 望加锡（印尼）
Malabo 马拉博（赤道几内亚）
Malacca 马六甲（马来西亚）
Malaga 马拉加（西班牙）
Male 马累（马尔代夫）
Malindi 马林迪（肯尼亚）
Malmo 马尔默（瑞典）
Malta 马耳他（马耳他）
Manama,Al 麦纳麦（巴林）
Manila 马尼拉（菲律宾）
Maputo 马普托（莫桑比克）
Maracaibo 马拉开波（委瑞内拉）
Mar del Plata 马德普拉塔（阿根廷）
Marseilles 马塞（法国）
Massawa 马萨瓦（埃塞俄比亚）
Matadi 马塔迪（扎伊尔）
Matanzas 马坦萨斯（古巴）
Mazatlan 马萨特兰（墨西哥）
Melbourne 墨尔本（澳大利亚）
Menado 万鸦老（印尼）
Mersin 梅尔辛（土耳其）
Messina 墨西拿（意大利）
Miami 迈阿密（美国）
Milford 米尔福德港（英国）
Mobile 莫比尔（美国）
Mogadisho[Mogadiscio] 摩假迪沙（索马里）
Mokpo 木浦（朝鲜）
Mombasa 蒙巴萨（肯尼亚）
Monrovia 蒙罗维亚（利比里亚）
Montevideo 蒙特维的亚（乌拉圭）

Montreal 蒙特利尔（加拿大）
Mokalla,Al 穆卡拉（也门）
Moulmein 毛淡棉（缅甸）

N

Nagasaki 长崎（日本）
Nagoya 名古屋（日本）
Naha 那霸（日本）
Nakhodka 纳霍德卡（俄罗斯）
Nampo 南浦（朝鲜）
Nantes 南特（法国）
Naples[Napoli] 那不勒斯（意大利）
New Orleans 新奥尔良（美国）
New York 纽约（美国）
New Castle 纽卡斯尔（澳大利亚，美国）
New Heaven 纽黑文（美国）
Nicosia 尼科西亚（塞浦路斯）
Niigata 新泻（日本）
Ningpo 宁波（中国）
Norfolk 诺福克（美国）
Nouakchott 努瓦克肖特（毛里塔尼亚）
Noumea 努美阿（新喀里多尼亚）

O

Oakland 奥克兰（美国）
Odessa 傲德萨（乌克兰）
Oran[Ouakran] 奥兰（阿尔及利亚）
Osaka 大阪（日本）
Oslo 奥斯陆（挪威）
Oulu 奥卢（芬兰）

P

Palembang 巨港（印尼）
Panama City 巴拿马城（巴拿马）
Papeete 帕皮提（波利尼西亚）
Paramaribo 帕拉马里博（苏里南）
Penang 槟城（马来西亚）
Philadelphia 费城（美国）
Piraeus 比雷埃夫斯（希腊）

Plaia 普拉亚（佛得角）

Ploce 普洛切（南斯拉夫）

Plymouth 普列茅斯（英国）

Pointe Noire 黑角（刚果）

Port-au-Prince 太子港（海地）

Port Elizabeth 伊利沙白港（南非）

Port Gentil 让蒂尔港（加蓬）

Port Harcourt 哈科特港（尼日利亚）

Port Headland 黑德兰港（澳大利亚）

Port Kelang 巴生港（马来西亚）

Portland 波特兰（美国）

Port Louis 路易港（毛里求斯）

Port Moresby 莫尔兹比港（巴布亚新几内亚）

Port Alegre 阿雷格里港（巴西）

Port of Spain 西班牙港（特立尼达和多巴哥）

Port Novo 波多诺夫（贝宁）

Port Said 塞科港（埃及）

Port Sudan 苏丹港（苏丹）

Port Victoria 维多利亚港（塞舌尔）

Portsmouth 朴次茅斯（英国）

Prince Rubert 鲁伯特王子港（加拿大）

Puerto Cabello 卡贝略港（委内瑞拉）

Puerto Cortes 科尔特斯港（洪都拉斯）

Punta Arenas 蓬塔阿雷纳斯（智利）

Puntarenas 蓬塔雷纳斯（哥斯达黎加）

Pusan 釜山（韩国）

Q

Qingdao 青岛（中国）

Qinhuangdao 秦皇岛（中国）

Quebec 魁北克（加拿大）

R

Rabat 拉巴特（摩洛哥）

Rangoon 仰光（缅甸）

Recife 累西非（巴西）

Reykjavik 雷克雅未克（冰岛）

Riga 里加（拉托维亚）

Rijeka 里耶卡（南斯拉夫）

Rio de Janeiro 里约热内卢（巴西）

Rostock 罗斯托克（德国）

Rotterdam 鹿特丹（荷兰）

S

Safaga 萨法加港（埃及）

Safi 萨费（摩洛哥）

Saigon 西贡（越南）

Salonica 萨洛尼卡（希腊）

Salvador 萨尔瓦多（巴西）

San Diego 圣跌戈（美国）

San Francisco 旧金山（美国）

San Juan 圣胡安（波多黎哥，秘鲁）

Sandakan 山打根（马来西亚）

Santiago 圣地亚哥（古巴）

Santo Dominga 圣多明各（多米尼加）

Santos 桑拖斯（巴西）

Savanah 萨凡纳（美国）

Seattle 西雅图（美国）

Semarang 三宝垄（印度）

Setubel 塞图巴尔（葡萄牙）

Sfax 斯法克斯（突尼斯）

Shanghai 上海（中国）

Shantou 汕头（中国）

Shekou 蛇口（中国）

Shenzhen 深圳（中国）

Singapore 新加坡（新加坡）

Songkhla 宋卡（泰国）

Southampton 南安浦敦（英国）

Split 斯普利特（南斯拉夫）

St.John's 圣约翰斯（加拿大）

Stockholm 斯德哥尔摩（瑞典）

Suez 苏伊士（埃及）

Surabaja 泗水（印尼）

Suva 苏瓦（斐济）

Sydney 悉尼（澳大利亚）

Szczecin 什切青（波兰）

T

Taipei 台北（中国台湾）

Tallin 塔林（爱沙尼亚）

Tamatave[Toamasina] 塔马塔夫（马达加斯加）

Tampa 坦帕（美国）

Tampico 坦皮科（墨西哥）

Tandjung Priok 丹戎不碌（印尼）

Tanga 坦葛（坦桑尼亚）

Tangier 丹吉尔（摩洛哥）

Taranto 塔兰托（意大利）

Tatus 塔尔图斯（叙利亚）

Tel Aviv 特拉维夫（以色列）

Tema 特马（加纳）

Tianjin 天津（中国）

Toamasina 图阿马西纳（马达加斯加）

Tokyo 东京（日本）

Toleary 图莱亚尔

Toronto 多伦多（加拿大）

Toulon 土伦港（法国）

Trieste 的里雅斯特（意大利）

Trineomalee 亭克马里（斯里兰卡）

Tripoli 的黎波里（黎巴嫩，利比亚）

Tunis 突尼斯（突尼斯）

Turku 图尔库（芬兰）

V

Vaasa 瓦萨（芬兰）

Valletta 瓦莱塔（马耳他）

Valona 法罗拉（阿尔巴尼亚）

Valparaiso 瓦尔帕莱索（智利）

Vancouver 温哥华（加拿大）

Verna 瓦尔纳（保加利亚）

Venice 威尼斯（意大利）

Veracruz 韦腊克鲁斯（墨西哥）

Victoria 维多利亚（塞舌尔，加拿大）

vila 维拉港（瓦努阿图）

Vladivostok 海参威（俄罗斯）

W

Valvis Bay 沃尔维斯湾（纳米比亚）

Wellington 惠灵顿（新西兰）

Wenzhou 温州（中国）

Wismar 维斯马（德国）

Wonsan 元山（朝鲜）

X

Xiamen[Amoy] 厦门（中国）

Y

Yantai 烟台（中国）

Yokohama 横滨（日本）

Z

Zanzibar 桑给巴尔（坦桑尼亚）

Zhanjiang 湛江（中国）

Zhuhai 珠海（中国）

参考文献

[1] Bowersox D. J., D. J. Closs. Logistical Management, the McGRAw-HILL Companies. Inc.1996.

[2] Chase R., N. Aquilano. Operations Management for Competitive Advantage. 北京：机械工业出版社，2003.

[3] Christopher M.. Logistics for Reducing Cost and Improving Service (2e),Prentice Hall. 北京：电子工业出版社，2003.

[4] Donald J. Bowersox., David J. Closs. Supply Chain Logistical Management. 北京：机械工业出版社，2002.

[5] Edward G. Hinkelman 著. 李健译. Dictionary of International Trade. 北京：经济科学出版，2002.

[6] FITZSIMMONS J. A., M. J. FITZSIMMONS. Service Management. 北京：机械工业出版社，2002.

[7] Gourdin K. N..Global Logistics Management. Blackwell Business.

[8] HEIZER J., B. RENDER. Operation management(6e). 北京：北京大学出版社，2006.

[9] Lambert D. M., J. R. Stock. Fundamentals of Logistics Management. Irwin McGraw-Hill.

[10] Kotler P., Marketing: an introduction. 北京：华夏出版社，2003.

[11] Helo P., B.S..Logistics Information Systems,an analysis of software solutions for supply chain co-ordination. Industrial Management+Data System, 2005.

[12] Russel R., B. Taylor III, Operations Management. Prentice Hall, Inc.1998.

[13] Shapiro J.. Modeling the Supply Chain. 北京：中信出版社，2002.

[14] 白世贞. 物流英语. 北京：中国物资出版社，2004.

[15] 程世平. 物流专业英语. 北京：机械工业出版社，2003.

[16] 程同春. 新编国际商务英语函电. 南京：东南大学出版社，2003.

[17] 甘鸿. 外经贸英语函电. 上海：上海科学技术文献出版社，2003.

[18] 侯荣华. International shipping operations. 上海：上海交通大学出版社，2000.

[19] 刘法公. 国际贸易实务英语. 杭州：浙江大学出版社，2002.

[20] 刘庆秋. 商务英语应用文写作. 北京：对外经济贸易大学出版社，2009.

[21] 秦志云，罗国梁. 国际商贸进出口实务英语. 上海：华东理工大学出版社，1997.

[22] 苏士哲. 英汉物流管理词典. 北京：清华大学出版社，2001.

[23] 王冰. 电子商务英语. 北京：电子工业出版社，2006.

[24] 王淑云. 现代物流（英汉对照）. 北京：人民交通出版社，2002.

[25] 翁凤翔. 图表单证详解. 杭州：浙江大学出版社，2002.

[26] 吴国新，李元旭. 国际贸易单证实务. 北京：清华大学出版社，2008.

[27] 余世明，丛凤英. 国际商务单证. 广州：暨南大学出版社，2003.

[28] http://china.alibaba.com

[29] http://www.npedi.com

[30] http://www.mhia.org

[31] http://tbw.teda.gov.cn

[32] http://www.wsntech.com

[33] http://www.dhl.com

[34] http://www.pbs.org/wgbh/pages/frontline/shows/wlmart

[35] http://www.ups.com